The making of the South African past

THE MAKING OF THE SOUTH AFRICAN PAST

Major historians on race and class

Christopher Saunders

Barnes & Noble Books: Totowa, New Jersey

First published 1988 in paperback in southern Africa by David Philip, Publisher (Pty) Ltd, 217 Werdmuller Centre, Claremont, Cape, South Africa

Published 1988 in hardback in the United States of America by Barnes &: Noble Books, 81 Adams Drive, Totowa, New Jersey, 07512

ISBN 0-86486-075-7 (David Philip, paperback)
ISBN 0-389-20785-3 (Barnes & Noble, hardback)

© 1988 Christopher Saunders

Library of Congress Cataloging-in-Publication Data

Saunders, Christopher.
    Making of the South African past/Christopher Saunders.
        P.   CM.
    Bibliography: P.
    Includes index.
    ISBN 0-389-20785-3
    1. Historians——South Africa——Biography.   2. South Africa——
Historiography.   I. Title.
DT765.5.S28   1988
968'.0072022——DC19   88-3956

Printed by Blackshaws (Pty) Ltd, Kinghall Avenue, Epping, Cape, South Africa

Contents

Acknowledgements

Many individuals and institutions aided my work on this book. Mrs Mona Macmillan very kindly invited me into her home at Long Wittenham to consult her husband's papers. Dr C. W. de Kiewiet consented to answer my many questions on three occasions, and Jay Naidoo gave me access to letters Dr de Kiewiet had written to him. The Human Sciences Research Council and the Ernest Oppenheimer Memorial Trust gave me generous financial aid, but are not to be considered responsible for anything I say. My visit to the United States was made pleasant thanks to the African Studies Center at Boston University and the Southern African Research Program at Yale, where it was a special privilege to work with Leonard Thompson. A Smuts fellowship at Cambridge enabled me to complete the project in the tranquil environment of Churchill College, where Anthony Low was most kind and Alan Findlay lent me a word-processor when I most needed one.

Eric Axelson, Bob Edgar, John Galbraith, Baruch Hirson, Arthur Keppel-Jones, Phyllis Lewsen, John Omer-Cooper, Jean van der Poel and Brian Willan were among those who supplied useful information. I am indebted to librarians at the Library of Congress and the following universities: Boston, Cambridge, Cape Town, Cornell, Oxford, Rhodes, Stellenbosch, Witwatersrand and Yale. Various friends and colleagues offered comments on parts of the manuscript. Russell Martin has been a meticulous editor and David Philip a patient publisher. Part 2 draws on my short monograph on C. W. de Kiewiet published by the University of Cape Town's Centre for African Studies in 1986. To all who have helped, my sincere thanks.

1 G. M. Theal, by Edward Roworth (South African Library)

2 Sir George Cory (Cory Library, Rhodes University)

3 C. W. de Kiewiet
(photo by Ansel
Adams)

4 W. M. Macmillan

5 Eric Walker
(University
of Cape Town
Archives)

6 Leo Fouché
(University
of the Wit-
watersrand
Archives)

7 J. S. Marais
(University
of the Wit-
watersrand
Archives)

8 Eddie Roux
(E. & W. Roux,
Rebel Pity,
London, 1971)

9 Sol T. Plaatje
(T. D. Mweli
Skota, *The
African Yearly
Register,* Johan-
nesburg, 1931)

10 S. M. Molema
(T. D. Mweli
Skota, *The
African Yearly
Register*)

11 Leonard Thompson
by Rupert Shephard
(University of
Cape Town)

12 Monica Wilson
(University of
Cape Town
Archives)

Introduction

'The struggle of man against power is the struggle of memory against forgetting': Milan Kundera, *The Book of Laughter and Forgetting*

'It is not the future which is unpredictable, but the past': after Jorge Luis Borges

Historical consciousness takes many forms. Man has always had some sense of history, and long before the first words were put onto paper, past events were remembered and information about such events was passed down to the next generation. This book is concerned not with historical consciousness in southern Africa in general, but with aspects of the history of historical writing on that country. Such writing, which has a history of over a century, is voluminous. An attempt at a comprehensive account of it would inevitably result in little more than a list of names and writings, with brief and invariably superficial comment. Such a 'who wrote what, when' account of the making of the South African past would be more an exercise in bibliography than in historiography. The approach adopted here is to focus on a (but also, I shall suggest, *the*) major thread in the long tradition of historical writing on South Africa: the way historians have viewed the South African past through the prism of race and class.

Earlier this century the term race was commonly used when relations between English-speaking and Afrikaans-speaking white South Africans were being discussed. How historians have approached such relations is not the concern of this work, except inasmuch as these relations are relevant to the other way in which 'race' has been used over the past century: to refer to relations between, on the one hand, those who can trace their origins to Europe – 'whites' – and on the other those who are in whole or part of African or Asian descent – 'blacks'. We shall not, then, be concerned with all forms of ethnic consciousness, but our focus will be on one particular cleavage: that between whites and people of colour. We shall explore how certain leading professional historians – all of them white – added to our knowledge and understanding of the role of the black majority in the country's history. We shall also consider the attitudes these historians adopted in their work to blacks and to the evolution of black–white relations over time. And we shall investigate explanations such historians have offered for the course of South African development. We shall note how historians at one time believed that white racial prejudice, or white racism, was a critical determining factor in South African history, the prime cause of the institutionalised and legalised racial discrimination for which the country became notorious. Other historians saw racial cleavages as less significant than those of class. As we approach the present, the interrelationship of race and class will become a major focus of attention. Changing attitudes to race, and the relationship of race and class, have formed the 'cutting edge of innovation'[1] in historical writing on South Africa from the 1870s, when the first major historian began to write his *History,* until the present.

* * *

To explain how historians have considered race and class it will be necessary to explore the context of their work. In this study historians will be discussed against the background of their times, and their ideas examined in the context of their lives and careers as a whole, following E. H. Carr's injunction: 'Before you study the history study the historian', to which he added: 'Before you study the historian, study his historical and social environment.'[2] We shall explore why certain major historians wrote as they did, and how thinking about the South African past has altered from generation to generation. As Carr pointed out, all works of history are themselves historical documents, and deliver up most meaning when most is known about the historical setting in which they were produced. The American historian Carl Becker has perhaps best expressed the lofty aim of such a study. It is, he once wrote, to find out

what men have at different times known and believed about the past, the use they have made, in the service of their interests and aspirations, of their knowledge and beliefs, and the underlying presuppositions which have made their knowledge seem to them to be relevant and their beliefs to be true.[3]

In a comprehensive survey of South African historiography, historical writing in Afrikaans would of course loom large. There are three main reasons why it does not do so here. It is not surprising that in a society as divided as South Africa, there should be a great divide in its historiography, as in Canada between English and French historians.[4] The great bulk of historical writing in Afrikaans either has been conceived in an Afrikaner nationalist tradition, inaugurated by S. J. du Toit's *Die Geskiedenis van Ons Land in die Taal van Ons Volk* (Paarl, 1877), or it has been highly descriptive and narrow in the range of topics it has addressed. There has been relatively little cross-fertilisation from historical writing in the one language to that in the other. Indeed George McCall Theal had, over many decades, far more influence on Afrikaner historians than any Afrikaner historian had on English-speaking writers. Secondly, Professor F. A. van Jaarsveld has written extensively about P. J. van der Merwe and other important Afrikaner historians.[5] Moreover, the crucial breakthroughs in the developing understanding of race and class were made by English-speaking historians, whether Theal, who set a pattern, or, say, Macmillan, Thompson or Legassick, all of whom, as we shall see, broke with existing orthodoxies. That no Afrikaner historian made any similar breakthrough may be explained at least in part by their more unquestioning acceptance of white supremacy.[6]

Professional historians were slow to investigate the history of blacks or to see South Africa from a radical perspective; the contribution of amateurs on both these counts has too long been forgotten, and separate chapters (10 and 13) try to rescue from obscurity some of the early work both on the history of blacks and on economic influences on the country's development. Above all, this study is concerned with the work of leading professional historians and of Theal, the great amateur historian, whose influence was enormous on generations of history students in South Africa. By examining a few individual historians in depth there is obviously the danger of seeming to exaggerate their importance, and of implicitly neglecting others who may be thought worthy of attention. Those treated here were chosen because they were at the forefront of historical scholarship in their time, or because their influence was greater than others. Only Macmillan among them has left us a published autobiography of any substance.[7] Others not only left no personal record but few, if any, private papers,[8] so that their careers, and the influences on their work, are now often difficult to recover in any detail. But their writings moulded the

historical consciousness of generation after generation of South
Africans, and, as they wrote in English, they were also read widely
abroad. At least as much as any other group of intellectuals, these
scholars, though relatively few in number, helped shape the view
of South Africa held in the outside world. The English tradition of
historical scholarship in South Africa deserves assessment, then,
to show something of how the South African past was 'made' over
time. Such an enquiry will help place present writing in perspective.

While most of these pages consider the way professional historians, all of them white, wrote about relations between whites and
blacks, and about the history of blacks, some attention will also be
given – in Chapter 10 – to those blacks who wrote about their
past, in English as well as in vernacular languages. Until very recently, there were no professional black historians. Had blacks
had the same opportunities to write about the South African past
as whites, the body of historical literature we possess would
almost certainly have been very different. As it is, the pioneering
contribution made by blacks to the writing of their own history
deserves to be remembered.

The history of historical writing on South Africa, and the social
history of the historical profession, both remain under-researched.
When this study was begun, the fullest account remained a revised version of an inaugural lecture given in 1961 by Van Jaarsveld.[9] As this study was under way, Van Jaarsveld's survey of
South African historical writing became available.[10] But the sweep
of his book is so broad that individual historians are inevitably
treated superficially, while his thread is the rather sterile one of
blame in ideological history-writing. There still exists no comprehensive survey in English of the history of South African historical
writing, and very little has appeared on the individual historians
in the English tradition. The brief historiographical article in the
official yearbook *South Africa*, which remained substantially un-
changed from the 1976 edition through those of 1977, 1978, 1979,
1980-1 and 1983, is extremely weak. In 1977 David Philip published the first book-length critical essay on South African history
in English. Harrison Wright's *The Burden of the Present* focused on
the contemporary 'liberal–radical debate', and not – as the present
book does – on the history of historical writing over a century.
Those who in the 1970s criticised liberal history from a radical
perspective usually looked back only to what was in effect a ste-

reotypical representation of 'liberal history' and they made little detailed reference to the century of historical writing that preceded their own, almost as if it was irrelevant to the new concerns. Neither Wright, in his mostly synchronic survey of liberal and radical history, nor Marianne Cornevin, in her rebuttal of the main apartheid myths about South Africa's past, considers change over time in South African historical writing in any depth, or attempts to set the earlier historians of South Africa in their social and intellectual context.[11] Only in her discussion of two of nine myths – that the blacks were migrants until they met the whites, and that the trekkers entered empty land – did Cornevin briefly consider the ways these myths evolved over time.[12]

* * *

In the pages that follow we shall investigate a range of themes in South African historical writing over the century between the publication of George McCall Theal's first major work – the *Compendium of South African History and Geography* (1874) and that of the first historical monograph to use class analysis – F. R. Johnstone's *Class, Race and Gold* (1976) – though some remarks will also be made about developments in the decade since then. One reviewer of *The Burden of the Present* expressed the hope that Wright's essay would help induce a degree of self-consciousness among historians.[13] The perspective obtained from a survey of trends over a century may, it is hoped, further this process. For just as all history helps provide perspective on current events, so too does the study of historical writing over time. As a famous American historian once put it, 'memory is the thread of personal identity, history of public identity'.[14] In the case of South Africa, the 'radical challenge' developed out of a critique of the 'liberal' approach, and the work of W. M. Macmillan in the 1920s was in turn largely a critique of what he called the 'authorised version' of South Africa's past, that of Theal and Cory. The later work can only really be understood with reference to what went before.

There are other reasons why the study of the history of historical writing is important. Historiography is cumulative as well as innovative: earlier work is not entirely overturned by newer scholarship; old ideas may sometimes live on, or may be rediscovered to good effect. Those who pioneered new ways of understanding deserve to be remembered. And all historical writing is part of the wider intellectual history of the country. Even if early historians are now seen to be wrong, their views of the past are revealing of their own time. South Africa's intellectual history mostly remains unwritten.[15] It is hoped that this study may contribute to the understanding of that history.

PART 1
G. M. Theal

1 A Canadian becomes South African

The South African War brought South Africa to world attention, and in 1902, as the fighting ended, a volume of biographies on *The Prominent Men of Cape Colony, South Africa* was published in Portland, Oregon. In it, appears this passage:

Happy is the nation that has no history, but very unhappy is the nation that has a history and no historian to write it. South Africa has a history, a great history; it also has a historian, a great historian. He is Dr George McCall Theal ... it is no exaggeration to say that the foundation of all that has been well and truly written on South Africa rests on Dr Theal's labors.[1]

In the first decades of this century, Theal's eleven volume *History of South Africa* and the numerous shorter histories he wrote together constituted the single most influential body of work on the South African past. When professional historians began to write detailed studies in the 1920s, they drew on his *History* for background, and the general reading public acquired much of its knowledge of the past from histories written either by Theal himself or by others who borrowed heavily from his work. Few may read him today, but his *History* is still the single most detailed general history of the country until the late nineteenth century, and the 'settler tradition' he fathered remains alive in South Africa. Yet for one so influential, Theal and his work have been relatively little explored. The first study of his work was a doctoral thesis presented to the University of Amsterdam by I. D. Bosman in 1931.[2] An unpublished master's thesis submitted to the University of Cape Town in 1962 by Merle Babrow (Lipton) provided a more critical view. The most recent and scholarly assessment, published after this chapter was written, is an article by Deryck Schreuder of the University of Sydney.[3] None of these authors used the full range of material on Theal now available in Cape Town and Stellenbosch.[4]

* * *

Theal was an immigrant to South Africa. He was born in Saint John, New Brunswick, in 1837, of United Empire Loyalist descent. His distant ancestors left Rye in Sussex, and settled in Connecticut. In the 1780s, when it appeared England would lose the American War of Independence, his great-grandfather moved north to the Canadian maritimes. Theal was to recall that in his childhood he was 'saturated with tales ... of the struggles of the pioneers', of what they 'had done for principle's sake' and had 'suffered in consequence'.[5] He learnt little history at school, but as he grew up he read the historical classics of Gibbon, Parkman, Motley and Prescott.[6] His father wanted him to enter the church, but he rebelled, left home at 17, worked in the United States, visited Sierra Leone, and was en route to Australia in 1861 when his ship called at Cape Town and he disembarked. He was never to get to Australia, and did not return to Canada until 1894, though he kept in touch with his friends and relatives there, and was Africa correspondent for the Saint John *Daily Telegraph* in the 1870s.

Theal became an historian via journalism and by a set of fortuitous circumstances. From Cape Town he travelled east along the coast to Knysna, where he taught and also began to learn Dutch. In the early 1860s he moved further east to what was then the separate colony of British Kaffraria, where he worked briefly as a bookkeeper and reporter in King William's Town. From 1863 he lived in the small harbour village of East London, the editor and owner of a weekly newspaper, *The Kaffrarian Record*, the first number of which appeared on his twenty-sixth birthday. When this venture folded, he started another newspaper, *The Kaffrarian*, but that too did not pay its way, and he had to move back to King William's Town, where in 1867 he became a teacher at the public non-denominational school, later Dale College. He was for many years to retain links with the world of journalism, contributing regularly to a wide range of newspapers, in South Africa and elsewhere, and he never lost his interest in the contemporary scene. But, while teaching in King William's Town, he began to read widely in the printed sources available to him there on the South African past, and began to think of writing a general history of his adopted country. At that time only a few amateur historians had turned their hands to the writing of the history of particular areas or topics: J. C. Chase, for example, a civil servant, had written on *The Cape of Good Hope and the Eastern Province*, the missionary W. C.

Holden had written a *History of the Colony of Natal* and Henry
Cloete, a judge, had given a set of lectures on the Great Trek to
the Literary Society of Pietermaritzburg in the early 1850s.[7] It was
not until 1869 that the first general survey of the history of the
Cape from its 'discovery' by Europeans was published: the *History
of the Colony of the Cape of Good Hope* by Alexander Wilmot and J. C.
Chase. The first fruit of Theal's wide reading was a sixty-page
pamphlet entitled *South Africa As It Is*, which he printed himself in
King William's Town in 1871. It seems to have been designed
mainly for immigrants, but its title was somewhat misleading, for
it contained considerable historical detail on the two British colonies and the republics in the interior.

Once that was published, Theal resigned his teaching job and
set out to try his luck in what he called 'the gigantic lottery' of the
Kimberley diamond fields, which attracted men from all parts of
South Africa like a magnet in the early 1870s. But he, like so
many, did not make his fortune there, and after little more than a
year he returned to the eastern Cape, where he found a job at the
famous Lovedale mission institution at Alice. There he was in
charge of the preparatory school and helped Dr Stewart, the principal, with the printing department.[8] At Lovedale he expanded
South Africa As It Is into a more substantial publication, the *Compendium of South African History and Geography*, which he printed on the
Lovedale press in 1873. A much enlarged edition appeared in
1876, and a third edition the following year. He included a long,
annotated list of the books he had consulted, which shows how
widely he had read in the secondary and printed primary literature on South Africa available to him in the eastern Cape.

The *Compendium* comprised more history than geography, and
amounted in fact to a general survey of his adopted country's past.
He had no access to archival sources, but did draw upon oral
material which he collected from Africans at Lovedale and elsewhere in the eastern Cape. It is unfortunate that he did not record
the interviews he conducted with Sarili, the Xhosa paramount, and
others, but they make him a local pioneer in the collection of oral
history. Besides historical information, he collected from Africans
what he termed folklore – stories, legends and proverbs – seeking
to emulate similar work carried out by the philologist Wilhelm
Bleek, the first great scholar of African societies in South Africa,
and by Henry Callaway among the Zulu.[9] The tales he began to
publish in the *Cape Monthly Magazine*. By 1877 he had collected

enough for a volume, and it was only because his career underwent a major change that his *Kaffir Folk-lore* did not appear until 1882.

* * *

In the latter months of 1877 the Cape eastern frontier was plunged into war, the last of the Cape–Xhosa conflicts. The 40-year-old Theal was mayor of Alice, the small town adjoining Lovedale, and a close friend of the civil commissioner Percy Nightingale. It was Nightingale who suggested to the government that Theal should be sent to try to ensure that Oba Ngonyama, a nearby Ngqika chief, did not take up arms against the colony. Theal accepted this potentially dangerous assignment and lived for some months with Oba. Oba did not rebel and Theal was able to persuade him to seek work for his people in Port Elizabeth. Theal accompanied him there, then travelled on to Cape Town in search of another commission in the public service. He was never to return to Lovedale.[10]

As the war drew to a close in 1878, the government rounded up several thousand Xhosa and transported them to the south-western Cape as indentured labourers. Most were women who had allegedly aided the rebels. Theal was given the post of labour agent, to supervise the hiring out of this labour to the farmers of the western Cape. He did not find it a congenial job, in part because he sympathised with those removed from their friends and relatives in the eastern Cape: one of the most moving passages in his *History* describes their longing for their own country.[11] But, stationed as he was in various country towns, with time on his hands, he began looking for historical records, and found, first in a magistrate's office at Stellenbosch, and then at Swellendam, Worcester and Tulbagh, the original archives of the districts of the early Cape, until then unused by any historian. He set about deciphering the old Dutch script, and decided to make his life's work the study of the original records of his adopted country, from which he planned to write its definitive history.

When his days as labour agent came to an end – many of the people he was supposed to be supervising absconded and returned to the east, for which Theal received some censure from the Secretary for Native Affairs – he obtained a junior post in government in Cape Town. The bonus for Theal was that there he had access to the main colonial archive – which was scattered in various government offices, was almost totally unsorted, and had been very little used.[12] In 1876, four years after the grant of full self-government, the Cape authorities had appointed a commission to investigate the establishment of a properly organised archive. From 1879 the government allowed Theal to call himself Keeper of the Archives and to work with the papers on a part-time basis. 'As soon as I saw the Archives at Cape Town', he recalled later,

> I perceived that they were of great value, that they could be made the means of bringing the Colony in contact with the great literary associations of Europe, that without any difficulty at all, without much effort, one could get into contact with the first literary men of Europe, and that there was buried in those papers a mass of information valuable anywhere in the civilised world. I saw a very brilliant and useful career before the man who took those papers in hand and put them in such a state as to make them valuable for people who wished to make researches, and that any man having charge of them could get information of an ethnological and philological character that would be valued throughout the world.[13]

Theal hoped to make an international name for himself as a scholar by using the Cape archives, because of the information he believed they would yield on 'primitive races'. And because his *History* would be based on the archives, it would, he believed, be definitive.

In 1880, after Theal had pressed for it, the government authorised a full-time post of Keeper of the Archives. Theal naturally expected to get the position, but it went instead to Hendrik Carel Vos Leibbrandt (1837–1911), a former Dutch Reformed Church minister, who had become an amateur archivist at Graaff-Reinet. Some observers suggested that Theal did not get the post because his *Compendium* was too anti-Dutch. Theal himself thought the government blamed him for reminding them of a promise it had made to Oba, and because it disliked the sympathy he had shown for the Africans brought to the south-western Cape.[14] Whatever the reason for Leibbrandt's appointment – the *Cape Argus* thought the fact that he was distantly related to the prime minister was significant[15] – there was strong criticism of it in the press, and a parliamentary motion in Theal's favour was lost by only one vote.[16]

The outraged Theal could not accept that Leibbrandt's experience in Graaff-Reinet qualified him to take charge of the colonial archives. He was to continue a kind of running battle with Leibbrandt for the rest of his life, on such historical issues as the Slagtersnek incident and the role and character of Willem Adriaan van der Stel, but also on how the Keeper of the Archives should spend his time. Theal was strongly critical of Leibbrandt's precis of the archives, published in many volumes from 1897, on the grounds that documents should be published in their entirety, and he produced numerous volumes of source publications to make that point. Leibbrandt's appointment was a personal affront which helped galvanise him to prove that he should have been given the post. Had he become Keeper of the Archives he would probably have remained in Cape Town, organising the archives and using them for his *History*. Instead, he had to carry out his research part-time for many years, and thereafter was to spend over ten years abroad. In those years he produced sets of documents which were to form a massive contribution to the source material available for later historians to use when writing their histories.

* * *

Theal not only lost his part-time archival post because of Leibbrandt's appointment but he was, to his great dismay, sent back to the eastern Cape as acting special magistrate at Tamacha near King William's Town, six hundred miles from the archives. He was soon pleading for transfer: 'the greater portion of my life', he told the government, 'has been passed in a study, and to undertake the management of natives involves a responsibility which I am glad to forgo.'[17] Fortunately for him there was soon a change of government and the new ministry thought he had been badly treated by its predecessor. His misery at Tamacha was ended and he was allowed to go to the Hague for ten months, where he revelled in the Dutch archives, transcribing documents and maps not available in Cape Town, and collecting material for his multi-volume *History*.

After his return to Cape Town in 1882 he worked as first clerk in the main office of the Native Affairs Department, rising to become chief clerk in 1893. During these years he was able to spend a good deal of official time on historical work of one kind or another: on his return from Europe he was instructed by J. W. Sauer, then Minister for Native Affairs, to collect together and publish all the material he could find on the history of Basutoland, for the Cape was then involved in discussions with the imperial government about handing the territory over. Three large volumes of *Basutoland Records* were published in 1883 and a fourth would have followed had not the transfer of the territory to imperial control taken place in 1884.[18] Theal then collected material on the various Transkeian territories, which the Cape was in the process of bringing under its formal rule. His accounts of their history were included, anonymously, in the *Blue Book on Native Affairs* in 1885, and after his death were reprinted in a volume of *Transkeian Territories: Historical Records* compiled by Frank Brownlee.[19] In 1886 Theal published an account of the early history of Natal. Then in 1887 appeared his very much larger and more important *History of the Boers in South Africa*, which was broader in scope than its title suggested; much of its contents was to be incorporated in his *History of South Africa*. A year later he published two volumes on the Cape under the administration of the Dutch East India Company. These volumes were written in the evenings after his office duties, and when he wrote of 'the first author at the Cape' in the late seventeenth century, he added, with some bitterness: 'at least he had no reason to complain of his labour not being remunerated'.[20]

The publication of these volumes did at last gain Theal widespread recognition as an historian, and in 1891 he was given the honorary title of Colonial Historiographer. A fire in the Native Affairs office in 1892 destroyed the manuscript of his history of 'the Kaffir [Cape–Xhosa] wars',[21] but in the following year he completed a genealogy of old Cape families, which appeared in three volumes in 1893. It was hardly surprising that by early 1894 he was suffering both from writer's cramp and from some kind of nervous breakdown. Though given leave to recuperate, when he arrived in England he spent his time in the British Museum, the India Office and the Public Record Office, finding material to copy for the Cape archives. He also took the opportunity to make his only return visit to Canada, his impressions of which were written up for a newspaper and later published under the title *Notes on Canada and South Africa*.

On his return to Cape Town in 1895, keen to escape his Native Affairs Department duties and to devote himself to full-time historical research and writing, he asked Cecil Rhodes, the prime minister, to give him a commission to return to the archives and libraries he had visited abroad, and to visit any others where there might be material on early southern African history. Rhodes wanted to learn more about the early history of the country north of the Limpopo River that had recently been given his name, and, like Theal, believed the 'early movement of the Bantu tribes' to be something in which 'we ... have a deep interest'.[22] He therefore agreed that Theal should visit London and Lisbon, and perhaps the Vatican archives, recently opened to researchers, and even Cairo and Constantinople.

Rhodes fell from office because of the abortive Jameson Raid, but the permission granted Theal to go overseas was confirmed by Rhodes's successor, though now it was agreed that, to justify the cost, Theal's main task should be to prepare for publication the records of the Cape Colony available in London. This Theal did very assiduously: between 1897 and 1905 thirty-six volumes of the *Records of the Cape Colony* – material from the British archives – were published, the last eighteen volumes in 1904–5 alone. During these years in London, working twelve hours a day, six or seven days a week, Theal produced much else besides, including nine volumes of the *Records of South East Africa* and a number of historical works, including *The Beginning of South African History* and *Progress of South Africa in the Century*. He also edited for publication a manuscript by the geologist George W. Stow (1822–82), written in the 1870s and entitled 'The Native Races of South Africa: A History of the Intrusion of the Hottentots and Bantu into the Hunting Grounds of the Bushmen, the Aborigines of the Country'. [23]

Theal enjoyed his time in London and the opportunity to visit European cities from time to time to tap new sources for the history of southern Africa. It would seem that he expected to remain based in Europe almost indefinitely. Then in 1904 he was told that because of the severe recession at the Cape, the government could no longer support his research abroad. [24] He was given another year in London to bring his edition of the Cape records to the end of 1827, but still felt very aggrieved at his recall. Accusing the government of trying 'to crush and disgrace me', [25] he retired to Rye Cottage, Wynberg, and only returned to Europe one more time, to arrange the publication in 1911 of the study by W. H. Bleek and Lucy Lloyd, *Specimens of Bushmen Folklore*, a book close to his heart. [26]

In retirement he continued writing and revising his *History*. Two further volumes took the story to 1884, except that he carried that of the Transkeian territories to the final stage in the process of annexation in 1894. His *The Yellow and Dark Skinned Peoples of Africa South of the Zambesi* (1910) became *Ethnography and Condition of South Africa*, and was later included as the first volume in his *History of South Africa* when the whole set was reissued. He also produced a catalogue of books and pamphlets on South Africa, a volume of documents on the Cape–Xhosa war of 1835, and a collection of historical sketches. George Cory, who became a close friend in his last years and was in Cape Town at the time of his death in 1919, says he continued working until ten minutes before he died.[27] A memorial fund was established after his death and the money collected went to erect a tombstone in the Wynberg Dutch Reformed Church cemetery, and to commission the portrait by Roworth which now hangs in the main reading room of the South African Library in Cape Town.[28]

2 The making of a settler historian

Theal liked to think of himself as a plain, narrative historian. 'The first object is to state nothing but facts that can be proved', he wrote, 'and the second to state them in plain language that cannot be misinterpreted. Ornamentation of sentences or paragraphs comes in nowhere.'[1] Elsewhere he said he had

> not tried to give polish to my writing, because I feel that for me to attempt to do so would be like a quarryman attempting to give the finishing touches to a statue. The duties of the various offices which I have held ... the labour of research ... and in past years the prolonged personal intercourse with natives ... would have unfitted me for putting a gloss on literary work, if ever I had the requisite ability. In this respect I am like the farmers whose wanderings I have followed [the trekboers], who had plain food in abundance, but no means of decorating their dinner tables. Recognising this, what I have kept constantly before me was to relate all events of importance, to arrange them generally in chronological order, to give dates for every occurrence, to furnish minute details of all subjects of interest to South African readers, to prepare an index....[2]

His was a narrative account of the past, concerned with describing what happened, rather than analysing why it happened; with events rather than processes. He tells us that his aim was to provide a comprehensive account of all important events relating to the history of South Africa. In places his *History* becomes a list of names – of early settlers, of those in the Retief party massacred by Dingane's men, or of members of the first Cape parliament and the Natal Legislative Council. Elsewhere it rises above the mere chronicle, but W. M. Macmillan was right to speak of his 'bald and unimaginative pages', devoid of any sparkle or sense of climax, and John X. Merriman was voicing criticism of Theal when he called for 'someone to give the soul of South African history – not the dry bones'.[3]

In Theal's *History* there was no probing, no attempt to ask profound questions of the past. If his work had a theme, it was the spread of white settlement and 'civilisation', and the moral and material progress that accompanied that process. But this theme was not explicitly developed in his *History*, and when he came to write a book specifically on progress in the nineteenth century, at the end of that era, he had to acknowledge that there was a problem about speaking of moral progress when, while he wrote, South Africa was embroiled in the most violent conflict in its history.[4] Without a clear thematic approach, his narrative merely progressed from one event to another, with no attempt to weigh the significance of events: those of no real consequence – shipwrecks, for example – were included alongside those of obvious importance. Nor did he incorporate much social or economic data; his work was largely political.

But that did not mean that it was objective. Theal did not give references to his archival sources, and professional historians – John Edgar, the first professor of history at the South African College, J. S. Marais, who taught at Cape Town and Witwatersrand universities and P. J. van der Merwe of the University of Stellenbosch[5] – who followed him through the records, pointed to numerous errors on matters of fact. In the early 1940s Marais maintained that Theal's work was flawed not only as a result of the haste with which he had worked, but also because of his prejudice: in particular that he had been blind to evidence which ran counter to his view that whites were right in their relations with blacks, and that those whites who were critical of the colonists' viewpoint were wrong.[6] In the early 1960s, Babrow went further, suggesting that, for all his protestations of impartiality, Theal had deliberately selected evidence to fit the case he wished to make.

When Theal began to write his *History* he knew of two opposing views on relations between whites and blacks in South Africa in the past. John Philip of the London Missionary Society had claimed that that past was largely a story of white oppression of blacks. This was the major theme of his two volume *Researches in South Africa*, published in 1828, a view rejected by most whites. Angered by Philip's *Researches*, a group of leading colonists persuaded the governor of the Cape to appoint Donald Moodie, a former protector of slaves, to search the then unsorted records of the colony to produce evidence to show that Philip was wrong. They then subscribed to the cost of publishing Moodie's collection of archival material, which he entitled *The Record, Or A Series of Of-*

ficial Papers Relative to the Condition and Treatment of the Native Tribes of South Africa.[7] Moodie's documents were selected to show that white–Khoikhoi relations had been relatively peaceful: there had been only two minor wars in the seventeenth century, involving little loss of life, and that of 1659 had begun when the Khoi attacked the Dutch. Disease, and not the whites, had been responsible for the large-scale loss of life among the Khoi.[8] Similarly, Robert Godlonton's *Narrative of the Irruption of the Kaffir Hordes into the Eastern Province of the Cape of Good Hope*, published after the frontier war of 1834–5, was a history of the origins and course of that war designed to demonstrate that the frontier settlers were in no way to blame for it.[9] The evidence such apologists advanced did not of course persuade those who, like Philip, observed racial oppression in the present and believed it was not new. Writing in 1853, the missionary David Livingstone criticised what he called the 'Van Riebeeck Principle', the idea that whites were always right and had the right to dominate and subjugate others. Livingstone went on to accuse the churches of failing to condemn racial oppression, such as the seizure by whites of the cattle and land of the indigenous peoples.[10]

The pro-colonist, anti-black stance which Theal adopted in his *History* was the common position among his settler colleagues. Alexander Wilmot, another amateur historian of the late nineteenth century, wrote: 'the barbarian outside our colonies and states must in all cases either conquer or be conquered, and to stop the flow of the tide of civilisation ... was as impossible as to curb and restrain the waves of the sea.'[11] But Theal did not start out with a full-fledged white supremacist approach, and unlike later historians who adopted his pro-colonist viewpoint, he remained deeply interested in Africans and always devoted considerable attention to them in his work. In 1877 he told a colleague that he thought his *Compendium* most important for what it said about black history.[12] Introducing the second edition of that work, he wrote as follows:

In the present edition, the chapters referring to early Kaffir history will be found to be much more complete.... The writer, finding it impossible to form a satisfactory conclusion concerning preceding events in any other manner, applied to various antiquarians throughout Kaffirland.... The first edition was read by some hundreds of natives, among whom were many of the teachers of mission schools on the frontier, and as it is confidently anticipated that this issue will have a still larger circulation

among them, it is but fair that anything in the history of their people –
even to the spelling of the names of the chiefs of old – should be accu-
rately given.[13]

And again, in his Preface to the third edition, he noted that comments by local Africans had been 'carefully considered'.

Though what is now known as precolonial history remained for
him more ethnography than history, he did not follow others in
ignoring entirely what had happened in South Africa before the
whites arrived. He wrote an entire volume on the *Ethnography and
Condition of South Africa before 1505*, saying that it was 'a necessary
preliminary' to his later *History* and 'may be regarded as the
nearest approach that is possible to a history of the country before
1505'. Though the rest of his *History* recounted what was essentially the story of white settlement, black leaders involved with
whites continued to be accorded some prominence, and altogether
Theal gave Africans more coverage than any other historian in a
general work on South Africa before the first volume of the *Oxford
History* appeared in 1969.

* * *

A number of those who reviewed his *Compendium* in the colonial
press in the 1870s believed Theal had been too concerned with ill-
treatment of blacks, and had exaggerated the violence done by the
early white settlers to blacks in the process of conquest. To talk of
'plunder and murder of Natives' by commandos was 'ridiculous'.[14]
Theal's reply was forthright: he said he could not ignore what the
commandos had done. What he had written was the truth. One
should ask:

was a system of constant warfare against natives by commandos permitted? Were the results such as are described in the numerous books
and official documents of the last century? If the answers to these questions be in the affirmative, the actions of commandos cannot be expunged
from our history.

And he added: 'hundreds of natives will in a very few years be just
as well able as we are to search the Records, or Sparrman or Bar-
row's works, and if they find us attempting to cheat them, what
respect will they retain for us?' Moreover, he denied that he was
anti-Dutch, admitting, 'I tried to avoid saying anything to offend
any section of the community', but repeating that he wrote what
he did because it was true.[15]

His *History of the Boers* offered a very different interpretation of what had happened, and he acknowledged in its Preface that his views had undergone a major change since publication of the *Compendium*. Theal explained that for the *Compendium* he had been forced to rely on books and printed materials, but that since then he had had access to missionary and other archival records, and these had shown his earlier views to be wrong. So he called the *Compendium* defective and inaccurate, and advised readers not to refer to it. His new work, on the other hand, was, he believed, above criticism because it rested on archival research. He now went out of his way to deny that instances of oppression of blacks by whites were at all numerous, adding:

One would not be justified in terming the Boers a race of oppressors on account of them, any more than in terming the inhabitants of London a race of pilferers on account of the pickpockets in their city.[16]

Such oppression as had occurred was the result of the weakness of the republican governments. He contrasted the missionary view of all men as being equal with a Boer view of difference in 'the intellectual capacities of races which mark some as inferior to others', a view he clearly accepted.[17]

In the course of advancing such ideas, Theal felt it necessary to keep stressing his lack of bias. He had tried to relate occurrences just as they took place, 'without favour toward one class of people or prejudice against another'.[18] As he had been born and brought up in Canada, 'no ties of blood, no prejudices acquired in youth, stand as barriers to my forming an impartial judgment of occurrences in South Africa in bygone times'.[19] He claimed his *Progress of South Africa in the Century* contained 'the indisputable truths of South African history.... As far as human power goes, it is absolutely free of partisan spirit.'[20] Much later, he did admit that sections of his *History* 'could be enlarged to advantage',[21] but he would not concede that anything he had written in it needed to be altered or corrected in any way. As he wrote with 'equal justice' to all, his was a 'true and absolutely unbiased narrative'. [22] One reviewer agreed: his work was 'painstaking and exact to a degree and runs but little risk of ever having even its slightest sentence controverted'.[23]

It was not access to the archival records, however, that was responsible for the new interpretation he advanced in his *History*. While living at Lovedale he had been influenced by his missionary environment, and had worked closely with Africans. Then came the shock of the frontier war of 1877–8, after which he moved to the south-western Cape and entered the official world of Cape Town. In the 1880s he wanted to write no mere compendium, but the great national history of his adopted country, which would be read in England and other parts of the empire, shaping the way South Africa was viewed from abroad, and be accepted as the definitive work of scholarship on the South African past. Such a history would also promote good relations between Boer and Briton within the country, and would further the goal of the development of a colonial nationalism. That in turn would be underpinned at the level of politics by unification of the various colonies and states in South Africa. He wanted to see the 'fusion' of Dutch and English in South Africa, so that the country might take its place as a leading member of 'a grand, strong, glorious [British] empire of sister States, in the very van of true progress throughout the world'.[24]

So he now emphasised that the two white 'races' were of the same stock: the Dutch were South Africa's Pilgrim Fathers, the pioneers of European civilisation in the sub-continent. The social manner of Dutch and English was sometimes different, Theal admitted, but their attitudes to labour and to race generally were, he claimed, the same.[25] His *History* did not follow most English-speakers at the Cape and adopt a critical approach to the trekboers and those he called the emigrant farmers, known to later historians as the Voortrekkers. Sir George Grey, he wrote,

knew how baseless were the charges of semi-barbarism so often made against the old colonists, and recognised in them as well as in the British dwellers on the same soil a sturdy, brave, liberty-loving people.[26]

The Dutch/Afrikaners were

men of our own race, they spoke a dialect which our great Alfred would have understood without much difficulty; their religion was that of the people of Scotland. That there was nothing of the nature of race antagonism between them and the people of Great Britain is shown by the readiness with which intermarriages have taken place ever since the colony came under our flag ... there was in truth hardly any difference in sentiment between them and a body of Englishmen or Scotsmen of equally limited education....[27]

As an exclusive Afrikaner nationalist sentiment grew, some in the republics found Theal's *History* insufficiently pro-Afrikaner, but F. W. Reitz (1844–1934), while president of the Orange Free State,

translated abridged versions for use in schools there.[28] When
Theal received an honorary doctorate from Queen's University in
Canada in 1895 the citation spoke of his seeing South Africa's
problems from a colonist rather than an imperial point of view,
and of his appreciating the importance of the Boer element and of
doing full justice to their virtues.[29] Theal was an ardent supporter
of the Rhodes–Hofmeyr wing of Cape politics before the Jameson
Raid, and when war came in 1899 he made clear his belief that
Kruger's government had no design to oust the British from South
Africa.[30] He ended his days as an elder in the Dutch Reformed
Church at Wynberg, and when he died *De Goode Hoop* praised him,
in Dutch, as 'an Englishman with an Afrikaner soul'.[31]

* * *

So far as his South African audience was concerned, then, Theal
aimed to use his writing to help reconcile Boer and Briton. He explicitly acknowledged that his goal was to promote the emergence
of one white South African nation through a common history.[32]
Popular histories then in print were regional or looked at events
from either an exclusively English or an exclusively Afrikaner perspective. When his *History* began to appear, a reviewer in the *Cape
Argus* wrote as follows:

The author may fairly hope that he will live to see 'South Africa' cease to
be like 'Italy', a geographical expression, but rather the name of one great
and unified country. When that consummation is brought about, let the
work of the writer have its meed of praise as well as the struggles of the
politician. Certain it is that the work of so absolutely impartial a historian
as Mr Theal will have borne no small share in teaching South Africas
that, after all, they are inhabitants of one country.[33]

Theal's 'one nation' approach was to be followed by many
others in what is usually referred to as the settler – as distinct
from either the British (or English), or the Afrikaner – tradition of
historical writing. Boer and Briton were reconciled in his writing,
both positively and negatively. Positively, there was the common
story of settlement. But white settlement in South Africa did not
merely reproduce what had taken place in Canada or Australia,
because the whites of South Africa had made a special contribution: they alone had brought, and were still bringing, the blessings
of civilisation to a large indigenous population. Theal's story was
of the triumph of civilisation in a country where the indigenous
people were neither few in number nor soon eliminated, but out-

numbered the white settlers. Negatively, Boer and Briton were reconciled through having common enemies: the meddling, blundering imperial government, advised by misguided humanitarians who had taken the side of the blacks against the colonists, on the one hand, and the blacks themselves on the other.

Theal was highly critical of the British annexation of the diamond fields, which took place while he was in Griqualand West in 1871, and of the annexation of the Transvaal in 1877. For his criticism of the British role in South Africa he was in turn to be strongly attacked, especially at the time of the South African War, when emotions ran exceptionally high. One critic – James Cappon (1855–1939), Professor of English at Queen's University in Canada – used Theal's own *Records of the Cape Colony* (which Theal, ironically, had sent to Queen's because it had awarded him an honorary degree) to write an entire book devoted to showing up Theal's errors.[34] One of Cappon's main arguments was that Theal had, in adopting a pro-Dutch position, shown himself anti-black.

In the 1880s Theal grew increasingly critical of humanitarians as enemies of the emerging new society of Dutch–Anglo South Africans. Their exposés of alleged white wrongdoing against blacks were an affront to his new patriotism. At the very time when, he claimed, Dutch and English had first come to appreciate each other – in the 1830s – John Philip of the London Missionary Society had taken up the issues of race and frontier relations, and sought to check white expansion into new lands. All the missionaries in the Philip tradition – Van der Kemp, Read, Livingstone, Mackenzie – were seen as outsiders who did not understand South Africa's problems, men who had sought to undermine the pattern of race relations established by the 'founding fathers' by preaching that people of colour were, in all respects except education, equal to the European colonists, and that they were being wrongfully oppressed by whites. For Theal, the only more serious enemy the colonists had had to face were the blacks themselves.

* * *

Theal did not doubt the importance of black–white relations in the country's history. When he reached 1657 in his narrative, only five years after Van Riebeeck's arrival at the Cape, he wrote: 'The Native difficulty had already become, what it has been ever since, a most important question for solution....'[35] He later commented that the theme of black–white relations was not a pleasant subject to write of, because its incidents have little or no variety except in the changed attitudes of the European authorities, and everything connected with it is petty and dull. But it is the subject that makes the history of the Cape Colony different from that of other British possessions, it is still, and must continue to be, a matter of vital importance to South Africans, and it is only by a knowledge of past events that such great mistakes as were made can be avoided in future.[36]

One of those lessons was that outside authorities – such as the British government – should not interfere, another was that agreements made with Africans were useless, because Africans, being barbarians, were untrustworthy. Their rulers had been despots, their motives totally evil. The Zulu king Dingane, for example, 'from the first was only seeking to lure the white men to destruction'.[37]

In Theal's eyes white settlement had always been beneficial for all concerned. Of the land on the Transkei side of the Drakensberg he wrote: 'If occupied by Europeans what a grand province would Kaffraria not be, what a fulcrum would the level of civilisation not have to rest upon. It would not wrong a single black man....'[38] The Europeans, as civilised people, had a duty to redeem Africans from barbarism and backwardness. In place of precolonial chaos and strife, the whites brought order and peace. In his *History* Theal forgot the violence of the commando raids, and stressed rather the violence, first of blacks against blacks in the precolonial era, and then of blacks against the whites. It had not been whites who had exterminated the Bushmen, but first 'the Hottentots' and then the Griqua, and that because the latter had been settled north of the Orange River by John Philip.[39] For blacks who had known Shaka, Natal under British rule was 'an earthly paradise'.[40]

Though he did not explicitly defend slavery at the Cape, Theal wrote that it

should not be judged solely by what civilised men and women would suffer if reduced to that condition, for even in its worst form it was ... an improvement ūpon the ordinary existence of millions of the children of Africa. In no other slave society had bondage sat so lightly: the work on the farms was not more severe than that performed by an English labourer. As far as food, clothing, lodging and abstinence from excessive toil were concerned, the slaves on the whole had nothing to complain of.

He quoted a 'common remark' that slavery 'was worse for the white man, who had all the care and anxiety, than for the negro, who had only manual labour to perform'.[41] One reviewer did wonder what 'the slaves' commentary' on that passage would have been,[42] and Cappon queried how Theal knew that 'the majority of Hottentots rather enjoyed prison life than dreaded it'.[43] The emancipation of the slaves, according to Theal, had turned useful individuals into paupers and social pests, with 'no concern for the needs of tomorrow'. Slaves 'of lighter blood' had shown themselves deserving of freedom, but the change was not beneficial to 'pure blacks'; 'a comparison between the negro slave of 1834 and his grandchildren of 1900 shows much in favour of the former.'[44]

Theal would have it that Africans welcomed white rule: 'The African, whose ancestors through all time had been accustomed to see the strong despise and trample upon the weak, felt no degradation in serving the white man, whom he instinctively recognised as his superior.'[45] Theal's *History* did not suggest that whites had invaded the lands of blacks, or that blacks might have had reason to resist such invasion. Instead, the blacks were depicted as robbers, who had taken the property of the whites and been responsible for the violence that ensued, whether on the Cape or other frontiers. Theal's readers would hardly have gathered that African societies were being undermined by white intrusion. Only very exceptionally, in the case of particular individuals, did he allow that whites might have acted incorrectly. Pretorius's execution of Dingane's messenger Dambuza, a man who had acted 'with the utmost calmness and dignity', was 'a great mistake as well as a great crime'.[46] But white rule meant progress: comparing the South Africa of 1800 and of 1900, Theal wrote:

The murderous rule of the Bantu despot has gone for ever, as even where the tribes are still intact under their chiefs, their power for evil on an extensive scale has been broken. The great progress of late years is due more to the several European communities being free to direct their own affairs in their own way than to all other causes combined, and certainly the native races, whose advancement in civilisation and prosperity must always be an object of the very first importance with the Caucasian settlers in the land, have benefited immensely by the change.[47]

Theal did not doubt that the imposition of white rule was right as well as inevitable. A Social Darwinist, he assumed that the strongest and fittest would win, and that might was right. Of the British invasion of Zululand in 1879, he remarked: 'The question was simply whether civilisation or barbarism was to prevail in the country.' Cetshwayo, though 'an exceedingly able man for a barbarian', had 'only a barbarian's idea of the sanctity of his word', and consequently he could not be dealt with 'in exactly the same way as a civilised ruler'. And when discussing the way the Cape government undermined the independence of the African societies east of the Kei in the 1870s, Theal commented: 'in the nature of things, a petty barbarous government could not be permitted to do whatever it pleased, even within the limits of its own territory, in opposition to the interests of a powerful civilised neighbour.'[48]

In the great 'struggle for survival' the fittest races naturally came out on top. The white race was clearly the great civilising force in modern history, its expansion overseas a progressive movement bringing civilisation to backward peoples. On the other hand, if left to themselves, Theal wrote of the Xhosa, no elevation in their condition would take place; faced by civilisation and 'the leaven of a higher life working in the minds of some of themselves, they must conform to the law of progress'.[49] As whites were superior, their conquest of others was justified. White expansion formed the vehicle of the spread of civilisation and its triumph over barbarism. That such expansion should occur was a law of progress, part of the way in which the principle of race worked in history. Theal spoke, for example, of 'the law that impels Europeans to struggle for knowledge and power'.[50] As Rhodesia was being conquered in the early 1890s, he saw that process as an opportunity to introduce civilisation to the Ndebele and the Shona. More white settlers were needed if the region was to have a brilliant future.[51] Africa's hope lay in copying the European mode of life. Natal was not as advanced as the other white states because it lacked European immigrants in large numbers, as well as European capital.

In the triumph of progress and modernity, indigenous peoples naturally lost out. Considering the fate of the San, Theal wrote: 'One may feel pity for savages such as these, destroyed in their creative wilds, though there is little reason for regretting their disappearance. They were of no benefit to any other section of the human family; they were incapable of improvement.' And of the Xhosa chief Maqoma's death in 1873, he wrote that 'it is impossible to feel sorrow for the unfortunate old man .... if one of another race sympathises with him, what must the Gaikas have felt when the tidings reached them that he had died as a dog dies. What must Tini, his son, have felt?' But Theal saw Maqoma's fate as 'an illustration of what must happen when civilisation and barbarism come in contact, and barbarism refuses to give way'. Any

barbarian ruler who resisted the progress of civilised neighbours
'must go under', for Africans had to be reclaimed from their 'heri-
tage of barbarism'. The Cape government could not be blamed.[52]
White rule represented a force of 'sheer necessity', and Theal
spoke of 'the right of civilised men to take possession of land occupied by such a race'.[53] To this justification for white colonisation, he added: 'to the present no-one has devised a plan by which
this can be done without violence.' When whites behaved like barbarians, their actions were justified: 'In dealing with barbarians
such as those they were at war with [the Ndebele], the farmers
had no scruples about adopting a barbarous mode of attack....'[54] In
his *History* he wrote that if 'real wrongs were perpetrated upon
Kaffir clans by military patrols or mixed commandos, they were
not regarded by the Kaffirs themselves as sufficiently serious to
leave a lasting impression'.[55] And he responded to Cappon's attack
on him by pointing out that English and Dutch in South Africa
both believed that Africans 'cannot be raised in the scale of civilisation without first being taught to work'. 'Whereas the Dutch had
said "You must work", we plan our legislation to compel them to
do so.... They are quite awake to our aims, and they have no more
real love for us than they have for our Dutch neighbors.'[56]

* * *

For all his concern with the history of blacks in South Africa,
Theal could on occasion write as if they did not exist, as when he
spoke of his hope for 'the reconciliation of the two kindred
peoples who occupy its soil', referring to English-speakers and Afrikaners.[57] Blacks were not equals in his eyes and their history and
that of their relations with whites were not as significant as the
history of white settlement. No other major historian – at least
before the 1970s – had more personal contact with Africans, or
more to do with their administration. Yet Theal, the pioneer, the
father of South African historiography, did more than anyone else
to establish a tradition of strongly pro-colonist, anti-black historical writing, and to create the racist paradigm which lay at the
core of that tradition and which served to justify white rule.

3   Race and class

Theal did not have a philosophical cast of mind. He did not stand back from his work and try to analyse, say, the role of race in history. Yet for all his talk about just 'telling the facts' about the past, his *History* and his other works are shot through with assumptions and comments that illustrate his ideas on race and class. Though given special shape by the local context in which he wrote, these ideas were not dissimilar from those of his peers in Europe. Theal's special interest in blacks and their relationship with whites ensured that he paid attention to current ideas of race. In describing people and events, he dwelt on the significance of such things as physical type and blood type, and assumed that they were directly related to culture, which explained why people acted as they had. For him, as for many European scholars of the late nineteenth century, race was all-important: race and culture, indeed, determined and shaped history.

Like his contemporaries, Theal believed that mankind was divided into discrete racial groups, with rigid, clearly defined boundaries. Races could, then, be discussed in stereotypical terms. Biologically determined, races could be ordered hierarchically in a 'great chain of being' and classified according to their position on a 'ladder of progress', which stretched upwards from savagery through barbarism to civilisation.

South Africa's 'true original inhabitants', the San, stood at the bottom of that ladder. These 'wild savages' were so primitive that 'one can hardly conceive of living beings entitled to be termed *men* in a lower condition than the Bushmen'. Theal shared the contemporary view that races had distinctive physical characteristics, and wrote of the San that their lower jaws were 'only surpassed in feebleness by that of the Australian black'. The 'wild Bushmen' were 'more like jackals than human beings....' Another contemporary way of ordering people was by skull size and Theal was quick

to bring forward alleged craniological evidence asserting that
hunters and herders had different skull sizes to explain why they
responded to whites in different ways.[1] The Khoikhoi pastoralists,
unlike the San, were 'capable of improvement', but their 'training
needed two centuries and a half to complete', and there 'is no instance on record of one of them having ever attained a position
that required either much intellectual power or much mechanical
skill'. 'Probably if intellectual enjoyment be excluded', he continued, 'the Hottentots were among the happiest people in existence.' But, he added, 'a more improvident, unstable, thoughtless
people never existed'. [2] On the other hand, he also remarked that
'they speculated upon objects in nature in a way that no Bantu
ever did, and their ideas on these subjects, though seemingly
absurd, at least bore evidence of a disposition to think'.[3]

Bantu-speaking Africans – and the term 'Africans' will here arbi-
trarily be confined to them – occupied a position above the
hunters and the herders, but below whites on the ladder of progress. Some of Theal's stereotyping of Africans was as crude as
that of the Khoisan people, but overall the picture he presented of
Africans was much fuller and consequently more nuanced and
complex. His generalisations about Africans as a group, though,
were negative ones. Thus, for example, they 'have great power in
imitating, but very little of inventing, so that they are highly conservative in character'.[4] They were 'so thoughtless and so indif-
ferent to the wants of future generations that such a thing as the
preservation of a forest never occurred to them'. Among them,
'sanitary arrangements ... were unknown and uncared for, as the
sense of smell was much duller with these people than with Europeans'.[5] Contradicting this, he wrote elsewhere that the Kwena
moved their towns 'for sanitary reasons'.[6] To his generalisations,
moreover, he admitted exceptions: not all Africans were the same.
The Kwena, for example, 'were for barbarians highly skilled as ar-
tisans'.[7]

Theal sometimes distinguished between the people of the
coastal strip – those whom scholars would later term Nguni – and
the 'people of the interior'. He claimed that the people of the
coast – whom he knew personally from having lived and worked
among them for some years – prided themselves on adhering faith-
fully to their promises. 'The word of an interior chief', on the
other hand, 'was seldom worth anything.' 'The man of the coast
was brave in the field; his inland kinsman was in general an arrant

coward. The one was modest ... the other ... an intolerable boaster.' And 'a kraal on the coast was a scene of purity when compared with one in some parts of the interior', where 'all that the most depraved imagination could devise to rouse the lowest passions of the young females was practised.' 'A description', added this late-Victorian, 'is impossible', so leaving it to his readers to think of the most depraved things they knew.[8]

Theal pointed to class and gender distinctions among Africans. Slavery did not exist among the coastal people, but 'there could be no more heartless slave-owners in the world than some of the people of the interior. Their bondsmen were the descendants of those who had been scattered by war....' Women were everywhere 'drudges performing all the severest labour', but 'were quite as cheerful as the men, and knew as well as Europeans how to make their influence felt'.[9] He also admitted that individual Africans whom he had met did not conform to his stereotypical picture. He could, he wrote, testify 'from personal experience' that 'the chief of our time who possesses the highest moral qualities of any in South Africa is Khama', the Tswana ruler, who 'was capable of acting with such generosity and good feeling as would do credit to any European'.[10] Other individuals received at least half-hearted praise. Ndlambe of the Ngqika was 'a splendid barbarian'. Sarili, Gcaleka paramount, whom he interviewed in the 1870s, 'possessed many good qualities'. Oba, whom he looked after in 1877, was 'good natured, witty, and generous ... sensible, strong in attachment and faithful to his promises'. Moshoeshoe of Lesotho, 'crafty as only one of his race can be', was yet 'the most intelligent Bantu chief ever known in South Africa' and 'one of the most cautious and prudent of men'. He could not be judged by the same standards as whites, because he shared the African vice of a lack of honesty and truthfulness, but he was nonetheless 'a great man'.[11] On Sandile's decision to give up strong drink in 1877, Theal commented: 'It would be hard to find an instance of a man having more command over himself than this changeable barbarian certainly had.'[12]

While Theal did allow, then, that 'on occasion individuals are capable of rising to a high standard', he was quick to add that 'the great mass shows little aptitude for European culture'. When they were young, African children could keep pace with European children, but after a certain point, 'the Bantu youth ... is found unable to make further progress. His intellect has become sluggish, and frequently he exhibits a decided repugnance, if not an incapacity, to learn anything more.' Even the exceptions were not really equal to Europeans: ministers of religion, for instance, 'as earnest, intelligent and devoted to their calling as average Europeans ... were very weak in everything that relates to finance'.[13] The ex-Lovedale teacher wrote of a stereotypical educated African:

With abundance of conceit, but devoid of perseverance, he does not attempt to qualify himself for some useful occupation, but goes about discontented or gives way to intemperance. It is possible that this class of man may prove troublesome in the future. They are certainly neither so useful to their race nor so comfortable and cheerful in their own lives as those who have had a good training in manual labour on a farm.[14]

Mhlangaso, an Mpondo sub-chief who had been to Lovedale, he described as 'just sufficiently educated from books to give him power for mischief'.[15] Such statements served in fact to justify contemporary racial discrimination, from which educated Africans were not exempt.

Though Africans were, in his eyes, capable of 'improvement', they were subject to the historical laws of social evolution. European habits of industry, for example, were the result of long generations of development. In his *Kaffir Folk-lore*, Theal spoke of Africans as inherently capable of joining the ranks of the civilised – their 'intellectual abilities are of no mean order', and their 'reasoning powers were quite equal to those of a white man'[16] – but he believed that African culture held individuals in the thraldom of unprogressive, irrational forces. Africans at missions had minds 'shackled by hereditary superstition'; even in third-generation Christians the old religion showed its presence, so that the profession of Christianity by an African only gave a Christian colouring to his inherited beliefs.[17] In the distant future, and given a decisive break with the old culture, Africans might become 'civilised'. But that transformation was so far off that Theal gave its consequences no attention.

When the slaves were emancipated in the 1830s, he claimed, the men and women freed had 'reverted to type': they had once been 'useful' but now became indolent paupers and social pests: 'a freed slave usually chose to live in a filthy hovel upon coarse and scanty food rather than toil for something better.... when sickness came he was a burden upon the public.'[18] The implication Theal wished his readers to draw was that blacks required the discipline of masters and should not be free to run their own lives.

Much of Theal's *History* recounted the story of the impact of a superior civilisation – that of the whites – upon an inferior culture. He did not agree that all men were equal, or that the law should treat them as such, as it did at the Cape. For him it was natural that the Cape colonists should not have wanted to see 'men of an inferior race' trained to use arms, and it was wrong for such men to be treated as equal under the law.[19] Little, he said, could be understood of the working of the minds of barbarians.

Like many contemporary writers, Theal paid close attention to blood types and the mixture of blood. He regarded purity of race as the key to white advancement; miscegenation brought about social decline. The fall of the Portuguese empire in Africa could be traced, he believed, to race mixing.[20] On the Cape frontier 'nearly every case of cruelty by colonists was committed by men who either had coloured blood in their veins or who had mixed with the uncivilised coloured people on terms of equality'.[21] The Griqua had inherited from their Khoi mothers 'an amount of restlessness, and want of frugality, that tended to prevent their advance'.[22] The pure 'Asiatics' who according to his ethnography had settled on the coast were grave and dignified; the mixed breeds, on the other hand, had 'all the superstitions of both races from which they were descended'.[23]

Miscegenation could involve the infusion of 'superior blood'. Theal probably knew of the work of R. J. Mann, Natal's first Superintendent General of Education, who claimed that the 'Kaffirs' were a hybrid race, 'a higher and nobler Arabian stock having been mixed with a coarse Negro stock'.[24] In turn Theal remarked that the Xhosa were capable of improvement because they had among their ancestors 'Asiatics of high intelligence'.[25] An admixture of 'superior blood' might also explain why an individual did not conform to the racial norm, but could approximate to the European 'level of civilisation'. That Cape colonial society included large numbers of people of mixed descent was something Theal did not face up to; he spoke of interbreeding between whites and people of colour as if it was something that occurred only on the frontier, and as if the offspring did not belong to the colony.

If race lay at the centre of Theal's categorisation of people, he also had a strong sense of class. Race and class were linked in his understanding; low class whites were, for example, those likely to mix with blacks. He reported that 'respectable burghers' had said that the whites who had joined Khoi on the raiding party which went from Stellenbosch to the east in 1702 were 'miscreants without families or homes, being chiefly fugitives from justice and men of loose character'.[26] Theal also spoke of the 'thousands of worthless characters of both sexes' who migrated to the Witwatersrand after the discovery of gold.[27] When he visited England in 1894, he was horrified by the 'ragged, unkempt, dirty and puny people' he noticed in the streets of Liverpool. Of poor whites in general, whether in South Africa or elsewhere, he could remark, 'the surplus individuals in this class are a nuisance and source of danger'. And he continued:

It is not prejudice against colour which causes inability to fraternise [between white and black], it is the same feeling as that which prevents a first-class artisan from associating in a workshop with untrained men of his own race: in both cases the individual with knowledge and skill must have authority over the others or all self-respect is lost.[28]

While he recognised class differences among whites, and despised whites of lower class who mixed with blacks, whites nevertheless in his eyes belonged to the superior race. All Africans, even the literate Christian class, were inherently part of an inferior culture. In Theal's way of looking at the world, race was more important than class.

4 Racial myths and Theal's legacy

Later historians often ignored Theal's crude and sometimes bi-
zarre views on race and class but took over from him certain central racial myths, which he did more than anyone else to
propagate. Before whites arrived, he would have his readers believe, there was 'almost constant strife and cruelty and misery'.[1]
He repeated again and again that war was the typical existence of
the savage tribes of Africa. 'As soon as one gets beneath the sur-
face of black traditions anywhere in South Africa', he wrote, it
became 'certain that the normal condition of things was pillage
and bloodshed'.[2] '"The man who plunders" would be almost an
ideal title of praise in the Bantu mind', he wrote, 'because it
would signify the power to do so, and by these people power is
more respected than anything else.'[3] The Mfecane was discussed
under the chapter heading 'Terrible Destruction of Bantu Tribes'.
The Zulu rulers were 'human hyenas', and in general Africans
were 'fickle barbarians prone to robbery and unscrupulous in
shedding blood'.[4] The Shakan upheaval was nothing new: 'long
before the time of Tshaka despots as clever and as ruthless as he
spread desolation over wide tracts of land' and 'cannibalism as
practised in the Lesuto and in Natal during the early years of the
nineteenth century was no new custom with sections of the Bantu
race'.[5]

Theal presented a near unmitigated picture of black barbarism:
blacks had accomplished nothing significant; everything of importance had come from outside Africa. He accepted the view of
R. N. Hall's *Ancient Mines of Rhodesia* (1900) that Great Zimbabwe
had been built by some mysterious, alien civilisation, rejecting
David Randall MacIver's argument (1906) that the structures that
remained were of indigenous origin, a view confirmed after
Theal's death by Gertrude Caton-Thompson in excavations begun
in 1929, and more recently by Peter Garlake. The ancient mine

shafts of Zimbabwe could not have been the work of Bantu-speakers, Theal wrote, because they could not have been dug without portable artificial light, and 'even the most advanced Bantu knew nothing of such a device'.[6] Blacks were – as barbarians – stupid and irrational. The cattle-killing of 1857 was 'a blunder such as a child would hardly have made'.[7] His picture of African societies was essentially one of changelessness; savage or barbarian societies, according to the Victorian view, were inherently incapable of significant change, and at best changed very slowly. 'The condition of the Bantu at the beginning of the sixteenth century', he wrote, 'is the condition of the great majority of them today'.[8]

Theal began writing his *History* in the 1870s as white rule was everywhere being consolidated in South Africa. But he remained very conscious of potential threats to white control. He did not share the view, held by many whites at the Cape in the mid and late nineteenth century, that the blacks would die out in the face of the advance of 'European civilisation'. 'The history of the Cape is already written in that of America', wrote one mid-century commentator, 'and the gradual increase of the white race must eventually though slowly ensure the disappearance of the black.'[9] Theal, on the contrary, referred again and again in his works to the 'amazing' growth in the numbers of Bantu-speaking people in South Africa, people whom he believed 'probably the most prolific people on the face of the earth', who 'multiply at a marvellous rate'.[10] Whites were 'too few in number to occupy and hold the great interior plateau' without much greater immigration, which he hoped for but did not expect. His visit to the country of his birth in 1894 prompted this reflection:

The European race has no guarantee of being permanently on South African, as it is on Canadian soil.... Great as the increase of white people has been of late years, the increase of the blacks has been enormously greater.... think where will the white man find himself a century hence if there is not a very large immigration. Swept away – at least from the open country – by the sheer passive force of the amazingly prolific Bantu people. If a leader of influence were to rise among them even today, and teach them their strength and how to use it for their own ends, there are many districts in South Africa in which such land difficulties as have already been experienced to a slight extent would be felt in a tenfold aggravated form. How will it be when the Bantu are three or four times as numerous as they are now?[11]

Theal also wrote of how the whites 'ought to be as one in the face of the great mass of barbarism beyond and among them'.[12] He believed the Bambatha rebellion in Natal in 1906 showed clearly that Africans still desired to be free of European control. A strong, united government over the whole region south of the Zambezi – Theal's 'South Africa' – was necessary to deal with this threat; in his last years Theal hoped that the lesser Union achieved in 1910 would go some way to meet that need.[13]

* * *

Theal's interest in early black history, first aroused at Lovedale and continued when he worked for the Native Affairs Department, was inspired in part by his wish to contribute to the work being done in Europe on 'primitive peoples', their habits and customs. But there was also, by the last years of the century, a political purpose to his work. From 1895, partly under Rhodes's influence, he became obsessed with the question of the early migration of Africans into South Africa. While he worked in London, Lisbon and other European centres between 1897 and 1905, he looked continually for information on early movements of 'the Bantu', as he called them, and after he returned to Cape Town he continued to read as widely as he could on 'Bantu origins', trying to trace them historically back to Egypt. Much of his latter-day interest in early black history, it is clear, arose from a concern to find evidence to prove that Bantu-speakers arrived in South Africa relatively late, and therefore had no more right to land in the country than whites. Reporting to the Cape government on the opening of the Vatican archives, he wrote: 'surely we, who have such a deep interest in tracing the movements of the Bantu tribes as far back as we possibly can, ought to avail ourselves of the information that is almost certainly to be found in them.'[14] In 1906 he told a parliamentary committee that the Mfengu 'were dispersed in Natal by the warriors of Chaka and came down into the Colony, and their ancestors came down from the Zambesi only a little more than three hundred years ago'. Then he added: 'What more right has the Fingo to privileges in South Africa than any member of the European family?'[15]

Theal was not the first to argue that whites and Africans entered southern Africa at approximately the same time in the seventeenth century. W. C. Holden's *The Past and Future of the Kaffir Races* (1866) had, for example, suggested a history of African settlement extending back many centuries. Theal powerfully reinforced the popular white view of the late arrival of Bantu-speaking people, and did more than anyone else to establish a pseudo-scientific basis for the myth of the empty land. Especially in his more polemical writing, but also in his *History*, he asserted that Africans arrived not long before the Dutch: migrating southwards and northwards at the same time, the two met on the Fish River in the eighteenth century. He rejected Cappon's assertion that Africans had lived in the Zuurveld for generations before whites arrived.[16] If black and white met on the Fish, Africans had no more right to land than the colonists.

In a speech given in Cape Town in 1909, when the process of political unification of the South African colonies was all but complete, Theal told his audience that the Ethiopian movement – the proliferation of independent African churches, which he saw as an oppositional, black nationalist unity movement – represented a potential challenge to white control. He went on to argue that Africans

like everyone else ... were learning that unity was strength, and when it came to the union of these people holding the idea that Africa should be for the Africans, the European people would have a difficult matter to deal with. He did not say it would be war, but these people would oppose us in every way they possibly could .... they really wanted to ... get rid of us altogether.

History could be used to combat this 'menace'. He recalled that when he had lived in the eastern Cape in the 1860s and 1870s, he had found that the Africans there believed their forebears had lived in the area for a very long time, whereas whites were seen as recent intruders. '"The land", said the Bantus, "belongs to us, we ought to govern ourselves."' They should be told the facts:

In reality this country was not the Bantu's originally any more than it was the white man's, because the Bantus were also immigrants.... most of their ancestors migrated to South Africa in comparatively recent times.

Dr Theal then, the newspaper report of his address continues, 'referred in some detail to the movement of the several tribes, in order to show that none of the tribes had been in South Africa for many centuries.... We must, he emphasised, prove to these people that we were no more intruders than they were, and that they enjoyed now as much as they were entitled to.'[17] Earlier, Theal had stated categorically,

the Bantu now in and south of Natal are very recent immigrants, their
ancestors having come down from the north less than four centuries
ago.... It was into this vast stretch of vacant land that white men moved
from the south and black men from the north almost if not quite simultaneously. Near its centre they met, and then a struggle began as to
which should go further. Bear in mind that it was not an attempt of white
men to take possession of land owned by black men, it was an effort on
both sides to get as much unoccupied land as possible....[18]

The evidence Theal produced for the relatively late arrival of
Bantu-speakers in South Africa was extremely flimsy. Much of his
argument was based on the assumption that the 'Mumbos' who
attacked the Portuguese settlements on the Zambezi in the sixteenth century were the same people as the Abambo of South
Africa. Monica Wilson was right to call Theal's speculation that
the Mumbo were the Abambo 'mumbo-jumbo'.[19] Theal's only evidence for his assertion that the Thonga arrived in the Delagoa Bay
hinterland in the fifteenth century was that a man on the Portuguese expedition of 1498 under Vasco da Gama could make himself understood to them in a West African Guinean language.[20]
Ironically, some of the very documents Theal published in his
nine volumes of *Records of South Eastern Africa* were used by Monica
Wilson, forty years after his death, to demolish the myth of late
African settlement in the Ciskei and Transkei.[21] These were the
accounts of shipwrecked sailors who mentioned the indigenous
people they encountered along the south-eastern coast. Theal got
the places of landfall wrong, enabling him to suggest that Bantu-
speakers lived further north than we now know to have been the
case.[22] But beyond that, he was blind to the fact that these accounts provide clear evidence of a stable and settled Bantu-
speaking population in the area by the seventeenth century. In his
histories – and especially the shorter ones, which were much more
widely read than the multi-volume *History* – he continued to argue
that African 'hordes migrated slowly, often remaining for two or
three years at favourable locations on the way',[23] and were still
moving southwards when the whites arrived. Theal was categorical
that Africans did not inhabit any part of South Africa when whites
first settled in the seventeenth century, outside the northern
Transvaal and Natal.[24] As the Khoisan did not count in his reck-
oning – the twentieth-century challenge came, of course, from the
Bantu-speakers – the land which the whites entered was therefore
empty. Africans and men of European origin had colonised South

Africa simultaneously. And where whites had entered land settled by Africans, this merely repeated the earlier intrusion of Khoi and Bantu-speakers into the lands of the San, the only true aborigines.[25]

When he reached the 1830s in his narrative, Theal claimed that the land the Voortrekkers entered was uninhabited, and a map in the 1891 edition of his *History* showed a large portion of the Transvaal and Natal to have been 'territory almost depopulated by the Zulu wars before 1834'. He had read W. C. Harris's *Wild Sports of Southern Africa* – it is included in his list of books in the *Compendium* – but he chose to ignore the evidence of Harris's sketchmap, based on his expedition through the highveld in 1836–7, of extensive African settlement there at that time.[26] In propagating a myth of an empty interior in the 1830s, Theal was legitimating white settlement.

* * *

The settler tradition established by Theal was directly continued by George Edward Cory (1862–1935), head of the chemistry department at Rhodes University College, and amateur historian. Cory very consciously saw himself as following in Theal's footsteps.[27] Like Theal, he sought to reconcile Boer and Briton: though his work focused on the 1820 British settlers, it was sympathetic to the Voortrekkers.[28] He also followed Theal in interviewing Africans, and, unlike Theal, left an invaluable transcript of his interviews. His misleadingly entitled *The Rise of South Africa* was quite as anti-black as Theal's *History of South Africa*. The frontispiece to the third volume, on the years 1834–8, depicted an African smoking a pipe with a peaceful rural scene in the background. Beneath is the caption: 'Meditating mischief'. Cory followed Theal too in deliberately seeking to show that whites in South Africa – English and Dutch-speakers – had not been ruthless in their treatment of blacks, contrary to what the missionaries had alleged.[29]

Apart from Cory's writings, Theal's racial myths were reproduced in the works of numerous amateur authors, ranging from S. Modiri Molema (1891–1965), the young African author of *The Bantu Past and Present* (1920), to Sydney Olivier (1859–1943), a social democrat highly critical of South African racial policy, and Gustav Preller (1875–1943), leading Afrikaner nationalist historian. In a book published in 1929, Olivier spoke of the colonists being 'confronted with competitive pastoral hordes of blacks coming down from the north as they came up from the south', and of the trekkers in the 1830s moving 'into unoccupied territories where they had every right to settle'; sometimes, he continued, they had 'to compete with a simultaneous counter-immigration of military Bantu tribes'.[30] Afrikaner nationalist historians of the 1930s and 1940s, for whom the main theme in the South African past was the epic story of Afrikaner survival and the struggle for unity, took over many of Theal's racial ideas, and like him blamed interfering missionaries for much of what had 'gone wrong'.[31] Theal's racial ideas are also to be found, say, in the series of articles on 'The History of the Bantu' which appeared in a conservative Johannesburg paper for Africans in 1932.[32]

In the first decade of this century the establishment of history departments in the colleges of higher education at Cape Town and Stellenbosch signalled the beginning of the professionalisation of South African history. The Prince of Wales Chair of History at the South African College in Cape Town was founded in 1902 because of the concern expressed during the South African War that the study of history be put on a sound footing, at a time when Theal's work was criticised as pro-Boer. Those who set up the history chair at Cape Town hoped for a different approach, and the first generation of English professional historians were to be strikingly pro-British in their approach. But Eric Walker (1886–1976), the incumbent of the chair from 1911 to 1936, took some time to break with the Theal mould so far as ideas about race were concerned. In his early work he reproduced many of Theal's myths. His *Historical Atlas* (1922) included a map headed 'Bantu Devastation and the Great Trek, 1820–48', which showed a large area, larger even than in the map in Theal's *History*, as 'depopulated'. In his most influential work, his single-volume *History of South Africa* (1928), Walker suggested that as a result of the Mfecane, the interior was 'cleared of most of its inhabitants', and he wrote of 'a whirling mass of tribesmen'.[33]

Those who accepted Theal's racial myths were often more Eurocentric than he, in that they devoted less attention in their work to blacks. Others did call for the study of the history of blacks. Among the speakers at a meeting held in London in January 1902 to promote the scheme for a chair in history at Cape Town was F. York Powell, Regius Professor of Modern History at the University of Oxford. He spoke of the need for the teaching of native history. They had in South Africa some of the finest native races, and these races had to be reckoned with and understood. The lack of understanding had been the cause of many of our troubles with the native races. He wanted to see a professor of history and a professor dealing with the history of native races established side by side; and the system would not be complete until they had them.[34]

Another supporter of the scheme pointed out that 'there was nothing in the shape of a history of the Bantu races and their institutions'.[35] As we shall see, however, it was to be more than a half-century before professional historians turned to the study of African societies.[36]

The racial paradigm of Theal's day underwent a major shift in the 1960s. According to Verwoerd's 'separate development' notions, blacks were no longer regarded as subordinate and inferior, but instead were to be excluded from the South African body politic and allowed their independence in their own 'homelands'. Similarly, they were excluded from South African history. C. F. J. Muller's *Five Hundred Years. A History of South Africa* (1969) – the very title an assertion of the length of time claimed for white involvement in South Africa – stood in the Theal tradition in that, unlike the work of Afrikaner nationalist historians, it tried to consider the history of English-speakers and Afrikaners in an impartial way. But it relegated Africans to an appendix, the year before the Bantu Homelands Citizenship Act provided the means to strip most Africans of their South African citizenship. In the year citizenship was restored to some Africans (1986), a new text attempted to bring Africans back into the South African story, but still not as if their history was as important as that of whites, and some of the old Theal myths remained.[37]

How long-lasting Theal's influence was may be seen, for example, from a textbook written by the leading Afrikaner historian, F. A. van Jaarsveld, and published in 1975, which explicitly acknowledged Theal as one of its major sources.[38] According to Van Jaarsveld, 'The Bushmen were eradicated in large numbers by the Hottentots, the Bantu and the Whites', which suggested, contrary to all the evidence, that whites had not played a larger role in that process than others. The early history of South Africa was, for Van Jaarsveld, 'one of migratory waves and conflicts among the Bushmen, the Hottentots and the Bantu'. 'White and Bantu met one another along the east coast as a result of independent movements in opposite directions.... Both Black and White were migrants.' 'The separate national groupings found among the Bantu ... are traditional ones and date from the time of the earliest immigration and settlement.' When black and white met, the former were 'uncivilised, primitive'. As a result of the Mfecane, the interior became 'one massive bloodbath' and the trekkers entered 'empty land ... unpopulated territory'. 'It was the whites who, after the Difaqane period of devastation and exterminatory war, brought peace and order to the Bantu nations.... the tribes eventually accepted the authority of the Whites and helped to tame the land as peaceful, law-abiding labourers.'[39]

* * *

Theal, then, the first great historian of South Africa, the influential proponent of a settler tradition in South African historical writing, helped create a picture of the past in which, if blacks were present at all, it was in a distinctly subordinate role. Blacks might rob whites and fight them, but they were not equal actors in the historical drama. The racist myths Theal employed were still being repeated by historians more than a half-century after his death. But in the very year of his death, an historian who began a very different tradition in historical writing on South Africa published his first important work.

PART 2
W. M. Macmillan and C. W. de Kiewiet

5 Macmillan: the South African years, and after

The revisionists of the early 1970s tended to attack a stereotypical representation of liberal history. But the early liberal historians of the 1920s and 1930s should be distinguished from those who wrote in the 1950s and 1960s, and the particular strengths and limitations of individuals also need to be defined and assessed. We begin with William Miller Macmillan (1885–1974), first and most important of the early liberals. His career is probably better documented than that of any other South African historian, for besides his autobiography of his South African years, which he recorded on tape late in life,[1] his papers survive,[2] his widow has written a biography of the years after he left South Africa,[3] and Jay Naidoo has written a dissertation on his career.[4]

* * *

Macmillan was, like Theal, an immigrant, and believed, as Theal had, that being an immigrant lent detachment to his view of South Africa and its past. But unlike Theal he did not arrive in South Africa as a grown man. He was born in Aberdeen, in Scotland, and was taken to Africa when he was 5. That he was born in Scotland always remained important to him: he lived in South Africa feeling he belonged elsewhere, and he tells us in his memoirs that he became increasingly of this mind. He was, he says, unrepentantly an expatriate Scot.[5] So in this respect too he was unlike Theal: he did not come to identify with the dominant white culture of his adopted country.

He grew up in the south-western Cape. His father, who had previously been a Church of Scotland missionary in India, became in effect housemaster in charge of a residence at Victoria College (later the University of Stellenbosch). In his memoirs Macmillan paints a picture of a relatively relaxed Cape society before the South African War.[6] Though a member of the English-speaking minority in the village of Stellenbosch, and often called a *rooinek*, he nevertheless got on well with the Cape Dutch, who were broadminded and inclusive in their nationalism. Yet he speaks also of an awareness, from the time of the Jameson Raid onwards, that the country was heading for civil war, and of a threat to the way of life he knew. This threat came from the north, from a more exclusive Afrikaner nationalism. There seemed to him to be two distinct traditions in the country: a liberal Cape one, with which his father and he identified, that 'gave an assured place to Coloureds and Africans',[7] and in the interior another tradition which he disliked mainly because it was, being exclusively Afrikaner, anti-British, but also because it was anti-black.[8]

As war approached, the teenage Macmillan naturally associated with the British cause: shortly before war broke out he became a bugler in the Victoria College Volunteers, and during it he served as a member of the Stellenbosch town guard. In the course of the war his father was dismissed from his post because, the family believed, he was British. This left his father so financially insecure that a few years later he asked his son, then at Oxford, for a loan of twenty pounds.[9] This impoverishment in his own family must have helped develop the young Macmillan's social conscience, and his determination to help right the world's wrongs.

Cecil Rhodes died in 1902 and left money in his will for scholarships to Oxford. At the local Stellenbosch secondary school Macmillan was runner-up to the man chosen for the first scholarship awarded to the school in terms of Rhodes's will. But Toby Muller, father of the historian C. F. J. Muller, so disapproved of Rhodes that he declined the scholarship. Macmillan was given it, and he sailed for England in 1903. He believed himself to be, with one possible exception, the only Rhodes scholar ever to have met Rhodes face to face, when the great man had visited Stellenbosch in the 1890s.[10] At Merton College, Macmillan expected to read classics, but his background in that subject was not thought good enough by his Oxford tutors, and he was advised to read history instead. In his autobiography he remarks that doubts about his capacity for abstract reasoning helped lead him to history. While at school his history had come from Henty rather than from anything taught in the classroom, where his teachers spoke of British misrule, of the Black Circuit and Slagtersnek. The first book he read from cover to cover told a very different story: it was a life of David Livingstone.[11]

When he read history at Oxford he had no expectations that he would become a professional historian, and he did not confine his intellectual interests to the rather narrow history course Oxford offered. He studied the Puritan Revolution as his special subject with the famous historian Charles Firth, but the lecturers who most impressed him were two political philosophers, Ernest Barker and A. L. Smith, Master of Balliol, men deeply concerned with current social issues. When asked to deliver an historical paper, he chose to write on the Highland clearances; he was morally outraged that his uncle, a crofter, had been forced to move so that a deer-park could be created for those he termed 'plutocrats'.[12] His friends at Oxford were men with strong social consciences; from them he heard frequently of Toynbee Hall, established to help the poor of the East End of London.[13]

He did not get a first for his degree, and unlike Eric Walker, who arrived at Merton when he was in his last year there and passed with a first, he did not begin teaching history when he left the university. Instead, as was expected of him, this son of the manse enrolled for a divinity course in Aberdeen, preparatory to entering the church. He was not to complete it, but Christianity always remained important to him. His widow remembers how influenced he had been by his study at this time of the Hebrew prophets, who impressed him as social critics.[14]

After the three years at Oxford followed what he calls in his memoirs 'four more varied and instructive wanderjahre'.[15] He soon developed doubts about the divinity course – one of his papers for it turned out to be more of a Fabian tract on current affairs than a treatise on theology[16] – and, having saved the thirty pounds needed, he returned to South Africa on what he rather oddly described, at the end of his life, as 'the first of my innumerable African expeditions'. Besides visiting Stellenbosch, he went to the eastern Cape and saw for the first time something of 'the greater South Africa'.[17] Back in Aberdeen, his unhappiness with the divinity course grew, and some pastoral work he did proved unsatisfying, so he began applying for history posts, among them a new chair in the Transvaal University College at Pretoria (which went to Leo Fouché (1880–1949), who was in 1934 to succeed him at Wits). Unsuccessful in his applications, he decided he should gain further historical training, and acquire it in Germany, that country then being regarded as at the forefront of historical scholarship. After first improving his German, he spent a semester at Berlin

University, where he was much influenced by Gustav Schmoller, the most eminent German economic historian of his generation and social critic. Schmoller taught Macmillan how necessary it was to see contemporary social issues in historical perspective.[18] Macmillan enrolled for a thesis on poor relief, but it was never to be completed. Back in Britain in 1910, needing money, he applied for the post of lecturer and head of a new dual department of history and economics at Rhodes University College in Grahamstown. In November 1910 he received a letter telling him to report there in the New Year. Before leaving England he joined the Fabian Society.

* * *

In the south-western Cape Macmillan had had, with one or two exceptions, no contact with Africans at all. He now found himself in the very self-consciously English town of Grahamstown, in an area where Africans constituted the overwhelming majority of the population. But he did not show any interest in their history: George Cory, Professor of Chemistry at Rhodes – who was in the audience at the first public lecture Macmillan gave in 1912 – seemed to have made the history of the eastern Cape frontier his own field, though Macmillan soon realised that the kind of history Cory was writing was deeply flawed. While at Grahamstown, however, Macmillan did not venture into any aspect of South African history. He taught European and medieval history, and at a meeting with fellow historians claimed that what South African students needed was more European and medieval rather than South African history, where the literature was so sparse and poor.[19] For his own research he decided to tackle – and one must remember that he was a lecturer in economics as well as history – a contemporary social problem.

A local medical man, Frederick Saunders, a fellow Scot who was Medical Officer of Health in Grahamstown, directed him to the inadequate sanitation in the town. Macmillan's first pamphlet, published anonymously in 1915, was on sanitary reform in the city. It led to his being approached by the local bishop to give a lecture to his clergy on what might be done to improve the wretched conditions and poverty in which some of their parishioners were living. At first Macmillan thought he would merely tell them about Rowntree's work on the scale and significance of poverty in York, but then he decided to see for himself how the poor lived in Grahamstown, and to discover the facts concerning their poverty. Using the concept of the poverty datum line developed by Rowntree in England, he worked out that between 450 and 600 of the 6000 whites in the town lived below such a poverty line. At this time blacks were entirely ignored in his work. His lecture led to the publication of another booklet, *A Study of Economic Conditions in a Non-Industrial South African Town*. 'Poor whiteism' had aroused considerable interest for some years, but it had been assumed to be a problem affecting Afrikaners. Macmillan's work attracted wide interest partly because he showed there were English-speaking poor, and because he was the first to use the techniques of social science to produce and analyse facts on the extent of poverty, while like the Fabians he also went on to suggest practical reforms. John X. Merriman, the former Cape prime minister, was one of those impressed by his work, and he suggested it ought to be extended to the Karoo; and the Dutch Reformed Church asked him to speak at one of its conferences on 'Poor Whiteism'.

Before he continued with his work on white poverty, Macmillan returned to Britain at the end of 1915. Like later visits – he went to Britain roughly every five years while he was in South Africa – this one was important partly because it helped him to see South African issues in perspective, but also because he was able to meet some of the leading British intellectuals of the time. He got to know A. F. Pollard, who did more than any other historian of his day for the professionalisation of the discipline, and through him met the Fabian socialists Beatrice and Sidney Webb, founders of the London School of Economics, and prolific writers on British social issues. The Webbs stressed that poverty had structural causes, and was not merely a sign of individual moral failure.[20] Sidney Webb reviewed Macmillan's Grahamstown pamphlet favourably in the *New Statesman*. Through the Webbs, he met R. H. Tawney and J. L. and Barbara Hammond, the most famous socialist historians of the day, who wrote much on the harshness of industrialisation and its impact on ordinary people.[21]

Macmillan went to Britain in 1915 in part to decide whether or not he should join up for war service. In Britain he listened to Philip Snowden and other pacifists, and concluded that there was no good reason to abandon his 'African work'.[22] He returned to Grahamstown more than ever committed, after meeting the Webbs, to the study of contemporary social issues. In 1916 he produced further pamphlets on post-war problems and on local government, then heard that the School of Mines in Johannesburg was advertising for a first professor of history. Despite the fact that he had not written any history, he got the post, and at the age of 32 became early in 1917 one of the founder members of the Arts Faculty of what in 1919 became a University College and in 1922 took the name of the University of the Witwatersrand. Grahamstown was too isolated and too small a place for someone concerned to play a role in the national life of the country. In Johannesburg, Macmillan wrote in 1919, one could, more than anywhere else, see the meeting of the old and the new, and the painful clash between them.[23] Economically, the Rand was very much the heart of the new South Africa, its strength based now not only on the mining industry but also on secondary industry, which had grown greatly during the war years. And at Wits a small group of able academics alive to this new social reality – Macmillan prime among them – forged in the 1920s a new form of liberalism.[24] Ironically, now that he was based in Johannesburg, Macmillan's research took him, first into the rural areas of the Cape and the Free State, and then back to the very eastern Cape he had moved away from. He was never to write about the process of industrialisation itself at any length, or about, say, the early social history of Johannesburg.[25] When Macmillan looked for the roots of South African poverty, he found them, first in the early history of the trekboer, and then on the Cape frontier in the 1820s, 1830s and 1840s, but not in the industrial process which, fuelled above all by gold, did more than anything else to transform South Africa in the first half of his life.

* * *

After moving to Johannesburg, where he was to spend his most productive years, Macmillan initially continued his work on white poverty, extending his interest to rural South Africa in general. He took up Merriman's suggestion that he investigate conditions in the Karoo, and he tried to find out where the poor whites flocking into Johannesburg came from, and why they had left the land. Though he looked at some Chamber of Mines records and those of the Johannesburg Public Relief Board,[26] he soon decided that the only way to understand the movement off the land was to discover for himself what conditions were like in the countryside. Now a professor of history, he recognised that the problem of rural poverty should be seen in historical perspective. So he read the little he could find relevant to the early agricultural history of the country, and then went to see for himself.

The most important secondary work he used was that of Leo Fouché on the emergence of the stock-farmers and their movement into the interior of the Cape in the eighteenth century. For Fouché that migration, which had opened up the interior for Dutch settlement, provided the key to understanding South African history.[27] As essential to Macmillan's intellectual development were the journeys he made every vacation to various parts of the country. In order to follow the route of white settlement, he went first to the Caledon district at the beginning of 1919, then to Oudtshoorn, where there were more well-to-do farmers but also more white poor, and then on to the Free State, where he suggested a minimum wage for white bywoners and was told that if such a wage were introduced, whites would simply be replaced by blacks, who would be paid less.[28] By May 1919 he was ready to present some of his findings in the form of a series of five lectures which he delivered in Johannesburg; they were printed later that year under the title *The South African Agrarian Problem and Its Historical Development.*

Macmillan's focus would probably have switched from 'poor whites' to 'the still poorer browns and blacks' by a natural progression in his thinking, and also because his eyes were opened through living in Johannesburg, where in the early 1920s, and especially after the Rand Revolt of 1922, he began to develop personal contacts with Africans. By then he had become convinced that a large black population was in the cities to stay, whatever a government commission might say about blacks being in them merely to 'minister to the needs of the white man'.[29] But the most important single reason why Macmillan was led to appreciate that he should be concerned with blacks in South Africa, past and present, was the 'lucky break' that came to him in 1920: he was given the use of the papers of Dr John Philip of the London Missionary Society.

By mid-1923 – four years after his lectures on the 'Agrarian Problem' – he made his first public statement on African affairs at another conference called by the Dutch Reformed Church. He now believed that 'poor whiteism' was primarily caused by black poverty, and that the fortunes of black and white were inseparably linked. 'The root of South Africa's ills was a disregard in the past for the place of the natives in the country.'[30] He spoke specifically about the effects of the Natives Land Act of 1913, and the failure in the decade since the passage of that Act to provide blacks with more land. To his Dutch Reformed Church audience he stressed that more land for Africans would help alleviate the 'poor white problem'. 'Poor whites' in the rural areas did not need more land, but fixity of tenure and greater control of the conditions on which they held it. On the other hand, if more land was given to Africans, and agricultural methods in the reserves were improved so that they could support a larger population, fewer Africans would move to the cities – there was then no rigid influx control – and the competition the poor whites faced in the cities would lessen. These ideas presented at the conference he elaborated in a series of articles in the *Star* the following year, reprinted as a pamphlet entitled *The Land, the Native and Unemployment*.

His political involvement grew as he worked on the Philip material. Soon after arriving in Johannesburg, he had made contact with white trade unionists, partly through teaching in Workers' Educational Association classes. But after the Rand Revolt of 1922 – on which he wrote what would be the first of many articles published in the *New Statesman* – he became increasingly involved with blacks: through contacts with the Industrial and Commercial Workers' Union, discussion groups, and especially his participation in the Johannesburg Joint Council of Europeans and Africans, where he learned at first hand from Africans of their disabilities. Some of the notes he took on the Philip material were written on the back of minutes of Joint Council meetings.[31]

Though by nature a retiring man, Macmillan was not shy to go out and do battle for what he believed. After Hertzog's triumph in the 1924 general election he arranged an interview with the new prime minister. He informed Hertzog of the overcrowding he had found in the African reserves, and argued that if Africans were not increasingly to compete with whites for scarce employment at low wages in the cities – which would inevitably cause conflict – they must be given more land. He added that if Hertzog thought he had misread conditions in the reserves, he would be happy to investigate any district of the government's choosing. Hertzog took him up on this, and suggested he investigate the district of Herschel, south of Basutoland, presumably because it was thought the results would show him to be wrong. Macmillan conducted a brief but intensive investigation of the Herschel district, with full access to the official records, and found that the official figures were unreliable. Production in the district was disastrously low. Between 10 and 25 per cent of Africans held no land. Food had to be imported to keep the people alive, and the population was overwhelmingly dependent on migrant labour, the district's chief export commodity. His report – entitled 'The Native as Producer and Consumer in the District of Herschel'[32] – was given to the government in 1926, and pigeon-holed.[33]

In June 1926 he left for England, with the notes he and his students had prepared on the Philip papers. It was only when he began to write up the material at All Souls College, Oxford, that he decided to make two books of it.[34] Within six months he had completed the first: the Preface to *The Cape Colour Question. A Historical Survey* is dated January 1927 and the volume was published later that year. Back in South Africa, he made several more journeys to rural areas: west to Tswana country, where he collected material on resistance in 1896; east to Swaziland; south to Basutoland; and again to the Transkei. Within another year he had finished writing the second book, based on his Philip material, concerned with what he called 'The Making of the South African Native Problem'. *Bantu, Boer, and Briton* was published in mid-1929. A few months later he suggested that the *swart gevaar* (black peril) election of that year had 'helped kill' his book.[35]

In the Preface to *Bantu, Boer, and Briton*, Macmillan mentioned his intention of providing, 'by way of commentary on the pages of history here dealt with', the results of his study of contemporary conditions in South Africa. By September 1929 he was beginning to plan a third book, which would give the facts of the current social crisis.[36] For this he collected together the material he had gathered over the previous eight years about contemporary social and economic conditions: the notes taken on his travels, the report he had submitted to the government on the Herschel district in 1926, and the newspaper articles. Modestly sub-titled 'An Economic Footnote to History', *Complex South Africa* was published in London in 1930.

* * *

Macmillan's decision to leave South Africa and settle in Britain, to which he was deeply attached, was made for a variety of reasons, some personal – on his way back from England in February 1931 he met the woman who became his second wife – some work-related, some political. By 1931 he was less than happy at Wits. He had a heavy teaching load, with little assistance, and wanted more time for his research and writing.[37] Within the university, he battled with some of those among his colleagues most interested in African studies: Mrs Winifred Hoernlé, lecturer in anthropology and wife of the liberal philosopher R. F. A. Hoernlé, and J. D. Rheinallt Jones, who wanted to become lecturer in a new department of Bantu Studies. To Macmillan their interest in 'decaying native customs' was dangerous: it exaggerated the differences between cultures, and could give support to segregationists who denied the common humanity of Africans.[38] What should be studied was the single political economy of the country, and its common history. As he wrote at the time:

Undue stress on the different mentality of the Bantu becomes too often an excuse for shutting the eyes to the unpleasant fact that the Bantu are ordinary human beings, and that the bulk of them are inextricably entangled in and dependent on our economic system.... At the present time it is more urgent that we see he is provided with bread, even without butter, than to embark on the long quest to understand the Native Mind.[39]

Macmillan's opposition to the anthropologically orientated Bantu Studies was unsuccessful. American funds, mainly from the Carnegie Corporation of New York, went to the conservative liberals on the advice of C. T. Loram, a former South African of cautious views who had become Professor of Education at Yale. It seemed to Macmillan that history was being downgraded. He disliked the new South African Institute of Race Relations which the conservative liberals established as a non-political, fact-finding body in 1929. He rejected the concept of 'race relations' – which he regarded as an inappropriate American import – because it implied a division between races which could only be bridged by some kind of diplomacy, and he feared the Institute would work to depoliticise and emasculate the Joint Councils, which provided an important forum for the voicing of African grievances.[40] He believed the government should be challenged politically, and while he remained in the country, he continued to put his energies into the Joint Council movement.

By 1931, with three books published, he had said what he wanted to say about South Africa. He now turned to a new project: a book on the political and economic needs of Africa north of the Union. He was already planning such a book when he visited England in 1930. That year Philip Mitchell, then Colonial Secretary of Tanganyika, told him of developments in British tropical Africa, and whetted his appetite for a look at the 'more hopeful Africa beyond the Union'.[41] He began to think that South Africa's racism should be challenged by advancing self-rule in tropical Africa, and that it was important to prevent the spread of any South African influence northwards. An insatiable traveller, he went north to the Rhodesias and Tanganyika in 1930, and in late 1931 he visited Basutoland, Bechuanaland, the Rhodesias and Nyasaland. At the start of his long leave at the end of 1932 he returned to Rhodesia. By mid-1931 he had decided on a tentative title for his book: 'Whence and Whither in Africa'. South Africa did not seem the best place in which to write it. This new project was under way when news reached him in Salisbury at the end of 1931 that a fire in the central block at Wits had destroyed the university library, into which he had recently moved the Philip papers. All that was left were the notes on the papers which he and his students had taken. A believer in predestination, he interpreted what he later described as 'my Reichstag fire'[42] as a sign that he had done the right thing in moving to another topic. In the revised edition of *Bantu, Boer, and Briton* he was to claim that he had intended writing a full biography of John Philip, but the contemporary evidence suggests otherwise.[43]

His departure from South Africa was precipitated by a clash with the government. He returned from England at the beginning of 1932 in a crusading spirit. The statutory colour bar in industry, the white labour policy, Hertzog's 'Native bills', all seemed to be leading the country towards the 'abyss'. He gave lengthy evidence to the Native Economic Commission, but its report, issued in 1932, disappointed him, for it spoke of whites and blacks as two quite separate peoples, held blacks responsible for their own poverty, and pleaded for caution.[44] An attack he made on the pass laws had already been condemned as 'un-South African' by a Nationalist Senator, but he was determined to make a last bid to influence the government to change its course. As chairman of the Johannesburg Joint Council he sent Oswald Pirow, the Minister of Justice, a letter concerning African distrust of the Hertzog bills, and complaining about the lack of consultation. When Pirow brushed him off, Macmillan let rip in the *Star* and the *Rand Daily Mail*. Pointing out that there was an African proletariat of one million in the cites, he said of Pirow, 'History, which I suggest is not his strong point, will tell him that even his strong government will have to take notice of what the proletariat itself has to say about it all.' A very annoyed Pirow demanded that Macmillan be restrained, and Macmillan received a letter from Raikes, the Principal of Wits, in November 1932 , informing him that members of staff should not take actions that might jeopardise relations with the government. It was a time of financial stringency, and Wits was afraid of government cuts. Fortunately for Raikes, Macmillan was about to go on leave, and he agreed to 'think things over' while overseas. In September 1933, believing that he might be given the task of writing a new general survey of Africa then being planned, and that he should be on hand in England for that task, he sent in his resignation.[45] He was not to return to South Africa for eighteen years, and never again for more than a short visit. For South African historical scholarship, as also for the liberal cause, his departure was a severe blow. His South African years were his formative ones. In Britain he played some part in persuading the British government to move its African colonies towards greater self-government, but what he wrote there on South African history was not as strikingly original as his earlier work.

* * *

Macmillan's first academic task when he reached England was to write the chapters he had promised for the eighth volume of the *Cambridge History of the British Empire*. Two went over ground covered in *The Cape Colour Question* and *Bantu, Boer, and Briton*, but he also wrote on political developments at the Cape to 1834, and on the Protectorates. He hoped to be given the task of writing the prestigious and well-funded *African Survey*, first proposed by Smuts in the Rhodes Lectures at Oxford in 1929, which would become the 'bible' of British administrators in tropical Africa. But he was passed over and an Indian administrator, Lord Hailey, who knew nothing about Africa, was asked to take charge of it. Macmillan did some work for Hailey, but fell out with the influential Round Table group in the mid-1930s over the question of the transfer of the Protectorates to the Union, which they favoured and he strongly opposed. He was critical of them for being too concerned with white politics in South Africa, for ignoring the blacks, and for being prepared to work with the South African government. As the years passed, he had to keep himself by writing for journals and newspapers and by examining for the Civil Service, for he was not offered another academic post until 1947.

What happened to his Wits chair confirmed him in his view that he had done the right thing to leave that university, for it was given, not to his brilliant student de Kiewiet, or to his loyal assistant Margaret Hodgson, but to Leo Fouché, whom Macmillan regarded as 'anti-native'[46] and who was certainly anti-Macmillan. Macmillan blamed the Bantu Studies people. Hodgson not only did not get the chair; she was dismissed from the staff after she married William Ballinger in December 1934. Raikes insisted that as a married woman she could not be kept on the staff; that she had lived with Ballinger, a radical, before marriage, and that she was closely associated with Macmillan, clearly counted against her.[47]

'Whence and Whither in Africa?' gradually turned into 'Africa Emergent'. Its completion was delayed while Macmillan wrote *Warning from the West Indies* (1936), the outcome of a visit there in 1935 paid for by the Carnegie Corporation of New York. The African book finally appeared in 1938. It was, the Introduction claimed, the result of eight years' research, travel and thought. Though the sub-title was 'A Survey of Social, Political and Economic Trends in Black Africa', sections of a number of chapters dealt with South Africa, and he used South African examples at numerous places in general chapters on such matters as land, labour, capital, and urbanisation. De Kiewiet reviewed it very favourably in the *American Historical Review*, and was later to suggest that it did not get the praise it deserved 'possibly because his manner of writing read nuanced and tentative, and therefore covered up the punch that really was obscured by his words' and perhaps also because the fact that he did not hold a prominent post may have lessened the attention reviewers paid him.[48]

Africa Emergent had various merits. Of all his books, it was perhaps the best written. It criticised an idealised picture of old Africa, and stressed instead the poverty of the continent. African backwardness, however, was not seen to be the result of racial inferiority, but was explained rather by environmental factors. The British government was charged with complacency: he believed the goal of self-government should be acknowledged for tropical Africa; that the future lay with educated Africans, not the indirect rulers; and that Britain should embark on planned economic development. In advancing such ideas Macmillan was ahead of his time. He saw South African policy colouring the approach taken by administrators in the north, and he criticised the South African road as the wrong one: the newer Africa should learn from the errors made in the south, and not repeat them. Tracing the growth of segregationist policy in South Africa, he linked it to racist attitudes. 'As a complete system', segregation was 'utterly impracticable'.[49]

Macmillan tried to keep up with relevant reading on South Africa by reviewing books on South African topics for the *New Statesman* and elsewhere, and in *Africa Emergent* he cited such recently published works as de Kiewiet's *Imperial Factor*, Monica Hunter's *Reaction to Conquest* and *We Europeans*, a semi-popular work on 'the myth of race' by Julian Huxley, A. C. Haddon and A. M. Carr-Saunders.[50] Nevertheless, especially when in West Africa during the war, he grew increasingly out of touch with South African scholarship. Cut off from sources in South Africa, Macmillan was not to conduct any primary historical research after leaving that country. Without a teaching job for over a decade, he produced no more students to work on South African history.

At the beginning of the war Macmillan produced a small book entitled *Democratize the Empire! A Policy for Colonial Change* (London, 1941), which defended much of the British record overseas as creditable, and went on to express the hope that the war might help move the empire in the direction of self-government. His years as a freelance finally ended when he was offered the post of Empire Intelligence Director for the BBC in 1941–3. From 1943 to 1946 he worked for the British Council in West Africa. In 1947 he finally obtained another academic post: Director of Colonial Studies – in practice merely a lectureship – at St. Andrews.[51] In 1949 he returned to South Africa, thanks to de Kiewiet, who suggested to the Carnegie Corporation that it fund his visit, and he gave the Hoernlé Memorial Lecture on 'Africa Beyond the Union'. In 1954 Eric Walker wrote to ask him whether he would like to revise his chapters for the new edition of the *Cambridge History* he was editing. Macmillan replied from the University of Jamaica, where he had gone from St. Andrews for a year as head of the history department, that 'this is not the place for fresh work on South Africa', adding,

I can't pretend to have kept a close watch on my 'period'. I'd much rather let well alone as far as possible. I'm not conscious of having been 'shot down' and am disposed to suggest leaving it to you and your editorial helpers to call my attention to any changes you think are needed.[52]

The chapter on the Protectorates was rewritten by Kenneth

Kirkwood, but Macmillan's other chapters were included unrevised in the volume which finally appeared in 1963. At St. Andrews and after his retirement, he worked on his last major book, *The Road to Self-Rule*, eventually published in 1959. In December 1957 he told Leo Marquard of Oxford University Press in Cape Town that the book was 'straight history of the mixed and black colonies, but I won't say it's not a bit of a Tract for the Times too'. He went on to mention that his publisher had agreed to call it *The Black Man's Burden*. Marquard replied that he had published a book with that very title during the war, and Macmillan agreed to give his book a new title.[53] *The Road to Self-Rule* was not based on new original research, but sought to explain the movement towards independence occurring as he wrote. Macmillan then revised *Bantu, Boer, and Briton*, long out of print, for the Clarendon Press. By the beginning of 1962 he had re-arranged the material, placing some of the footnote material into the text, and giving greater attention than in the first edition to Philip himself. The new edition, which briefly surveyed developments in South Africa to 1948, appeared in 1963. No new edition of *The Cape Colour Question* appeared, but a reprint was issued in 1968 with a new foreword contributed by de Kiewiet. Macmillan turned to the dictation of his memoir on his South African years. This was published in 1975, the year after his death.

6   The revisionist historian

Macmillan's view of history was quite different from that of Theal, who died the month before the first of the five lectures on 'The South African Agrarian Problem' was delivered. Macmillan brought to his historical work the critical sense of the professional scholar, a concern to be rigorously analytical. But he was not a historian of the same mould as Walker, his colleague in Cape Town. He never showed any interest in writing a general history textbook for white South Africans. Instead, he was concerned to disclose the facts about relevant social issues so that people would understand better the nature of the society in which they lived, and work to transform it. History should not be a mere matter of record, a chronicle of past events, but should involve the study of the origins of contemporary social problems. So Macmillan wrote on the 'Agrarian Problem', and 'The Making of the South African Native Problem' and began *The Cape Colour Question* by quoting Benedetto Croce's remark – made in response to those who declared the historian should tell 'what had actually happened' – that 'every true history is contemporary history': historians choose what to investigate in the past, and that choice is determined by present interests. As a social critic, Macmillan sought through his historical writing to draw lessons from the past for the present. He was interested in a relevant, usable past. He hoped, too, his historical writing might influence the making of policy.

* * *

The Agrarian Problem was a short book of only a hundred pages. It was not well written or structured; Macmillan was never a stylist, and always found writing difficult.[1] Perhaps partly because it consisted of printed lectures, and was not better written, it did not attract much attention at the time of publication, and was not to be rediscovered until the 1970s, when it came to be recognised as an important pathbreaking work.[2] For it began the task of investigating the history of agriculture in South Africa and of changing social relations in the countryside. Macmillan was the first historian to try to chart the growth of social stratification between wealthy farmers on the one hand and landless tenant farmers (bywoners) on the other. He was also the first South African to plead for the study of social history, the history not of politics and of elites but of the common man and his day-to-day existence. For him,

the South African history which is really significant is that which tells us about the everyday life of the people, how they lived, what they thought, and what they worked at, when they did think and work, what they produced and what and where they marketed, and the whole of their social organisation.

'Such a history of the people of South Africa', he added, 'remains to be written.'[3] It would be over fifty years before other historians took up the challenges he threw down in this work. Only the second of the lectures in *The Agrarian Problem* was primarily historical, but the book as a whole represented a study of a particular social issue in historical perspective: it took a contemporary problem and investigated its historical roots. Macmillan sought to explain, for example, the relationship between rural impoverishment and the move to the cities which was occurring as he wrote. His one-man enquiry into rural poverty and landlessness anticipated much of what the large-scale, well-funded Carnegie commission into white poverty was to find over a decade later. The author of the first volume of the Carnegie Report, J. F. W. Grosskopf, was to pay tribute to Macmillan's pioneering research.[4]

Like the Carnegie enquiry, Macmillan focused on 'poor whites'. When he spoke of 'the people' or 'South Africans', he usually meant whites; some of his population figures related only to whites, as if blacks did not count.[5] 'The native question' was listed as but one of a number of causes of white poverty, and under that heading he included the widely held view that only blacks should do unskilled work, the legacy of slavery, and the competition whites faced from blacks in the urban areas. The main causes for the movement of 'poor whites' to the towns he found in their lack of legal rights as tenants, the repeated subdivision of farms, and the environmental difficulties facing pastoral agriculture in much of the country. Only after *The Agrarian Problem* was published did his focus switch from the study of poor whites to that of poor blacks, as he came to realise that in his early work he had 'dealt with only the tip of the iceberg'.[6]

* * *

At the beginning of the 1920s the accepted version of South African history was the Theal–Cory one, a pro-colonist representation of the triumph of white power over African people. For Theal, and even more so for Cory, perhaps the main devil of the drama, the chief mischief-maker, because he took the side of the 'weaker races', was John Philip of the London Missionary Society, who was blamed for most of the colonists' troubles in the 1820s, 1830s and 1840s. Cory had tried to gain access to the voluminous Philip papers held by the family but had been unsuccessful, for they knew what he felt about their ancestor.[7] Philip's missionary son had begun to write his father's biography, and a grandson had carried it further, but it had not reached publishable form. The papers, including the draft biography, had then been left to a great-grandson, who was persuaded in 1920 to entrust them to Macmillan.[8] Macmillan was an extraordinarily suitable person to work on them: like Philip a Scot, with some divinity training, he was an active member of the Scottish church. Philip had ministered in Aberdeen, Macmillan's birthplace, from 1804 until he left for South Africa in 1818, and had married there. Moreover, to the Philip family, Macmillan seemed the ideal biographer because he was a professor of history who had shown himself of independent mind, and prepared to speak out on issues of the day, as Philip once had.

The first instalment of the papers arrived shortly before Macmillan left for England in 1920. In London he had a cursory look at the relevant London Missionary Society papers. On his return to Johannesburg in 1921, two large packing cases of papers were awaiting him. Of the great historical significance of this material there was no doubt: it was a treasure trove to which no other historian had had access. Philip was not only head of the London Missionary Society in South Africa, but also in overall charge of the Paris Evangelical Missionary Society and the American Board missionaries, and the papers contained a mass of correspondence from all over South Africa. Philip, moreover, had been in close touch with leading government figures both at the Cape and in England. The papers were probably the single most important source, outside the government archives, for the early 1820s,

1830s and early 1840s. But inasmuch as working on them meant labouring over documents, and focusing on an early period of South African history, the project did not suit Macmillan, who never had any wish to bury himself away in an archive and who regarded the past as only important if it helped explain the present.

There were various reasons, however, why Macmillan went ahead and produced his two classic volumes based on the Philip papers. Firstly, these papers could be kept in his own office, and lent out to helpers. An inspiring teacher, Macmillan attracted an extremely able group of students at Wits in the early 1920s, and he asked them to go through the documents for him. Philip's handwriting was execrable and many of his letters were almost illegible. Each student was given a bundle of papers and a theme, and told to make notes from the documents on that theme. The two students who graduated to advanced work in history, C. W. de Kiewiet and Lucy Sutherland, researched for Macmillan in the public archives in Cape Town and London, which he never visited himself.

Secondly, Macmillan used the papers to present an alternative view of South African history to that so authoritatively given by Theal and Cory. He decided to write, not a biography based on the draft by Philip's descendants, but a much wider study deliberately intended to challenge and overturn the Theal–Cory interpretation of South African history by taking 'full account of the weaker peoples as an essential part of the whole'.[9] He was concerned with 'the predicament of the natives', which, he rightly pointed out, 'has never been taken into account'.[10] He realised that blacks had not been merely robbers of cattle as Theal and Cory usually suggested, but had had their own interests to defend. Macmillan sought to view them sympathetically and on their own terms.

Seeing through Philip's eyes, Macmillan realised that the key issue in South Africa's past, as also in its present, was the role of the blacks and their relationships with whites. Historians and politicians alike had been too narrowly concerned with intra-white politics, with Briton versus Boer. Theal and Cory had regarded relations between black and white almost exclusively in terms of frontier conflict. What interested Macmillan was the way in which blacks had entered white-ruled society, and the relations that had existed and should exist in a single multi-racial society. He argued that it was exactly in Philip's time that the way in which blacks were to be treated in a white-ruled society had first been tackled – with the grant of rights to the Khoi, the emancipation of the slaves, and the beginning of the incorporation of Africans. Since then, though politically divided by the Trek, South Africa had essentially formed one country, and the dominant theme in its history was increasing interaction between black and white, interaction that had from the start involved co-operation as well as conflict, and had become more 'co-operative' with the growth of a single economy.

Philip had spent much of his time travelling to see conditions for himself, and so gained an unrivalled knowledge of the Cape and the territories beyond. Macmillan believed that in order to understand the Philip material he should continue his own travels and see what had happened to the people about whom he was writing. Concerned as he was with the present as well as the past – and now above all with black poverty – he wanted to go out and establish the facts. Philip had warned against stripping Africans of their land east of the Fish River in the 1830s, for example; Macmillan wanted to discover the consequences, by field-work in the Ciskei of the 1920s.

* * *

The Philip papers taught Macmillan that what he called 'the larger Native question' could not be understood historically without looking first at what had happened to those he termed 'the Cape people', the 'Eurafricans' or 'browns', who had been Philip's first concern. He was to admit in his memoirs that because he thought he knew the condition of the Coloured people from his Stellenbosch childhood, he paid less attention than he should have to what had happened to them,[11] though he did note on his travels that the missionaries had failed to secure adequate protection of their land rights at mission stations such as Hankey and in the Kat River Settlement.

The main theme of *The Cape Colour Question* was the way the missionaries had, under Philip's leadership, ameliorated the lot of people of colour at the Cape in the early nineteenth century. Its central chapters were devoted to Philip's struggle to have the laws that discriminated against 'Hottentots and other free persons of colour' changed, a struggle culminating in what Macmillan called 'the emancipation of the Hottentots' by Ordinance 50 of 1828, which removed legal inequalities affecting them, as well as by the Order in Council which Philip subsequently obtained in London to prevent the colonists from undermining the provisions of that Ordinance.

But Macmillan's books on Philip were designed to influence current government policy and he very explicitly linked what he wrote of the 1820s, 1830s and 1840s to his own times. *The Cape Colour Question* concerned the story of how the 'Hottentots' had been brought within the law, of how 'the descendants of the nomadic aborigines, a physically inferior stock, originally less well endowed than the Bantu ... have come to achieve a measure of civilisation deemed sufficient to entitle them to a full share in European privileges', thanks to Ordinance 50 and the non-racial franchise of 1853.[12] Only in passing did he point out that the grant of legal and political equality had not guaranteed economic well-being, and that most Coloureds had become members of a rural and (latterly) urban proletariat; he was later to admit that he should have stressed this more than he had.[13] Writing in the mid-1920s – when the Hertzog government was promoting a 'New Deal' for those called Coloureds – Macmillan saw them as 'irrevocably a part of the European community', accepted as 'an inevitable part of the South African whole'.[14] His central message in the Philip books was that as the Coloureds had been 'emancipated' in the nineteenth century, so could Africans acquire their freedom in the twentieth. 'If by general agreement the "Eurafricans" ... rank today as a civilised people', he wrote, 'this is the result not of a policy of restrictions, but of the measure of freedom allowed them.'[15] Just as the problem of the 'Eurafrican' had been 'solved' by the grant of legal and political equality, so the 'Native problem' could be solved. The common citizenship once given to Coloureds should now be granted to Africans.

* * *

Macmillan's major concern – contemporary as well as historical – in the 1920s was policy towards Africans rather than Coloureds. In 1921 he travelled into the Transkei and in 1923 he returned to the eastern Cape, to try to find the causes of landlessness, overcrowding and lack of development. He collected some oral information for his history, but not systematically. More important for that work, he saw with his own eyes the lie of the land: it was not until he visited the Kat River Settlement, for instance, that he realised how the Xhosa had used the Fish River bush as a strategic defence to guard the fertile valley of the Kat.[16] And it was through his travels that he became convinced that the frontier wars had been fought for land, and in defence of land, and not for cattle.

In his second Philip book, Macmillan turned to Philip's attempts to influence African policy on the Cape eastern and northern frontiers in the 1830s and the early 1840s, and his protests against Governor D'Urban's plans for 'extermination', i.e. stripping the Africans east of the Fish of their lands. *Bantu, Boer, and Briton* then followed relations between black and white on the Cape frontier from the time of the Great Trek, through the treaty system of the late 1830s and early 1840s, to the British abandonment of the lands north of the Orange in the early 1850s, which left white-ruled South Africa politically divided.

Macmillan believed that he wrote at a crucial moment in the elaboration of policy towards the African population. In the mid-1920s, Hertzog was securing for South Africa full Dominion status and was working out a comprehensive policy for Africans in the Union as a whole. South Africa's whites, in the full bloom of 'young nationhood',[17] seemed to Macmillan to be taking the wrong road in elaborating racial policy. Instead of removing restrictions on Africans, such as access to land, the government was imposing new ones, such as a colour bar in industry by means of the Mines and Works Act of 1926. Hertzog was not proposing to extend rights to Africans, but to segregate them: to remove the Cape Africans from the common voters' roll, and to give Africans throughout the country separate, communal representation.

Smuts told Macmillan in 1926: 'Our feet are on the edge of an abyss.'[18] Writing *The Cape Colour Question* in England a few months later, Macmillan began the last paragraph: 'Our feet are in truth on the edge of an abyss', and suggested how it might be avoided:

white South Africa must carry its child races along with it on the way of progress. There can be no vision of a 'Civilization' that will rest on a base of serfdom and live. The policy for the future is to be judged according as it stands by those principles of Freedom which have been tried in some measure and have not been found wanting.[19]

He recognised that because there were far more Africans than Coloureds, their incorporation posed a much more difficult political problem for the whites, but he rejected any idea that because they were so numerous they should be accorded separate treatment. Segregation in the sense of separation was no longer possible, and were Africans to be totally excluded from the body politic, and whites to take all important decisions relating to them, white interests alone would be considered. It was therefore crucial that the non-racial franchise should be maintained and extended.[20]

Macmillan was not unaware of the pressures exerted on Hertzog by whites to adopt an anti-African policy because of the apparent threat to white jobs in the cities. But he explicitly denied that there was any political danger for whites in a non-racial franchise. It was, after all, a qualified one, and only a few thousand Africans, he pointed out, were politically conscious. The real danger would come if, denied the vote,

these few, who are still eager and willing to be led – content with a humble place in the One South African society – were to be driven into increasingly bitter racial opposition. There is no solution which denies to this little group of progressive and dispossessed Bantu full rights of citizenship in the Union which is their only home. Given such rights they may easily be led and won.[21]

Elsewhere in *Bantu, Boer, and Briton* he wrote:

Nowhere is there such danger of political disaster as in a country, constitutionally democratic, which denies political rights to a section of its own people.... The Natives ready to qualify [for the vote] increase all too slowly. Wisdom demands that White South Africa bind this handful to itself and secure their co-operation in devising a policy for leading up to civilization the great backward masses who must, for many years, remain incapable of independent political thought and action.... For the Union – in blindness born of fear – to baulk or retard their progress will be to sow dragons' teeth that must soon spring to dreadful life in the not infertile seed-plot of South Africa.[22]

Talk of segregation evaded the reality of the contact between 'advanced' and 'backward' peoples in one country. What was needed was a policy to raise – he did not doubt their capacity to be so raised – the mass of landless blacks from the 'backwardness' that made them a 'problem'.

Macmillan blamed the follies of the policy-makers on white racism. He expressed his admiration for the independent spirit of the Voortrekkers, granted that they had 'carried civilization over a wide area', and remarked that he did not want to make light of 'the hardships stoutly endured by the European pioneers, or to minimise their sufferings at the hand of the natives'.[23] But they had 'set and confirmed the disastrous fashion of ignoring the very existence of a native population, and of looking at South African problems with eyes exclusively for European interests'.[24] The Great Trek had been a disaster because of the political disunity it brought, which allowed the establishment of a divergent racist tradition in the north. Macmillan recognised that British settlers as well as trekkers had 'stoned their prophets' – 'the critics [such as Philip] who rightly strove all they could to prevent wholesale "extermination" of the native population and to temper the process by which, all over north and central South Africa, "civilization" and "barbarism" were brought into such close and inextricable contact'.[25] Had the colonists allowed Africans to retain more land, segregation might have been possible. Indeed, Philip had advocated a kind of segregation in the 1830s. But the wholesale appropriation of land had left fully half the African population directly dependent on white landowners, and so an inseparable part of the South African whole. Given the extent of economic integration that had occurred, segregation in the sense of separation was now impossible. Edgar Brookes and those liberals who believed in a protective form of segregation were wanting the impossible.[26] In practice, segregation would mean repression of blacks.

* * *

Macmillan's books based on the Philip papers challenged Theal and Cory at various levels. They sought to raise questions which those amateur historians had left unasked about the central themes in South African history. Macmillan was the first historian to ask how and why a racist South African society had come into being. Theal merely accepted that races were clearly defined and hierarchically ordered, and that whites would conquer and rule; he did not attempt to analyse the roots of South African racism. Macmillan realised that racism was something that had developed over time, and he advanced – though did not elaborate – the idea that the white racism which developed in the pre-industrial eighteenth century was the same as that of the twentieth century, and explained the segregationist policies of his own day. This idea was taken up by Eric Walker, who made it into a general thesis about the course of South African development, one which asserted the critical importance of the frontier in the emergence of South African racism.[27] In the late 1930s C. W. de Kiewiet would further explore Macmillan's idea that the frontier was not only the scene of conflict, but also – and more significantly – the place where black and white became intertwined economically.

In his two classic books of the 1920s Macmillan tried to understand what had happened in the early nineteenth century from the point of view of blacks. He did this not because he was anti-colonist but because he believed that the historian should not merely see from one side, and he accused Theal and Cory of having been anti-black. He realised that many of Theal's arguments had served to justify white domination, and were not substantiated by any evidence. Theal had been wrong on many points. Africans had not arrived in the country relatively late in time, but had been a settled population when whites began to enter the country. Blacks had not been fighting continually among themselves before white pacification. It was not a lust for colonial cattle that had led Africans to war with whites so often on the Cape eastern frontier, but rather a concern to maintain their land and way of life in the face of efforts to dispossess them. The Voortrekkers had not advanced into an empty interior in the 1830s. The African population had been larger in the early nineteenth century than Theal had imagined, so there had been no dramatic increase in population later in the century. In such ways, Macmillan began to undermine the pro-colonist, anti-black view of South African history Theal had presented.

And in opposition to the Theal–Cory view of Philip as the devil incarnate, Macmillan represented him as 'the best South African of all'. Social critic, prophet, pioneer of liberal thought in South Africa, Philip was for Macmillan an immensely sympathetic figure. A racial egalitarian, for whom all men were equal before God, he had concerned himself with blacks and their needs, had grappled with the problem of creating a single multi-racial society, had realised that the problems of black and white were intimately connected, and, more than anyone else in his day, had seen the 'total picture' during 'the thirty formative years of the Cape'.[28] Almost a century before Macmillan wrote, Philip had pointed out what Macmillan came to believe in the early 1920s: that South Africa could not survive half slave, half free; that legal and political rights, and access to land, should be granted to all; and that blacks should be paid adequate wages, so that they could become both producers and consumers, so that the one economy might grow and all prosper.

* * *

Macmillan is an ambiguous figure.[29] He could write that 'the long series of Kafir wars ... [were] mere stages in the triumph of the robust young colonial community over the forces of barbarism which hemmed it in.'[30] He accepted the Victorian notion of a great dichotomy between the 'civilised' and the 'barbarous' or 'savage', between the advanced and the backward, and in his writing that divide often seemed to correspond with the racial cleavage. He believed it the white man's duty to help uplift the African masses, whose backwardness he regarded as an inherent condition rather than the result of white conquest and exploitation. Like Theal, he wrote of 'races' as discrete, hierarchically ordered entities, and he spoke, in the idiom of the day, of 'child races', of 'weaker peoples', of 'five million savages'. 'Civilisation' was something whites had carried into the interior.[31] At times Macmillan became self-conscious about his own racism – perhaps when he remembered blacks he knew – and put 'civilisation' and 'barbarism' in inverted commas. When he came to revise *Bantu, Boer, and Briton* in the era of African independence, he omitted reference to Africans as 'primitive' and to their 'savage' existence. But even in the early 1960s he still spoke of 'civilised races'.[32]

Yet a forthright rejection of racial discrimination was an essential part of Macmillan's liberalism. Those who rose out of backwardness should be accepted as equals. 'Civilization, being of the East as well as of the West, knows no Colour Bar.'[33] Macmillan's service with individual Africans on the Joint Councils taught him something of what Africans suffered from racist legislation. He disliked the 'obsession' of white South Africans with race, and the weight they put on 'the abstraction of colour'.[34] He disapproved of the new term 'race relations', as applying to relations between whites and blacks – 'race' had earlier been used for relations between English-speakers and Afrikaners – because it suggested that colour was the crucial cleavage setting people apart.[35] Wishing to see racial distinctions in the present removed, he began to discover that racial categories might not always be the most appropriate ones to use historically. In his historical work, he frequently remarked how unimportant race was: black and white in the interior, for example, had faced the same difficulties from a hostile environment.[36]

Macmillan did not try to analyse the dynamics of African societies. Few individual blacks received attention in his narrative, and besides a couple of pages on 'customs and institutions' in the second chapter of *Bantu, Boer, and Briton* blacks featured in his books only as the object of missionary concern or government policy. They tended to be discussed in generalised, sometimes romanticised terms, or, more commonly, he followed Philip in dismissing African societies as barbarous and inferior. For he considered the early history of African societies as of mere antiquarian interest.[37] As his purpose was to influence policy, he wrote for whites and had no sense of giving blacks back their history, a project he thought of little relevance to contemporary struggles. Nothing the anthropologists had written seemed relevant to the history he was writing, and he even ignored the work of A. T. Bryant, his colleague at Wits in the early 1920s, on the Zulu.[38]

* * *

Macmillan's dual post in history and economics at Rhodes University College encouraged him to take account of economic considerations, and he was much influenced by Tawney and others who stressed the importance of economics in history. While he emphasised political and legal freedom in his Philip books because of the nature of the material he was working with, and in order to make a political point, he did not believe, as later liberals did, that the franchise and constitutionalism were all-important. He spoke of South African opinion being absorbed with the political aspect of a problem that was in fact 'one of administration, and, above all, of economics'.[39] Knowing how obsessed whites were with the 'danger' of racial mixing, he pointed out that if blacks were uplifted economically, such mixing would be less likely to occur. In the mid-1930s he spoke of the 'race relations' movement being 'evasive, by its emphasis on race, of issues which are by their nature economic, and have acute political realities. Colour, though unquestionably an important psychological factor, is only one element.'[40]

Though he emphasised the importance of economics – of land, for instance, in explaining trekboer history – he did not develop this insight, in part because his Philip books were mainly on missionary and government policy. As we shall see, it was left to de Kiewiet to flesh out the importance of the economy in historical development. Macmillan failed to observe, say, the economic pressures for Ordinance 50,[41] or the economic drive behind British imperialism.[42] He asserted the importance of the process by which blacks had over time entered the white-controlled economy, but did not himself explore in detail the dynamics of that process.

In devoting considerable attention to social differentiation within Dutch/Afrikaner society, Macmillan was a pioneer. But he did not extend his sensitivity towards class to his study of Africans, who were mostly dealt with as a blanket category. As he presented his material on class empirically, and did not think in conceptual terms, he failed to explore the relationship of race and class as historians of the 1970s were to do. And his work would be criticised in other ways as well: he overstated the influence of Philip and the humanitarians on the making of British policy; economy, it has more recently been argued, was in fact the chief concern of the British policy-makers.[43] He failed to see that the imperial factor was more destructive than protective of African societies,[44] or that the missionaries had served as agents in conquest. He had, in other words, been an apologist for British imperialism.[45] He exaggerated the backwardness and stagnation of the countryside, and did not see it as a site of racial conflict.[46] His concern to influence state policy led him to draw ahistorical lessons. The importance he attached to the 'freedom' won for the Coloureds made good polemics, but was bad history, for it inflated the significance of legal equality and the non-racial franchise. His remark that 'the coloured people now present little difficulty' was meant to suggest that the Cape franchise had been a success, and therefore should be extended to all Africans, but it grossly misrepresented the lot of the mass of Coloureds in his own day.

* * *

Macmillan's work on South African history was not all that wide-ranging. The Philip papers limited him to the early nineteenth century, and the books based on them constituted his only major historical work. He produced no general synthesis. Though his *Agrarian Problem* pointed to the importance of the eighteenth century, his Philip books spoke of the early nineteenth as the seed-plot for South African history. His remark that the 'native problem' of the 1920s was the product of the disruption of the 1850s overplayed the continuity between his period and the present, and ignored the great transformation wrought by the mineral discoveries.

Yet Macmillan is important, as pathbreaker and ideas-man. He challenged successfully the 'authorised version', the pro-colonist, anti-black view of South African history propagated by Theal and Cory. More than any other historian of South Africa, he was a pioneer, in his rejection of the settler tradition and his sympathy for people of colour, in beginning to move away from racial categories, in insisting that there has come about a single South African economy, in realising the significance of economics, and of interaction between black and white as a central theme in South African history. And because his books made sound empirical use of the Philip papers, they are still valuable to anyone seeking to understand the country's early nineteenth century history. De Kiewiet said of *Cape Colour Question* that it contained 'the fertile seeds of other books and studies'.[47] The words Keith Hancock used of the Canadian economic historian Harold Innis can be applied to Macmillan: 'his difficult prose was full of smouldering coals that burst aflame in other people's minds.'[48] One of those minds was that of his student, C. W. de Kiewiet.

7 De Kiewiet: from Johannesburg to America

Cornelis Willem de Kiewiet was, like Theal and Macmillan, born outside South Africa, but unlike them his first impressions were not of another country, for he was under a year old when his parents took him from Holland – where he was born in May 1902 – to Johannesburg. He grew up in a prejudiced, narrow environment in the Golden City, and much of his later career can be seen in terms of an escape from that background.[1]

Having won a scholarship to the University College in Johannesburg, de Kiewiet first registered there at the beginning of 1920. Unhappy with the major course he began, and because of Macmillan's reputation for intellectual excitement, he switched to history, which became his passion. Macmillan had a crucial intellectual influence on the young de Kiewiet. From him, de Kiewiet recalled later, he learned how 'to hunt out information for myself, how to find the essential meaning and [how to] set it down in clear English'.[2] Before he completed his undergraduate degree, de Kiewiet was being asked to help mark essays, and sift through batches of documents from the Philip papers; from them de Kiewiet learned the excitement of working on manuscript sources. Macmillan did his writing at home, and allowed de Kiewiet to use his university office, and it was there an important episode in de Kiewiet's liberation from his restricted upbringing occurred: for the first time he conversed on equal terms with an African interested in history.[3]

After completing his degree with distinctions in history and Dutch, de Kiewiet went to Cape Town to search in the archives for Macmillan, as well as to begin research for an Honours long essay based on work he had carried out for his mentor on the Philip material. He broadened his Honours essay into a master's thesis, entitled 'Government, Emigrants, Missionaries and Natives on the Northern Frontier 1832–1846'.[4] After another month's work in the Cape archives, he completed the writing of his thesis in August 1924 in Salisbury, Southern Rhodesia, where he had taken a teaching post to earn enough money to supplement a scholarship he had won from Wits for overseas study. When Macmillan received the thesis, he called it 'capital' and sufficient for the degree, but suggested he carry out further research to take the story to the annexation of the Orange River Sovereignty in 1848, or even to Britain's abandonment of that territory in 1854.[5] As de Kiewiet lacked the money to return to Cape Town, he did not follow his supervisor's advice. Eric Walker, the external examiner, agreed with Macmillan that he should not have stopped in 1846, but nevertheless recommended a distinction, which was duly awarded him in April 1925.[6]

De Kiewiet recalled that it was Macmillan who led him

to see the historic tragedy of the colored folk, and then the Indian community. Only some time later did the fullness of South African history come through, because he spoke of the black man as an economic phenomenon, and quietly and thoroughly dispelled the false mythology of 'Kaffir wars'.[7]

His letters from Rhodesia confirm Macmillan's strong influence. He not only joined him in criticising the Theal version of South African history, but also explicitly made clear his agreement with his mentor's views on matters of contemporary concern. Were the reserves developed as Macmillan advocated, de Kiewiet told his friends, fewer Africans would flock into the towns and enter into competition there with 'poor whites'.[8] By 1924, if not earlier, de Kiewiet shared the liberal position on race which Macmillan had acquired since moving to Johannesburg, and in Southern Rhodesia he began to follow Macmillan in giving practical expression to his views, taking the white high school boys he taught to an African school, and preparing evidence for a commission on 'Native education'.

Such activity came to an end with his departure from southern Africa. As he was leaving for England in 1925, Macmillan advised him 'to go to [A. F.] Pollard if you can', adding:

As for Research.... You must consider the London supply of material, and be guided so as to make good use of that.... you might find as good a subject as any the Attitude and Influence of His Majesty's Government towards or on Native Policy in SA over a term of years – thirties to fifties, especially 1852 and 54, or ... in some ways better still, after it left the

Republics to go their own way, e.g. 1854–77. I think, in fact am sure, that is your cue.[9]

He told de Kiewiet of the recently published *History of Native Policy in South Africa* by Edgar Brookes, who taught public administration and political science at the Transvaal University College.[10] But Macmillan did not have much respect for Brookes's weighty tome, in part because it supported segregationism. Brookes claimed to have read 'every scrap of printed matter' on 'Native affairs' in the Cape archives,[11] but Macmillan was dismissive of his historical chapters, informing de Kiewiet that what Brookes said about history 'need not worry you – it is very sketchy for the most part and some of it is bad, or wrong'.[12]

Macmillan was correct in anticipating that his star student would be constrained in his choice of topic for his doctorate by the source material in London. It was inevitable that de Kiewiet would use the Public Record Office, and all theses in imperial history completed at the University of London at this time investigated some aspect of the 'official mind' and the making of official policy. A. P. Newton, the Rhodes Professor of Imperial History at the University of London, became his supervisor and helped steer him in that direction. It may be that he did not follow Macmillan's advice to focus on 'native policy' in part because he learned of the Oxford B.Litt. thesis which J. A. I. Agar-Hamilton (1895–1984) had completed on 'The Native Policy of the Voortrekkers'.[13] De Kiewiet chose instead to investigate British policy in general towards the Afrikaners in the interior until the discovery of diamonds and the return of British rule across the Orange. The doctorate, published in 1929 under the title *British Colonial Policy and the South African Republics*, would be followed, some years later, by a successor volume which took up where the earlier monograph had ended, and also had imperial policy as its focus.

Despite de Kiewiet's move overseas, Macmillan continued in one way or another to play an important role in shaping his career. They kept in close touch and de Kiewiet, for example, compiled the index for Macmillan's second Philip book. After completing his doctorate, he travelled first to Paris, and then, following in Macmillan's footsteps, to the University of Berlin. It was while in Berlin that he received 'out of the blue' an invitation to teach in Iowa. He had long been worried about finding a permanent post. He had told Macmillan some years earlier that he thought he might 'plunge into native work' and to equip himself for this might 'go to the States, do some rural sociology, administration and teaching'.[14] It was, he believed, because he delivered 'the Macmillan line' at a lecture in London that he was blacklisted by the South African High Commission in the city, and that pressure was applied to have withdrawn an invitation to act as leave replacement for Eric Walker in Cape Town.[15] As he left for Iowa in 1929, Macmillan advised him that the chair at Rhodes might soon fall vacant, adding: 'We want you back in this country, which needs all the enlightened youth it can produce.' But Macmillan then proceeded to describe the Nationalist government which had been returned to power in the 1929 election as 'harder and narrower' than before – hardly an encouragement to the younger man to return.[16] Nevertheless de Kiewiet did not plan to remain in North America, and even after marrying an American, informed Macmillan 'I shall have no difficulty in persuading her to leave the United States when the time comes.'[17]

When Macmillan resigned his Wits chair in 1933, de Kiewiet expected, as his leading protégé, to be offered it. He was only 32, but S. Herbert Frankel, another of Macmillan's students, had been appointed to an economics chair at Wits in 1931 at the age of 28, and it was almost certainly not de Kiewiet's youth, but his association with Macmillan, who was regarded as a radical, that counted against him.[18] After he failed to win the Wits chair, de Kiewiet still considered returning to South Africa, and when he applied for the Cape Town chair in 1936 he asked Macmillan for a testimonial, joking that he should perhaps tell the university: 'If you have heard the awful news about the redness of Professor Macmillan, it is not true.'[19] Cape Town, like Wits, made a 'safe' appointment, and de Kiewiet, whose doubts about returning to South Africa had led him to withdraw his application even before the decision was known, remained in America.

* * *

De Kiewiet applied for the Cape Town chair from London, where he was on sabbatical from Iowa. Working in the Public Record Office in 1936, he completed the research for his second monograph, *The Imperial Factor in South Africa*, which Cambridge University Press published the following year, after it had been much praised by Newton.[20] He then turned to writing an economic history of the self-governing dominions from 1783 to 1935, but had not advanced far with that project when Oxford University Press asked him to write the South African volume in a new series of histories of the dominions designed to replace Charles Lucas's volumes on the *Historical Geography of the British Colonies*, which had appeared between 1887 and 1920. De Kiewiet's first reaction was that he had 'been away too long to have a properly balanced and decently informed view' of South Africa, but on reflection he decided to take on the assignment, which was one he could complete in Iowa. So he set aside the economic history of the dominions, which would never be completed, and instead wrote what was to be his most influential work, still the most famous of all the single-volume histories of South Africa.

As his *History of South Africa Social and Economic* was with the Press, de Kiewiet moved from Iowa to Cornell University in Ithaca, New York. During the war, he was active in teaching in a programme for army officers, and at the end of the war he entered the world of administration when he became Dean of Cornell. He moved up progressively in the administration, and was being considered for the position of president of the university when he was asked to become president of nearby Rochester University, to which he moved in 1951. He remained there for a decade, before ill-health and family tragedy, along with a desire to spend more time on African educational projects, led to his early retirement.[21] In his years as an administrator, he hoped to continue academic writing, and long cherished a project to write a history that would begin where *The Imperial Factor* had left off in the mid-1880s and take the story through to the end of the South African War, based on documents in the Public Record Office. But this did not materialise for various reasons: the long delay in completing a collection of documents on Canada which he edited jointly with Frank Underhill, pressures of administration, his distance from the sources, and the fact that J. S. Marais chose this topic for himself.[22] All de Kiewiet produced on South Africa in the 1950s was a set of general, somewhat polemical lectures on South Africa, published under the title *The Anatomy of South African Misery* in 1956, and the beginning of what would be a series of semi-popular articles on contemporary South Africa for the *Virginia Quarterly Review* and other journals.[23] His *History*, published in 1941 when he was under 40, thus remained his last major work on the country's history.

8 The master historian

It was owing to Macmillan's teaching in the 1920s, de Kiewiet later recalled, that 'the whole unhistorical architecture of Theal and Cory broke down, so that I began to see that really there was no South African history. It had to be rewritten, round a fresh architecture.'[1] Like Macmillan, the younger man set out deliberately to challenge the prevailing dominant interpretation of South African history. Both the method and the content of the old work were faulty. Of Theal's *History*, de Kiewiet wrote in his first book: 'Its value is greatly diminished by a concentration on local events. There is consequently little unity of treatment. Theal adopts the traditional point of view of the colonists.' George Cory's *The Rise of South Africa* was likewise 'so overburdened with detail that the main issues tend to get lost. The author, like Theal, tends to adopt the traditional colonial point of view.'[2] Macmillan and de Kiewiet sought to advance a different point of view, and to do so analytically, as befitted professional historians: they set out to write critical history 'that instead of grubbing seeks to understand and evaluate'.[3]

British Colonial Policy and the South African Republics, both explicitly in its introductory pages and implicitly throughout, challenged the Theal–Cory view of two fundamental themes in South African history: the role of British policy, and relations between white and black. For Theal, 'the chief interest' of the 1850s and 1860s had been 'the struggle of the settlers for self-expression against a misunderstanding and interfering Home Government'. De Kiewiet was not prepared to condemn Britain in that way. He spoke of 'a certain inevitability of conflict and misunderstanding', so that 'no single man, nor party, idea, nor set of principles was solely responsible either for effecting any solution, or producing any tangle'.[4] Blame for what he regarded as South Africa's tragic past lay with no one group. At the head of his first chapter he placed the Latin tag, 'Iliacos intra mures peccatur et extra': sins are committed within the walls of Troy as well as without.

A few years before de Kiewiet wrote, A. P. Newton had called
for South African history to be rescued from local bias by being
set in a wider context.[5] De Kiewiet introduced his book by asserting that to understand British policy in South Africa one had
to place it in the context of developments both in Britain itself
and in the other British colonies. He pointed out that events in
New Zealand, for example – the kinds of policy that had been
adopted towards the Maoris, or the constitutional developments
set in train there – had helped shape 'native policy', or constitutional development, in South Africa. The same Colonial Office
officials dealt with all colonies; their minutes demonstrated that to
a considerable extent they regarded the empire as one. Beyond
this, however, de Kiewiet was aware of the similarities displayed
by all white settler societies, whether within or outside the empire.
He called Frederick Jackson Turner's seminal essay 'The Frontier
in American History' 'an illuminating and suggestive analysis of
the expansion into the middle and far west, with interesting parallels for South Africa', and he cited it in his book as evidence 'that
the frontier process in South Africa was essentially the same as in
America or indeed in any colony of settlement'.[6] But he did not
follow Turner to the extent of believing that South Africa's white
settlers had advanced into 'free', i.e. vacant, land – which had
formed one of Theal's myths – and he was aware that the similarities between South Africa and other settler societies should not be
overstressed.

Useful though the comparative context might be, he was to
repeat again and again that South Africa stood out as distinctive
among the British dominions because its aboriginal population
had not been 'swept aside' as in North America, or 'greatly outnumbered as in New Zealand'. The crucial fact was that 'the
Bantu remained in the land and multiplied'.[7] Previous historians
of South Africa had not sufficiently realised the importance of the
role of the African people in the country's history. De Kiewiet
wrote his first book before either of Macmillan's major historical
works based on the Philip papers had been published, but he borrowed what he knew to be Macmillan's position: that relations between white and black were 'much more significant than the
relations of English and Dutch colonists'. South African history
was not mainly, let alone entirely, the history of the white man; in

it 'Europeans, natives and Home Government are interlocked and inseparably intertwined'. Indeed, the process of white conquest had 'caused the dispossessed natives to transform European society by entering its midst as bondsmen'.[8]

He both refused to blame the British government alone for South Africa's ills and attempted to remain impartial between settlers and indigenous peoples. Thus he rejected Theal's view that Moshoeshoe of Lesotho had deliberately led the Free State into war in 1858: Theal had overlooked 'the part the farmers themselves played in arousing the antagonism of the frontier natives.'[9] In the late 1920s such writing constituted a revolutionary challenge to the existing historiography.

British Colonial Policy was not centrally focused, however, on the theme of black–white relations. Nor did de Kiewiet attempt in its pages to draw out analogies with the history of other dominions at any length. His statements concerning the importance of such analogies and of the processes of social transformation making 'the dispossessed natives ... bondsmen' remained assertions in this book; they could not be elaborated in a work that had as its main theme British colonial policy towards the republics. Today the book is still worth consulting for the quality of its writing, for the sources used (the Wodehouse papers, and especially the Colonial Office minutes), and the way de Kiewiet brought out the complexities of the story he told. When it appeared, however, *British Colonial Policy* was not uniformly praised. Under the heading 'A Useful History', an anonymous reviewer in the Johannesburg *Star* thought it conscientious rather than brilliant, adding: 'The natives are pawns and suffer as such, but the author does not forget ... their importance, ethnically and practically'.[10] A reviewer in the influential *English Historical Review* was closer to the mark when he spoke of it as an excellent monograph, though limited in its range – it was sketchy on the internal history of the republics – and betraying its origins as a doctoral dissertation.[11]

* * *

De Kiewiet's supervisor was one of the general editors of the multi-volume *Cambridge History of the British Empire*. In 1928 Newton asked him to contribute to the eighth volume, which was conceived as a definitive history of South Africa. Newton suggested they collaborate on a chapter to be entitled 'The Period of Transition', which would survey South African events during the years de Kiewiet had examined for his doctorate, and that de Kiewiet write a chapter on his own dealing with 'The Economic and Social Development of the Native Peoples in South Africa 1795–1921'. On the latter, all Newton could say was 'I imagine that you will be concerned mainly with the Bantu living under tribal conditions.'[12] De Kiewiet accepted the commission, which was a highly prestigious one, and worked on the chapters in Iowa and during a return visit to England in the summer of 1930. By early the following year he had finished them. The one chapter became two, on 'The Period of Transition, 1854–1870' and 'The Establishment of Responsible Government in Cape Colony, 1870–1872', the latter covering new ground for de Kiewiet. Other contributors took years to produce their chapters, so the South African volume was not published until 1936. When he received his copy, de Kiewiet found that though Newton had made no alterations to his text, he had allowed his name to appear as co-author, much to the younger man's disgust and annoyance. These two chapters were concerned largely with imperial policy and local politics, and their approach did not substantially differ from that de Kiewiet had pursued in his doctoral dissertation.

The third chapter he wrote was quite different. Entitled 'Social and Economic Developments in Native Tribal Life', it broke with an 'imperial history' approach. His reading of two books published in 1930 helped him identify with the plight of South Africa's blacks in the nineteenth century: Macmillan's *Complex South Africa*, which pulled together his mentor's work on the roots of African poverty, and *The Age of the Chartists* by the socialist historians J. L. and Barbara Hammond. De Kiewiet drew upon many of the major printed sources for African affairs in the British colonies in the nineteenth century: the Natal Native Commission of 1852, the Cape Native Laws and Customs (Barry) Commission of 1883, and Maclean's *Compendium of Kafir Laws and Customs*, as well as sources of less obvious interest to the historian, such as Warner's *Native Appeal Court Cases*. He used these, not merely to discuss policy towards Africans, as Edgar Brookes had in his *History of Native Policy*, but in an attempt to understand what had happened to African societies, and in particular the progression from 'barbarism to pauperism'. In a mere twenty-page chapter de Kiewiet could not produce more than a sketch of broad trends, but he nevertheless charted the emergence of an African proletariat over time in a way that no historian of South Africa had done before.

Much in this chapter would now be criticised: its picture of in-cessant strife among African societies before European intrusion; its failure to distinguish clearly between a fully fledged 'proleta-riat' and a migrant labour force; its view of the 'proletariat' as being 'without independence or initiative'. He said nothing about twentieth-century developments. For all that, his chapter, perhaps to a greater extent than any other piece of historical writing on South Africa published before the 1960s, pointed to themes of social and economic change which Africanist scholars would not begin to pursue until the 1970s: the environmental effects of over-grazing, the importance of diet and disease, the social conse-quences of Christian marriage, the origins of migrancy. And de Kiewiet now began to follow Macmillan in exploring the causes of African poverty. The picture he painted was one of 'continuous depression and disintegration'. The Xhosa cattle-killing of 1856–7 marked 'the collapse of an order that had been undermined and honeycombed for half a century by an aggressive European colo-nization'. The new black proletariat of the second half of the nine-teenth century harboured 'the resentment of men convinced there is something false and degrading in the arrangement and justice of their world'.[13] Leonard Barnes, a radical critic, condemned the *Cambridge History* as uniformly weak on colour policy, but in the *Spectator* Basil Williams drew special attention to de Kiewiet's con-tribution as 'far the most interesting chapter on the ['Native'] problem.... The whole chapter should be carefully read and pon-dered for its wise and sympathetic attitude to the natives' point of view.'[14]

* * *

De Kiewiet did not pursue the Africanist insights so tantalisingly revealed in his *Cambridge History* chapter. For his next project, he returned to the accessible, and more familiar, sources available in London on British policy. He now continued the story from where his first book had left it at the beginning of the 1870s, and took it to the mid-1880s. Periods of leave in 1933 and 1936 were spent in the Public Record Office in Chancery Lane. He was not the first to use the South African despatches for the early 1870s: Newton had arranged for C. J. Uys to be affiliated to King's College while he worked on his doctorate for the University of Pretoria. This was published by Lovedale Press in 1933 under the title *In the Era of Shepstone. Being a History of British Expansion in South Africa*

(1842–1877). Uys had one major advantage over de Kiewiet: for the
events leading to the British annexation of the Transvaal in 1877
he drew not only upon the London records but also upon the
valuable and previously unexploited Shepstone papers available in
Natal. De Kiewiet's argument that the annexation of the Transvaal was not without benefit for the white Transvaalers had been
anticipated by Uys. De Kiewiet referred his readers to 'the em-
phatic pages of Professor Uys' at one point,[15] but Uys lacked de
Kiewiet's flair, his rather pedestrian book was published obscure-
ly, and it was never widely used. De Kiewiet's main source was
once again the official despatches – and where the originals had
been destroyed, he was often able to use the copies printed for the
cabinet, the Confidential Print – but he also drew extensively on
the semi-official and private papers of Lord Carnarvon, Secretary
of State for the Colonies from 1874 to 1878. After his *History*, *The
Imperial Factor* was the most influential of his works, an inspiration
to later historians who saw themselves as working within the liberal tradition of historical scholarship on South Africa.

In *The Imperial Factor* de Kiewiet was again concerned to argue
that Theal had wrongly accused Britain of ignorant meddling in
South African affairs, and of bad faith. He pointed instead to the
intractable problems which British officials had been compelled to
face in South Africa. British policy was ambiguous and contradic-
tory, sometimes ill-informed, its shortcomings 'many and
grievous', but it was not malign. It had helped protect Africans in
their rights and their lands. Where it had failed, that failure was
one of 'high motives and worthy ends'.[16] While most reviewers
welcomed his reluctance to apportion blame, one commented that
his 'praise balances censure so continuously that the reader is apt
to become confused'.[17] And writing in the *New Statesman*, Macmillan agreed with de Kiewiet that the imperial government had
had good intentions but added that the trouble was that in practice trusteeship had counted for little.[18]

In introducing his book de Kiewiet expressed his belief that it
had contemporary relevance: though treating South Africa of the
1870s and 1880s, it was also about the South Africa of his own
day. In the 1870s, he remarked in his Preface, the attention of
whites was already too much focused on the issue of Boer versus
Briton. As in his own day, there existed 'the pretence that a dangerous native problem was miraculously unrelated to the fortunes
of the white population'. His book was designed to show the inter-

relatedness of South African problems, and how black–white relations lay at their heart. But the historical record had been
distorted by racism. The most distinctive feature of the history of
blacks and whites was not the clash of races, the 'endless Kaffir
wars' chronicled in such detail by Theal and Cory, but rather the
development of a close economic association, a theme those
earlier amateur historians had almost entirely ignored. This important revisionist perspective, first pointed to by Macmillan, had
been developed by H. M. Robertson in an article in the *South African Journal of Economics*[19] but no one more effectively propagated it
than de Kiewiet. In the introductory pages of *The Imperial Factor*, he
spoke of frontiers, not as Turner had, but as gateways through
which Africans were incorporated into 'European society', incorporated not as equals but as a migrant proletariat. The dependence of the whites on black labour represented 'the greatest
social and economic fact' in nineteenth-century South African history, and that history had produced one economy, 'a single society
in which the main line of division was not one of race and culture,
but of possession and authority'. Nineteenth-century attempts at
segregation had all failed. In stating this, de Kiewiet was again
speaking to his own day: the segregationism then being introduced in South Africa would, he implied, likewise fail. Adopting
the central idea in Eric Walker's Oxford lecture on 'The Frontier
Tradition in South Africa', de Kiewiet now saw segregation as the
result of frontier race-attitudes, and twentieth-century policies as
'the Great Trek coming out of exile and avenging itself'.[20] But
such policies were doomed because they ran counter to the process of incorporation he charted in his book.

The Imperial Factor was not narrowly confined to colonial policy.
Sub-titled 'A Study in Politics and Economics', its pages on the
economic problems of the frontier reflected de Kiewiet's now
keener awareness of the importance of material realities in
shaping the course of history. An entire chapter was devoted to
'The Economics of War' and much of the book dealt with the way
in which Africans, especially in the eastern Cape and the
Transkei, were deprived of their lands and forced into migrant
labour. De Kiewiet wrote, for instance, of the 'sheer hopelessness
of social and economic conditions in the Ciskei' in the 1870s.
Macmillan gave special praise to the way the book both dealt with
increasing landlessness and drew attention to the congestion
already existing in the 1870s in African areas.[21]

Imperial policy nevertheless remained the central focus. For all its vivid recreation of events 'on the ground', through the skilful use of detail – and de Kiewiet made especially good use of the annual Cape bluebooks on Native Affairs to that end – the picture of African societies that emerged in his pages was a highly generalised one. There was no attempt to see Africans as actors on an equal footing with whites, or to understand African societies from the inside in the way white communities were analysed. Some of his remarks about Africans, moreover, might have found a place in a work in the settler tradition of South African historiography. 'Among savages with no government save the intermittent one of councils', he wrote, 'the party of action and violence must always prevail.'[22] He told his readers that his tale was one that would be told again, and when in fact it was de Kiewiet would be shown to have erred not only on points of detail but also on interpretation: writers of the 1970s and early 1980s agreed with Uys rather than de Kiewiet in their appreciation of Carnarvon, but also argued that the Colonial Secretary had been motivated by economic considerations. De Kiewiet had realised the new importance of African labour in the 1870s, and linked it to the disturbances of that decade, but he did not argue, as Norman Etherington and others would in the 1970s, that the emergent need for African labour lay behind the adoption of the confederation policy.[23] But for its insights, style and sweep, *The Imperial Factor* would remain a classic of South African historiography.

* * *

That de Kiewiet's vision of South African history not only embraced certain decades of the nineteenth century but ranged more widely was confirmed by a paper he presented to a meeting of the American Historical Association in 1937, the year the one hundred and fiftieth anniversary of the United States constitution was commemorated. He was asked to survey the constitutional development of South Africa. Written with his usual elegance, 'The Frontier and the Constitution in South Africa' was brief, but full of insight. Referring to parallels between the American and South African frontiers, he focused especially on sectionalism, the importance of which Turner had stressed for American history. Contrary to the American case, sectionalism was a fortuitous development in South Africa, for colonisation had developed from a single centre, and the country was climatically and geographically uniform. So it was 'the political workings of men that superimposed upon this basic uniformity of climate and soil a disastrous political disharmony'. Given this disharmony, de Kiewiet implied that a federal constitution would have been more appropriate than the unitary one adopted in 1909.

South Africa had adopted a unitary constitution, he suggested, because of the need to rule the African majority with a firm hand. His survey linked a century of constitutional developments with the 'frontier tradition' of repressive policy towards blacks. 'White civilisation' had set out deliberately to create a black proletariat. 'Its legislation sought to restrict and to bind, not to relieve or to liberate.... Economically it drew the natives deeply into white society. Socially and politically it cast them forth.' He bemoaned the withdrawal of Britain and the 'metropolitan point of view' concerning 'the rights of civilised men'. The grant of self-government to the Cape in 1872 had come at the cost of the possibility of a 'wider liberty' embracing Africans as well. The frontier tradition of repression and inequality in church and state had triumphed, first in the Treaty of Vereeniging which ended the South African War in 1902, and then in the Union constitution itself. Surprisingly, de Kiewiet did not mention the abolition of the Cape African franchise in 1936, but he did point to the racial inequalities in legislation passed since Union. Though industrialisation had given them new means of physical coercion, the whites remained 'fearful', and had chosen a path of repression to avert any challenge to their supremacy. De Kiewiet ended by quoting, with obvious agreement, the remark made by Lord Selborne, British High Commissioner before Union, that the path of repression was one 'few nations had trod before ... and scarcely one trod with success.'[24]

* * *

Oxford University Press 'want a new sort of pie', he told Macmillan in November 1937, referring to the commission they had offered him for the *History*, 'one third history and two thirds economics, sociology and current comment.' Macmillan advised that the historical section stop with Union in 1910, and the second part tackle contemporary developments. The 'native question' – Macmillan expressed his dislike of the term – should not be dealt with in separate chapters, but form an integral part of the analysis throughout. Political issues were not as important as economic ones, he suggested, citing the dependence on mining and the comparative poverty of the land to make the point. De Kiewiet agreed with these comments when they were sent him, and told the Press he would not write specifically for a South African audience, but with other readers in mind, and that he would attempt to stress analogies with other dominions.

By March 1938 he was hard at work on the project, but although friends in South Africa sent him articles, and the reports of the Native Economic and other major government commissions were available in the United States, the sources still posed problems. 'I find I have to do a great deal of blue book reading to get up to date', he informed Macmillan.

I am appalled at the absence of decently organised information ... about the country.... I must keep comparisons and contrasts with the other dominions before the reader. Some of these are obvious, such as Australian and South African rainfall and desert conditions.... the social and socio-economic problems are a different job altogether. Here quite obviously the poverty of the country in an agricultural point of view, the emphasis on mining, and the universal and unusual dependence on mining, the still more unusual dependence on black, poorly paid labor, are among the leading problems. I am going to try to discuss the natives as they really are, indissolubly part of the whole society. That will get rid of what is arrant nonsense, the usual treatment of white progress and conditions in three chapters and the 'Oh and then of course there is the Kafir' sort of final chapter.... Maybe I had better keep the story sober, and not break any obvious lances. It after all is to be an explanation, something of a textbook, and thus should not belabor men and matters too hard. Anyhow, even a quiet and modest account will be shocking enough.[25]

He told the Press of the difficulty of not seeming to indict, explaining: 'so much of South African life is an indictment that a pure impartiality will not be possible. Wage legislation that would be unobjectionable in New Zealand becomes a two-edged sword in South Africa....'[26]

Teaching modern European history as he did, and reading the contemporary German press, he became increasingly concerned about events in Europe, but he pushed ahead with the book nevertheless, and when he put pen to paper he wrote quickly, soon filling a hundred sheets of paper with his small, spidery script. In his first draft, the book was divided into the two parts suggested by Macmillan and the publisher, the second of which, headed 'The Modern State', opened with the chapter on 'Poor Whites and Poor Blacks'. The book had much less to say on contemporary developments than the Press had originally intended, however, and in the end the chapters were run on without a break. Some material was rearranged – paragraphs transferred from 'The Witwatersrand and the Boer War' chapter, for example, to that on gold mining, which was placed after the one on Union, written last.[27] Altogether, however, remarkably few changes were made to the original draft before it was published in July 1941.

In *The Imperial Factor* de Kiewiet showed that he was not merely content to follow the established tradition of imperial history, which was political and constitutional, and that he was aware of the importance of social and economic change 'on the ground' in the country about which he was writing. His *History* moved right away from the imperial policy theme of his first two books, and had as its central concern broad themes in social and economic history. In addressing such themes he was in part returning to, and elaborating on, ideas pioneered by Macmillan, especially in his *Agrarian Problem* and *Complex South Africa*.

The *History* was written with grace and lucidity, and many of its short sentences are full of pregnant meaning. One of his students at Iowa, later himself an imperial historian of distinction, remembers de Kiewiet reading from his manuscript in a seminar on imperial history. The student was at once 'entranced by the clarity of his thought and the charm of his writing',[28] as so many have been since. It was de Kiewiet's literary gifts as well as his unmatched ability to synthesise that made his *History* a best-seller and therefore extremely influential, reaching a far wider audience than Macmillan's trilogy.[29]

The *History* could be so readable because it did not include a mass of undigested detail. It was 'an interpretation rather than a textbook'.[30] De Kiewiet knew that Eric Walker had produced a largely political *History* which had tried to be comprehensive, and provided so much detail that the wood was lost for the trees. De Kiewiet's much shorter and more analytical work – less systematic than, say, Keith Hancock's *Australia* (London, 1930), which he cited – comprised a set of linked essays on what he considered the most important themes in the social and economic history of the country. It revealed him at the height of his powers as an historian who could synthesise the best insights of others and offer new insights distilled from the massive detail of bluebook material.

Hancock had begun his history with 'The Invasion of Australia',[31] but de Kiewiet followed Walker in beginning his with 'The Foundations of a New Society' – the coming of the Portuguese and the Dutch to the Cape. Like Hancock and Walker, he gave minimal attention to precolonial indigenous societies. But in later chapters he picked up and elaborated ideas from Macmillan's writings and his own earlier works. 'The leading theme of South African history', he wrote, was 'the growth of a new society in which white and black are bound together in the closest dependence upon each other.'[32] The frontier was the sieve through which Africans passed into such a society; frontier wars were civil wars between people already associated economically. And these wars were not just about land; they were also about labour. He headed his second chapter, on the early nineteenth century, with an apt quotation from Montesquieu's *The Spirit of the Laws*: 'From the right to kill in conquest, politicians have drawn the right to reduce to servitude.'

Yet the frontier which gave birth to a new society was also seen as the seedplot of white racism. Though de Kiewiet cited neither Walker's *Frontier Tradition* (1930), nor MacCrone's *Race Attitudes in South Africa*,[33] he followed them in suggesting that the white racism of the eighteenth-century frontier had somehow been carried over into twentieth-century South Africa. The Union constitution represented 'the triumph of the frontier.... It was the conviction of the frontier that the foundations of society were race and the privileges of race.' In recent decades, 'the equality which had been denied the natives in the churches of the rural Republics was again denied them in the temples of labour.'[34] Just as Frederick Jackson Turner had argued that the American frontier gave the history of the United States its distinctive character, so de Kiewiet was now implying that the South African frontier had shaped the country's past and contemporary development.

Throughout the *History* comparisons were drawn with the other dominions – as befitted what was intended to be one of a number of companion studies of dominion histories – or with North America. But whatever the parallels suggested – between, say, the 'poor whites' of South Africa and the 'crackers' of the Old South[35] – in the end de Kiewiet came down on the side of South Africa's uniqueness: the language of the other dominions, or of the United States, he concluded, could not be applied to South Africa, where the 'native people' had not been 'swept away'. It was its large black population that made South Africa distinctive. Unlike Australia or Canada, it had not drawn most of its immigrants from without, whites who were able to claim a vote and a decent wage.

South Africa's immigration came from within. Her immigrants were conquered people and they were black.[36]

Reviewing the *History* in the October 1942 issue of the *American Historical Review*, Paul Knaplund rightly called it 'a real history, not a tract', but in places it did almost read like an anti-segregationist manifesto. Though de Kiewiet admitted that some segregationists sought protection for blacks as well as whites, and spoke of their 'genuine effort to improve native life and administration', he argued that history showed that the segregationist measures recently implemented in South Africa gave no answer to the country's problems. He did not view segregation, as recent historians have done, as 'the highest stage of white supremacy', something created deliberately in the early years of the twentieth century. He used the term vaguely, usually to mean any attempt to keep blacks apart from whites, and so traced the history of attempts at territorial segregation back to the beginnings of white settlement at the Cape. All such attempts had failed; segregation was 'a myth, a fancy, anything but a fact'; the growth of the single economy formed the main theme of South Africa's history. Thus, 'to unwind the woven cord of native and European life is simply to require history to retrace its steps', and he implied that that was impossible. He allowed that other countries had adopted protectionist policies in recent years contrary to sound economics, and that 'in their company South Africa's insistence that its economic life must be organised to secure the dominant position of the white man is not seriously out of place', but he nevertheless asserted that on economic grounds the case against segregation – and here he was probably thinking especially of the colour bar in industry – was 'unanswerable'.[37]

Though he strove to present a balanced picture, he emphasised South Africa's poverty more than its wealth, which even in the form of gold was, he stressed, fragile. The boom that had followed the abandonment of the gold standard in 1932 was 'born of international confusion' and was precarious. It was the essential poverty of the country that helped explain why the whites were so determined to protect their privilege.[38] One reviewer admitted to finding his book 'rather pessimistic. The reader is left with the impression that to find a solution of the South African problem is beyond the wit of man.'[39]

Many other professional historians have published single-volume histories of South Africa – J. A. I. Agar-Hamilton and Alan

Hattersley in the 1930s, for example; Arthur Keppel-Jones in 1949 – but no other had the power of de Kiewiet's masterpiece, which in its emphasis on social and economic themes anticipated so much that was to concern the historians of the 1970s and 1980s. Macmillan had written about the early nineteenth century, and about his own time too, and had been the first to adopt the anti-Theal perspective which de Kiewiet developed in his work. But unlike Macmillan, de Kiewiet did not stress changes on the land to the extent of failing to give due emphasis to the process of industrialisation. On the foundation laid by Macmillan, de Kiewiet was the first to build a general structure, in which such themes as the origins of migrant labour and the emergence of the colour bar in industry fell clearly into place in the overall history of the country. In this there was genius, for again and again a phrase or a sentence encapsulated a process which no historian before him had written of, and opened a new world of understanding of the country's past. The praise which A. J. P. Taylor, who would become the most-read English historian of his generation, lavished on the book was not overdrawn: 'The scholarship and penetration give the reader that exhilarating intellectual pleasure which one gets only once or twice in a decade; a mature mind has been stretched to the full and one's own mind has to be equally exerted.'[40] In many cases over two decades would elapse before other professional historians – some called 'liberal Africanists', others 'radicals' – began to research in depth topics which de Kiewiet had opened up in his *History*. In 1985 the president of the South African Historical Society called for 'a new de Kiewiet' to provide 'a vision as bold and brilliant and stimulating as his was in his own day and, indeed, continues in surprisingly many respects to be almost half a century later'.[41] In 1986 there was still no really new, or better, 'broadly interpretative essay'[42] ranging over most of South Africa's history.

9 Race, class and liberal history

The Progressive historians – Frederick Jackson Turner, Charles A. Beard and V. Parrington – dominant in American historiography in the 1920s and 1930s, believed that a new history was needed in the interests of reform.[1] Macmillan and de Kiewiet thought likewise. Unlike Theal and Cory, they were profoundly disillusioned with contemporary South Africa, and sought through their work, not to help create a charter for the existing social order, but to challenge it. Like the Progressives, too, they believed the new history should embrace a social and economic dimension, that it should include the history of 'the common man', in their case whether he were white or black. But in other ways, their approach did not parallel that of contemporary historical writing overseas. In Britain those whom Herbert Butterfield would call Whig historians believed in history as a story of progress towards the present and what they assumed would be an even better future.[2] Macmillan and de Kiewiet were as ready as their British counterparts to moralise, but for them South Africa had done anything but progress; on the contrary, in its racial policies, it was moving backwards. South Africa's history was not a story of advancing liberty, but rather of retrogression, as chances were missed and unfortunate policies adopted. They began to do what later liberals would engage in more explicitly: they tried to identify 'what had gone wrong', 'where we had taken the wrong turning', sometimes laying the blame at the door of particular individuals. By contrast with the Progressives in America, the early liberal historians of South Africa stressed co-operation rather than conflict in the past. The conflict on the Cape eastern frontier in the nineteenth century, about which Theal and Cory had written at such great length, did not mainly concern cattle, as those historians had suggested, but was essentially a struggle for land. As liberals, Macmillan and de Kiewiet strove to achieve evolutionary change and co-operation across the colour line rather than conflict in the South Africa of their day, so it was natural that they should stress co-operation in the past. Through their rewriting of the South African past, they hoped to be able to influence the contemporary situation in their country. Both men believed Afrikaner–English relations had been given too much attention in South African history, and that 'race relations', meaning relations between white and black, formed the key thread in that history. But de Kiewiet also shared Macmillan's view that race as such – though critically important – had been overplayed in South African historical writing.[3] There had been much inter-racial co-operation in the past; racial differences had not been as important as had been claimed. This is what the radicals of the 1970s were to argue, though unlike Macmillan and de Kiewiet they would once again stress conflict in the past, conflict between classes and not races.[4]

* * *

In beginning to pioneer social and economic history in South Africa, Macmillan directed that country's historiography towards themes that would not be explored in depth until the 1970s. De Kiewiet chose to work on imperial policy – the main subject of his first two books – and in so doing helped take South African historiography squarely into its imperial phase, parallel to that of the other dominions, whose historians, like him, travelled to London to work on the documents in the Public Record Office, and so wrote works on imperial policy.[5] The Imperial Factor can indeed be seen as one of the finest products of that kind of writing in South African historiography. But in this book de Kiewiet revealed that he was no 'mere' imperial historian, that he sought to incorporate Macmillan's concern for social and economic change 'on the ground', drawing upon local records and a feel for the 'lie of the land'. Broad social and economic themes – which he first tackled in a much more limited way in his Cambridge History chapter on African societies in the nineteenth century – became the main focus of his History, and thereby provided what Macmillan had not, an overall outline of South Africa's social and economic development. So there was in de Kiewiet's work a broadening of approach, and a move towards greater attention to social and economic history.

De Kiewiet did not use the dichotomy between the 'civilised' and the 'barbarous' to be found in Macmillan's pages; he did not call African societies 'uncivilised', 'primitive' or 'backward'. Yet while he followed Macmillan in challenging many of the myths in Theal and Cory, other myths – including the assertions that African agriculture was backward, or that African societies remained egalitarian – survived intact in his pages. His *History* gave the impression that all blacks were semi-nomadic, and a map after his text reproduced the myth of the empty interior at the time of the Great Trek.[6] He spoke of the 'unscientific and wasteful [agricultural] methods of the natives',[7] and was too ready to forget how less than successful some white farmers had been. Though his picture of the essential poverty of African societies in the eastern Cape by the 1870s was confirmed in the early 1980s in the work of Jack Lewis,[8] some of his other judgements have been shown to have been quite wrong: the Khoi societies of the south-western Cape, for example, did not collapse 'undramatically and simply'.[9] He began *The Imperial Factor* by saying how difficult it was for a historian to judge, but remained quick to moralise and apportion blame. Sir Owen Lanyon, administrator of the Transvaal, was one for whom de Kiewiet had nothing but scorn; he not only 'acted stupidly as a politician ... his conduct as a soldier was conceited, fatuous and shortsighted'.[10]

In his old age de Kiewiet reflected on his early career in this way:

I am the last surviving member of the group that labored in Johannesburg in the early '20s to bring the native problem, as it was then called, into a credible historical, economic and social focus. It was a lonely, and, to some of us, a costly exercise. We developed the history that put the African population in its proper place as the central element in South African society. We laid the groundwork of economic and social perception that displayed the role and the condition of the African in society.[11]

This was too large a claim. To be sure, in the Theal–Cory tradition which Macmillan and de Kiewiet challenged, Africans did not occupy a central role in South African history, and later historical work in that white-supremacist tradition took the process of excluding Africans much further than ever Theal or Cory did.[12] But the liberal historians of the 1920s did not elaborate an Africanist perspective in their historical work. It was only in the 1960s that those who would come to be called 'liberal Africanists' really began to 'put the African population in its proper place' as a central element in South African society. De Kiewiet, and before him Macmillan, did not investigate African societies in the same depth as white-ruled ones; blacks were essentially passive in their pages; and they brought few individual black actors to life. De Kiewiet did not take South African history into an Africanist phase, though in his brief *Cambridge History* chapter, for the only time in his oeuvre, he focused directly and exclusively on the history of Africans, and showed himself open to new approaches to the study of their societies. But he thereafter returned to the study of imperial policy. Considerable traces of Eurocentricity remained in his writing: in his *History*, for example, he spoke of South African society being 'complicated by the presence of other races and societies'.[13] Lacking close personal relationships with Africans, he very clearly directed his writing at a white audience, and he never appreciated the need for detailed work on the history of African communities, work that would explore them 'from the inside', as Africanists attempted to do in the 1970s. The black history of South Africa could not easily be studied either from the prairies of Iowa, or from the finger-lakes of up-state New York to which he was to move after completing the *History*. It was only after the Second World War that the climate of anti-racism, the decolonisation of tropical Africa and the growth of new universities in West, East and Central Africa would together provide the context and stimulus for the new African history. De Kiewiet was involved in those great changes, but as administrator, educationalist and political commentator, not as historian.

When revisionist criticism of 'the conventional wisdom' in historical scholarship began to be heard in the 1970s, de Kiewiet was one of those liberals taken to task for arguing that economic growth and segregation were incompatible, and that economic growth would undermine segregation. Colin Bundy, for example, spoke of his assumption that 'economic development (that is the growth of the modern sector of a dual economy) has served, and serves still, to minimize social conflict and to ameliorate social and economic disabilities. This approach posits a fundamental and historical dissonance between racism ... and economic growth.'[14] De Kiewiet was later to argue that proposition, and he continued to believe that *in the long run* economic growth was both 'rational' and race-blind, and that the needs of a modern economy would force changes in South Africa's system of legalised racial discrimination, even while he came to realise that there was no necessary incompatibility between industrialisation and segregation in the short run.[15] That relationship was far from a major concern of his historical writing, however. Only a few sentences in his *History* spoke of a contradiction between capitalist development and racial segregation, and they were introduced to make an essentially political point, to put forward an argument against the segregationist policies being introduced in the South Africa of his own day. When he wrote his *History*, secondary industrialisation was a relatively new phenomenon, and the evidence that it could proceed in tandem with, and even be supported by, segregationist policies was not yet clear.

Martin Legassick, writing in the early 1970s, and more recently John Cell, have both argued that segregation was a product of the early years of the twentieth century, and was intimately linked to the mineral revolution. For de Kiewiet, segregation had roots that went back to the very beginning of the establishment of white domination in South Africa.[16] Yet he recognised that the emergence of the diamond and gold mining industries in the late nineteenth century marked a new era in South African history, and that another was beginning as he wrote the *History*, for manufacturing industry was for the first time becoming significant. De Kiewiet hoped that secondary industrialisation would bring the racial segregation of which he disapproved to an end. Segregationist policies were, he asserted, out of date in the 'modern world' South Africa was entering in the 1930s.[17]

Another major criticism directed against his work in the early 1970s related to his view of British imperial policy. In a powerful critique of previous writing on imperial policy in South Africa entitled 'The Imperial Factor in South Africa in the Nineteenth Century: Towards a Reassessment', which appeared in the *Journal of Imperial and Commonwealth History* in 1974, Anthony Atmore and Shula Marks claimed that de Kiewiet, along with other historians of imperial policy, had over-emphasised the formal imperial framework, and been overly concerned with individual motivation and the importance of day-to-day policy making. He had paid insufficient attention to the penetration of capital and to the economic imperatives driving British colonial policy, and had failed to probe the impact of British expansionism on the African societies affected. In all this there was undoubtedly much truth, though the kind of imperial history de Kiewiet wrote was less blinkered and narrow than most written before the 1970s. De Kiewiet himself later acknowledged that in the 1930s he had not distanced himself sufficiently from the imperial records.[18]

The charge that de Kiewiet, along with the other early liberal historians, ignored class, is unfounded. Macmillan, as we have seen, devoted much attention to the poor whites – and hence to accumulation and stratification – before he turned to the 'poor blacks', who were more of a blanket category. Eric Walker noted in his *History* that the existence of 'poor whites' was not a recent phenomenon: he traced them back at least to the time of the Great Trek.[19] De Kiewiet developed Macmillan's insights on the inequalities in white society, which like his mentor he traced back to the trekboer and the Trek. Like Macmillan, too, he tended to discuss 'native life' in general terms, and he sometimes assumed an undifferentiated ethnic collectivity, the Afrikaners. In their landlessness and their lack of industrial skills, he found 'poor whites and poor blacks ... close indeed'.[20] But he did not go on to chart stratification in African societies, or the emergence of a black petty-bourgeoisie in his own day. The early liberal historians did not conceptualise class, or its relationship to race or to the state, nor did they identify it as a major factor (let alone *the* major factor) in South African history. But they were not oblivious of its importance, and they presented the evidence they found, even if it ran counter to their ideological assumptions.

If de Kiewiet was indeed a liberal historian – the label was not one he himself used, but came to be used for both Macmillan and himself – then his liberalism cannot be defined negatively by reference to his failure to stress the primacy of class, or the functionality of segregation and economic growth. Nor should the spotlight fall on the incorporation into his writing of the idea of a frontier tradition of racism as a major explanatory concept. Following Macmillan, de Kiewiet believed material factors were important in history, though as a liberal he rejected any notion that they were always and necessarily more important than all others. His liberalism meant, in other words, that he was no rigid determinist, but a pluralist, who, for instance, attached considerable weight to the role of the individual in history, as witness his treatment of Rhodes in his *History*.[21] Macmillan and de Kiewiet stressed the importance of environmental and economic determinants more than their challengers in the 1970s were to allow, but both men did believe that individuals could make important choices and that ideas crucially shaped historical processes. Take the cause of the Anglo–Zulu War of 1879 for example. Theal had seen the war as a struggle between civilisation and barbarism, and others had regarded it as an event satisfactorily explained by Zulu aggressiveness. De Kiewiet was aware that economic pressures and drought had brought the Zulu to a desperate state. He did not anticipate the kind of argument about the capitalist origins of the war made by Etherington and Guy in the 1970s, but he did recognise that Sir Bartle Frere, the Cape Governor and High Commissioner, bore a major responsibility for the war, as have most historians since he wrote.[22]

Macmillan and de Kiewiet were 'friends of the native', who attempted to be sympathetic to blacks as well as whites, who rejected the colour prejudice which suggested blacks were inferior, and whose humane vision embraced all the inhabitants of South Africa. If, for all their 'modernism', their approach now often seems paternalistic and limited, it must be understood in the context of the time at which they wrote. When it appeared, their work was highly challenging to the prevailing historical orthodoxy. Today's platitudes were then novel, and only became platitudes because of their work. That it retains its importance today, in a very different historical climate, is a mark of their scholarship.

PART 3
Amateurs and professionals

10 Early Africanist work

In their work Macmillan and de Kiewiet recognised blacks as important, but did not take account of African societies on equal terms with those of whites. Nor did other professional historians who wrote in the 1930s, 1940s or 1950s move any further towards an Africanist perspective. Yet long before the 1950s there were a few amateur white scholars who took an interest in African societies, and some Africans themselves who began to write about their past.

Some of the most important early Africanist work was done by A. T. Bryant (1865–1953) (Father David), a Trappist missionary based at the Mariannhill monastery near Pinetown between Durban and Pietermaritzburg. Having compiled a Zulu–English dictionary, published in 1905, he wrote a series of articles on Zulu history in the Mariannhill periodical *Izindaba Zabata* between 1911 and 1913.[1] His appointment as research fellow and lecturer in Zulu ethnology at the university in Johannesburg in 1921 enabled him 'to give his whole time to the collecting of fast-disappearing historical material'.[2] With money donated by the Native Recruiting Corporation and the Witwatersrand Native Labour Association, Wits appointed C. M. Doke to a lectureship in Bantu philology in a new Bantu Studies department, and it was under the auspices of that department that Bryant in 1923 gave a series of lectures at Wits which he then incorporated into *Olden Times in Zululand and Natal, Containing the Earlier Political History of the Eastern-Nguni clans*, published in 1929.[3] This classic was written in a style which he thought would be entertaining for white readers but which now appears to be insufferably patronising. Though Bryant saw himself as no more than a collector of information about Zulu history, he rightly said that his book laid 'the very foundation on which all future "Zulu" history must be based'.[4] The first professional historian to analyse his work in depth in the 1960s found it 'the essential starting-point' for 'any reconstructions of the Nguni past'.[5]

James Stuart (1868–1942), a magistrate in various Natal districts, wrote the official history of the Bambatha rebellion of 1906, published in 1913, and, much later, assembled the writings of one of the first white traders in Natal, Henry Francis Fynn, which helped promote an image of Shaka as a bloodthirsty monster.[6] But Stuart's major contribution lay in the mass of valuable oral material he collected on the history of Africans in Natal–Zululand. When Stuart's papers were returned to South Africa from England in 1944 after his death, there was a flurry of interest in the history of Africans, and an editorial in the *Daily News* (Durban) called for the establishment of a chair of Zulu history at Natal University.[7] That came to nothing and the significance of Stuart's work only became generally recognised when the publication of his archive began in the mid-1970s.[8]

Other officials pursued important work within an 'antiquarian tradition' of Africanist scholarship. Any survey of that tradition would have to include such works as *The Story of the Zulus* by the magistrate J. Y. Gibson, which first appeared in 1903 and was issued in a revised edition in 1911; *The Native Tribes of the Transvaal*, compiled by Major R. H. Massie for the British War Office after the South African War and published in 1905; the six articles by W. C. Scully under the title 'Fragments of Native History' in *The State* in 1909; and 'An Account of the Bapedi' by D. R. Hunt, a Native Commissioner in Sekhukuniland, who used oral testimony to construct a brief history of the Pedi from their origins to 1930.[9]

* * *

The new Christianised African elite that emerged in the eastern Cape in the last part of the nineteenth century soon began to write works with a historical content. The first book one of them published in English was a biography of the earliest Christian convert among the Xhosa. Though John Knox Bokwe's life of Ntsikana[10] read 'like a novel'[11] and was totally uncritical, it was nevertheless an original work of history and one of the first biographies of a black South African.[12] In Cape Town Francis Peregrino – son of the more famous F. Z. S. Peregrino, the Ghanaian editor who settled at the Cape in 1900 and founded and edited *The South African Spectator*[13] – published the first general work of history by an African in South Africa. His *Short History of the Native*

Tribes of South Africa, which appeared in 1899, drew heavily upon Theal, but presented a far more balanced account than was to be found in Theal's pages.

Other histories which are known to have been written by Africans have not survived. Alan Kirkland Soga of East London, former editor of the Xhosa–English newspaper *Izwi Labantu*, wrote a large work of over 500 pages, which was on the verge of publication in Boston and East London in 1906. A pre-publication notice in *Izwi Labantu* of 30 October that year gave details of the contents of 'The Problem of the Relations of Black and White in South Africa'. Among its over twenty chapters on historical subjects were ones on 'The Ancient Bushman', 'The Hottentots or Khoi-Khoin', 'Kafir Patriots' and 'The Origin of the Fingoes'. The prospectus spoke of it as 'the only work that attempts to give the real story of the South African aborigines.... It tells the plain and pathetic story of the early owners of African soil....'[14] Why it was not published is not known. Soga's colleague Walter Rubusana (1858–1936), also of East London and later to be a member of the Cape Provincial Council, is said to have completed a 'History of South Africa from the Native Standpoint' early this century, and to have obtained an honorary doctorate for it from 'McKinley University, USA',[15] but no such work has ever been traced. His interest in the history of his people is, however, attested to by his massive anthology of praise-poems and other historical items in Xhosa which he published in 1906.[16]

During the First World War two considerable works of history were written by Africans in English. Solomon T. Plaatje, editor of *Tsala ea Batho* (The People's Friend) newspaper in Kimberley and first general secretary of the South African Native National Congress, had shown 'great mastery' of Tswana history as early as 1895, when he was 18.[17] In 1916 he published the classic *Native Life in South Africa before and since the European War and the Boer Rebellion*. In part a polemic, it was also a work of contemporary history and a source-book, which contained chapters on 'Armed Natives in the South African War' and 'The Boer Rebellion' of 1914, a sketch of the history of Thaba Nchu which went back into the early nineteenth century, and a masterly description of the effects of the Natives Land Act of 1913 in the Orange Free State.[18] When he was in England in 1919–20, Plaatje began a sequel on the effects of the Land Act, and the history of the Native Labour Contingent in the First World War. There is evidence that it began with the same events he described in his novel *Mhudi*, which he wrote at the same time.[19] The novel, an account of the war between the Ndebele and the Rolong in the 1830s, was eventually published in 1930, but the other work never appeared.

It was also during the war that Plaatje's friend Silas Modiri Molema (1891–1965), then a young medical student in Scotland, wrote *The Bantu, Past and Present. An Ethnographical and Historical Study of the Native Races of South Africa.* This uneven attempt at a general survey was eventually published in Edinburgh in 1920. It was based in part on personal information, but also used Theal and other Eurocentric sources, and reproduced their myths. According to Molema, blacks had arrived in South Africa in the sixteenth century; the Shona had not built Zimbabwe; the Bantu 'remained an indolent, lethargic and dreamy race of men, and their history one dull dreary, featureless scene of barbarism and incompetence'; the Zulu revolution was a war of extermination, Shaka a tyrant and Mzilikazi a drinker of blood. The Khoisan 'stole Dutch property on a grand scale', the Mfengu were 'delivered from bondage' by the colonial forces in 1835 and the Xhosa cattle-killing of 1856–7 was mere superstition. In Molema's eyes it was the missionaries who had brought progress and light, and his work was designed to show how Africans could, under white tutelage, emerge from their dark past. In 1951, when he was an office-holder in the African National Congress, he published a somewhat more scholarly biography of *Chief Moroka*, but even then a reviewer with some justification called it 'a worthy product of George McCall Theal' and 'an INSULT to the African people...'[20] Once again, before the missionaries arrived, 'the mind of the people was a blank, an utter void, a howling vacuum'. The Rolong were

rude in their manners, totally illiterate, ignorant of the arts of peace, polygamous, sunken in superstition, without the light of any true religion, so degraded in morals as to be almost unmoral, intellectually undeveloped, content with a life of indolence and oblivion, and without ambition beyond the satisfaction of the immediate physical needs, regardless of the past and careless of the future.[21]

Magema M. Fuze, an early Christian convert in Natal, wrote in Zulu a general history of 'the black people' shortly after the turn of the century. Published in Pietermaritzburg in 1922, *Abantu Abamnyama* opened with the history of 'Bushmen and Hottentots', and was much concerned with the origins of different black groups. In part ethnographical, it presented a Zulu view of Zulu history. Only when, translated into English, it was published by the University of Natal Press in 1979, did it receive wide attention.[22] Other histories, written in the vernacular and published on mission presses in the 1920s and 1930s, have never been translated, and have remained unused by professional historians, though Monica Wilson cited some of them in the first volume of the *Oxford History*.[23] Only recently has an historian of the Xhosa drawn upon, say, what Samuel Mqhayi (1875–1945), poet and biographer, wrote about the history of his people.[24]

Of the miscellany of papers D. D. T. Jabavu, academic and son of J. T. Jabavu, published under the title *The Black Problem* in 1920, none were strictly historical, but in his Preface Jabavu called for 'native history, written by black hands' because

however sympathetic and good a European may be, he cannot undertake such a task with the minute knowledge and enthusiasm that can belong only to the Native African, who must himself be the victim of the untoward circumstances and difficulties under discussion.

Any book on African history by whites, Jabavu went on, was inevitably biased because such writers 'must take care of their own interests first'.[25] Other members of the African petty-bourgeoisie made appeals to their people to 'dig out their own history',[26] but the missionaries controlled the main presses and would not print anything they disagreed with, which hampered the production of historical as well as other works.[27]

One work the Lovedale Press refused to publish was a massive survey in Xhosa of the history of all the Xhosa-speaking people by John Henderson Soga (1859–1941), brother of A. K. and a medical missionary. Fortunately in this case, the editors of the Wits journal *Bantu Studies* heard of Soga's work, arranged for him to translate it into English, and published it as *The South Eastern Bantu* (1930). Soga's history drew extensively on oral testimonies he had collected, but also on Theal and other printed sources, so that it repeated many racial myths.[28] A few years later, Lovedale did publish a book by Soga on the Xhosa, written in English. Part historical, part sociological, it included a finely drawn portrait of Sarili, the Gcaleka ruler who saw his country fall under white rule.[29]

An autobiography written by Clements Kadalie (c.1896–1951) of the Industrial and Commercial Workers' Union was not published during his lifetime,[30] but other Africans in the inter-war years found the means to publish historical commentary of a more indirect variety. H. I. E. Dhlomo (1903–1956) helped T. D. Mweli

Skota (1890–1976) compile his remarkable *The African Yearly Register* (Johannesburg, 1930), which included biographies of such past leaders as Shaka, Moshoeshoe and Moroka as well as of contemporaries.[31] From 1943 Herbert Dhlomo helped his brother Rolfes edit *Ilanga Lase Natal* and that Zulu–English newspaper printed historical articles by Herbert Vilakazi and others.[32] Both Dhlomo brothers wrote on Shaka and Dingane in the 1930s, and Herbert completed plays on Moshoeshoe and Cetshwayo as well. Like Plaatje's *Mhudi*, and before that Thomas Mofolo's novel *Chaka*, published in Sesotho in 1925 but written much earlier, the novels, plays, poems and articles written by the two Dhlomos offered a view of the past very different from that in the textbooks written by whites. Mofolo went to Natal to research his book, which deliberately sought to make Shaka a more human person. When published in English it was described as 'a serious contribution to history'.[33] Plaatje's *Mhudi* told of the violence of the trekkers, and sought to debunk the myth of Ndebele bloodthirstiness. When Plaatje, Mofolo and the Dhlomos wrote of the past, they were addressing the present as well: Herbert Dhlomo's play on Cetshwayo was an attack on both Shepstonian and Hertzogian segregationism.[34] Contemporary professional historians did not take note of what such writers said; their work headed in quite other directions.

* * *

In the 1930s and 1940s most professional historians assumed that the study of Africans – as distinct from policy towards them – 'belonged' to the discipline of anthropology, because African societies had been changeless and there was no evidence to allow historians to recover the history of African lives. While anthropologists did study African societies, they were essentially synchronic and structural–functionalist in their approach. Most accepted A. R. Radcliffe-Brown's ahistorical idea that kinship was the key to social structure.[35] Some of the most famous South African anthropologists, including Max Gluckman and Hilda Beemer (Kuper) read history under Macmillan at Wits, and Monica Hunter (Wilson) read history as an undergraduate at Cambridge,[36] but none went on to advanced training in historical method, and the few who were interested in social change over time did not exploit the written sources used by historians. Isaac Schapera, professor at the University of Cape Town and doyen of the South

African anthropologists, always had an interest in history, and he brought together work on Africans across a number of disciplines in two major collections of commissioned essays, *Western Civilization and the Natives of South Africa. Studies in Culture Contact* (London, 1933) and *The Bantu-Speaking Tribes of South Africa* (London, 1937). The former set out in its preface the need for the study of relations between white and black in the past. Only the chapter by J. S. Marais in the second volume was primarily historical in its focus, however, and that was a study of policy towards Africans. Schapera's earlier monograph on *The Khoisan Peoples of South Africa* (London, 1930) had contained a chapter entitled 'The History, Distribution and Tribal Divisions of Bushmen and Hottentots', but there was very little about change over time in it in fact, and in his other work there was no real sense of the historical evolution of African societies. Many other fine works of ethnography were produced, but they did not challenge the idea of 'unchanging Africa'. Eileen Krige's *The Social System of the Zulus* (London, 1936) and Brian Marwick's *The Swazi* (Cambridge, 1940) both began with a brief historical sketch, drawing on A. T. Bryant, but both were essentially ethnographic, ahistorical works. No professional historian before the 1960s thought that the writings of anthropologists could be of any use to his or her work.

11   Walker and other historians of the 1930s and 1940s

If Macmillan and de Kiewiet were the giants of South African historiography in the inter-war years, it was because other professional historians did not make significant breakthroughs either in an Africanist direction or in tackling economic issues and the relationship between the political and the economic. There were still relatively few historians – only from the 1960s did the ranks of those writing on South Africa's past begin to swell significantly – but it is worth asking what was being written by those who might otherwise have carried forward what Macmillan and de Kiewiet had begun.

Eric Walker held the Cape Town chair of history from 1911 until he left for Cambridge in 1936. Soon after arriving in Cape Town he met Theal, whom in 1913 he invited to become the first president of the newly founded South African Historical Society[1] and whom he clearly held in high regard as the Grand Old Man of South African history. Walker was to be almost as prolific as Theal, and by the early years of the war was already planning to write a general history of South Africa in a single volume suitable for students and general readers. Because of the war, he did not begin the actual writing of his *magnum opus* until 1921.[2] For this task he read widely in the printed literature, and Theal's *History* as well as his *Records of the Cape Colony* were major sources for the volume which was finally published in London in 1928. For over forty years, Walker's densely packed *History* – reissued with additions in 1935, published in a second edition in 1940, and in a third, enlarged edition in 1957 – remained the basic text in English, providing the circumstantial detail and the political narrative which de Kiewiet's much briefer synthesis lacked.

In the Preface to the first edition Walker observed that his *History* made neither 'the struggle between British and Afrikanders' [*sic*] nor the achievement of self-government or closer union the main theme. The principals of his story were 'Western civilisation, tribal Africa and, to a less degree, theocratic Asia'. But his account, which began with the Pharaoh Necho, who according to Herodotus sent ships to circumnavigate Africa, was essentially Eurocentric in focus. He briefly described 'the Bantu tribal system', but only when he got the trekboers to the Zuurveld; he showed little appreciation for a 'Bantu point of view'; and he reproduced many of the myths to be found in Theal, even after Macmillan had criticised them in print.

A conservative and a romantic – for whom the Great Trek, the subject of his most popular book, was 'a great adventure'[3] – Walker was also a liberal. In the early 1920s he wrote of the life and times of Lord de Villiers, who had presided over the National Convention of 1908–9 as chief justice of the Cape. In the 1930s he published another biography, this time of W. P. Schreiner, brother of Olive and prime minister of the Cape from 1898 to 1900. Schreiner was a congenial subject for Walker because he had come to 'see the light' and been converted to a liberalism which took him to London as leader of the delegation protesting against the colour bar in the South Africa Bill of 1909. Walker was no political activist in the Macmillan mould, and he was only gradually aroused to the wrongheadedness of South African policy: while Macmillan baited Hertzog in the late 1920s, Walker spent time designing a possible flag for the Union, and his revised *History* was to call the late 1920s 'The Good Times'. But then followed 'The Bad Times' of the early 1930s. In the early months of 1936 Walker played an active role in opposition to the removal of Cape Africans from the common voters' roll. A series of articles he wrote on 'The Cape Native Franchise' for the *Cape Argus* soon appeared as a booklet.[4] The removal of the Cape African vote was the exclusion of 'human beings from full citizenship' merely because of the colour of their skins, and meant that 'the recognition of the rights of men as men will hardly survive in our national administration outside the courts'.[5] As the Cape African vote was removed, Walker heard that an application he had made for the chair of Imperial and Naval History at Cambridge University had been successful. He was not to return to South Africa until long after his retirement from that chair in 1951; his appointment to head the Union War Histories project in 1944 fell through when he suffered a severe mental breakdown.[6] In retirement in Cambridge in the 1950s he both revised and expanded his *History* for a third edition and served as editor of a new edition of the South African volume in the *Cambridge History of the British Empire*. His *History* did use some of the newly available radical and Africanist work available by the early 1950s, most notably Eddie Roux's *Time Longer Than Rope*, discussed below, but by the early 1960s Walker's work was justly criticised for its Eurocentricity.[7]

Today the most remembered of Walker's writings is *The Frontier Tradition in South Africa*, which was originally given as a lecture at Rhodes House, Oxford, in March 1930, when he was on sabbatical leave from Cape Town. His *History* was so full of detail that broad themes, such as industrialisation, got lost. In *The Frontier Tradition* he offered an explanation for the course of South African development. The roots of the thesis he advanced in the lecture lay partly in the writings of late nineteenth century imperialists who saw the struggle of the Transvaal against Britain as that of the eighteenth century against the modern world, of pastoralism against industrialism.

But Walker also drew on ideas advanced by Fouché and Macmillan. The first professional historian to offer a single key to unlock the South African past was Leo Fouché – once called the Frederick Jackson Turner of South Africa.[8] For Theal mere description of the course of white settlement had been explanation enough. Fouché found the key to lie in the evolution of the trekboer in the eighteenth century, which explained all that followed. Fouché stressed the relative isolation, as stock-farmers, of the trekboers and their need to look to their own resources, but not their racial ideas. It was Macmillan who first, in passing, claimed that white racism had developed on the frontier, and that it was the 'die-hards of colour policy' who had left on the Great Trek in the 1830s rather than accept the implications of the Enlightenment, with its principles of legal and political equality, which Britain brought to the Cape.[9]

While not adopting Macmillan's sympathetic attitude towards people of colour, or his stress on interaction, Walker took from him the idea of a frontier tradition of white racism. While preparing his Oxford lecture, he told Macmillan that he wanted to respond to the support for segregationism which Smuts had voiced in lectures at Oxford the previous year.[10] For Walker, the white racism that lay behind contemporary calls for segregation was the product of the early frontier, something out of place in the modern world. More than Fouché, he wanted to do for South

Africa what Frederick Jackson Turner – whose famous lecture on the American frontier had made a great impression on him – had effected in American historiography: to provide an argument which would account for the unique course of its history. In effect Walker turned Turner on his head: whereas Turner argued that America owed its democracy to the frontier, Walker asserted that South Africa owed its racism to the frontier. In each case the frontier had bred what was seen to be most distinctive about the particular country, but while the frontier in America was responsible for what was best in American life, in South Africa it had created misery and conflict. So the trekboers and the trekkers were at the same time both those who had set out 'to blaze the trail for civilisation far into the interior of Africa'[11] and the source of South Africa's current problems, because of the archaic racist ideas, forged on the Cape frontier, which they had carried with them.

Concerned to find the source of white racism, Walker and other early liberals ignored the history of non-military interaction between the trekboers and the trekkers, on the one hand, and the people of the interior on the other. Walker lacked Macmillan's close contact with Africans and strong sense of South African history as the story of people being drawn into a single economy. Walker talked, as Macmillan never would have done, of Africans having experienced a quite separate history from whites. 'Since first contact', he wrote in a short article published in 1935 in *The Critic*, a University of Cape Town journal, whites and blacks 'have in great measure lived each their own life apart'. He then referred to the 'big opportunity' awaiting someone to write 'Bantu history'. Walker anticipated that such a history would be a story of dispossession, and that it would, for example, depict Sarili (Kreli) and Sandile, not in negative terms, but as 'rulers who tried to save Xhosa society'. His article proceeded to publish a Zulu account of the massacre of Piet Retief and his party in 1838: Kosana's story of the killing of Piti.[12] But Walker never really accepted that the history of Africans was of equal importance to that of whites.

* * *

Johannes Stephanus (Etienne) Marais (1898–1969), Walker's junior colleague at Cape Town in the early 1930s, was more influenced by Macmillan's work than was Walker. Born on a farm outside Paarl, and educated in that town, Marais proceeded to the University of Cape Town – where he majored in classics – and there and at Oxford, where he studied history from 1920 to the end of 1924, he became a firm adherent of liberal values. After completing a second undergraduate degree at Oxford, he stayed on to write a doctorate under Reginald Coupland, Beit Professor of Colonial History. He chose as his subject the colonisation of New Zealand, so becoming the first South African historian to make a significant contribution to the historical writing of another country. The thesis was published in 1927 and was long recognised as 'one of the most useful books on New Zealand history'.[13] After three months at the Sorbonne, and another three at Heidelberg, Marais returned to South Africa, first as a temporary lecturer in the Wits department while Macmillan was away, and then, from July 1927, as senior lecturer in the Cape Town history department. Within a few years, much encouraged by Walker, he had decided to write a major study of 'White, Black and Coloured in the Cape Colony – a history of the origins and growth of a heterogeneous society'.[14] He contributed a masterly chapter on 'The Imposition and Nature of European Control' over Africans in the eastern Cape to a collection of essays edited by Isaac Schapera,[15] then decided to turn his work on the Coloureds into a separate book, which he completed in 1938 and called *The Cape Coloured People 1652–1937* (London, 1939). In his Preface, he paid tribute to Macmillan's *Cape Colour Question*, but also remarked that Macmillan had overstated his case against the colonists and officials and had sometimes lost 'sight of the inexorable realities of the Colonial situation', in particular that 'Coloured backwardness and apathy have often helped to frustrate the best efforts on their behalf'. But Marais's work was not as Eurocentric as those phrases suggest. He went on to present his standpoint: 'that justice, which has rightly been represented as blindfold, does not allow the use of two measures, one for ourselves and our own people, and another for those who differ from us in nationality, or race, or the colour of their skins'.[16] His book itself began by describing the miscegenation that had created the Coloured people, themselves living proof that South African society had not been segregated in the past, and it ended by speaking of the 'philosophy of blood and race ... held by most Afrikaners' as 'Nazilike' and by concluding, pessimistically: 'History seems to show that the beneficiaries of privilege do not voluntarily surrender their rights.'[17]

Besides being anti-segregationist, Marais's book was also a pioneering study of many previously neglected aspects of nineteenth-century Cape history, including the history of the Griqua, of the colonisation of the north-western Cape, and of the emergence and decline of the Kat River Settlement. But it was mainly a study of white policy towards people of colour, not of their history from within. Marais could still write of the 'South African nation' as a white nation, though he wanted to see 'civilised' Coloureds and Africans enter 'the society of [their] European peers'.[18] Marais's next book took the form of a very detailed and meticulous study of the first decades of interaction between whites and Africans on the Cape eastern frontier in the late eighteenth century. He presented a mass of evidence from the Cape archives to 'convict Theal of bad workmanship' and to vindicate H. C. D. Maynier, a leading white official, in much the same way as Macmillan had vindicated Philip. Marais depicted the frontiersmen, not in heroic terms, but as violators of the rule of law. Another study of what whites had done to blacks, his book did not attempt to see the events it described from a Khoi or Xhosa perspective.[19] But Marais did make a plea for scholars to return to the records, for only on the basis of detailed monographs would 'some future historian ... be in a position to write a *History of South Africa* worthy to stand beside the important works of European and American scholarship'.[20]

* * *

Neither Walker nor Marais was much interested in economics.[21] Macmillan's stress on the importance of economics was missing in later work carried out in South Africa, in part because at the leading South African universities economic history was not taught in history departments, but in departments of economics. At the University of Cape Town Michael H. de Kock, a Harvard graduate, was appointed in 1923 to a new post in the economics department set aside for the teaching of economic history, and he produced the first general textbook on the subject dealing with South Africa. It was a mostly dry, descriptive account of economic development looked at from above, with little attention paid to the role of individuals.[22] De Kock left academic life to pursue a career which would culminate in the governorship of the Reserve Bank. His successor, D. M. Goodfellow, published an uneven *Modern Economic History of South Africa* in 1931[23] which was mainly concerned with the various branches of economic production. In 1930 Goodfellow was in turn succeeded as senior lecturer in economics responsible for teaching economic history by Hector Menteith Robertson (1905–1984).

English-born, Robertson completed a doctorate at Cambridge which was published as *Aspects of the Rise of Economic Individualism. A Critique of Max Weber and His School* in 1933 and won international recognition. Soon after arriving in Cape Town, Robertson grasped, as Goodfellow had not, the importance of Macmillan's work. He was also much impressed by an article which Macmillan's assistant at Wits, Margaret Hodgson, had published in 1924 on 'The Hottentots in South Africa to 1828: A Problem in Labour and Administration'.[24] Her title suggested an entirely Eurocentric approach, but in fact she considered what happened to the Khoi themselves. She wrote of how 'the two races [whites and Khoi] drifted into a state of mutual dependence which, by 1769, seems to have been complete'. That passage, and not anything in Macmillan's work, led Robertson to take up the theme of growing economic ties between black and white.[25]

What Robertson wrote was originally intended for a volume of essays edited by his colleague Isaac Schapera on *Western Civilization and the Natives of South Africa*. His paper turned out to be too long for that collection, and instead became a two-part article in the *South African Journal of Economics* entitled '150 Years of Economic Contact Between Black and White'.[26] Few historians – de Kiewiet was an exception – read that journal, and Robertson's article did not receive as much attention from historians as it might have enjoyed had it appeared elsewhere. It was a brilliant general synthesis, 'the skeleton of a work that was never written – yet the book was written'.[27] He himself did not continue writing on the theme of economic co-operation, except for the first years of the Dutch settlement; his later work was very disparate and had little impact on historians.[28] But 'the book [that] was written' was by an outstanding student of his, whom he directed to the topic of African labour, a subject he had only touched upon in his article.

Sheila van der Horst had studied economics in Cape Town, but turned to economic history for her doctorate at the London School of Economics, where she was supervised by Arnold Plant. Robertson remained her mentor, and provided her with much material when she was in London in 1938–9.[29] Her thesis, published as *Native Labour in South Africa* in 1941, was perhaps the most important single study of policy towards blacks to be completed in these decades. As a study of policy it elaborated on aspects of Edgar

Brookes's *The History of Native Policy in South Africa from 1830 to the Present Day* (1924), which had defended segregationism, and J. A. I. Agar-Hamilton's *The Native Policy of the Voortrekkers* (1928). But Van der Horst took up the theme of economic interdependence from Robertson's paper and traced the particular strand of labour in rich detail from 1652 to the present. Implicitly throughout, and explicitly in her conclusion, she argued against segregation, which must, she contended, damage an economy based on African labour. A caste system, she wrote, could only be maintained by force, and that promised 'racial and social strife'.[30] It was not until the 1970s that more detailed studies, which drew upon archival material (she had used only printed papers), significantly carried further knowledge of how and why African labour was obtained and employed.

* * *

An attempt to move away from policy towards blacks and to study 'the other side of the frontier' was made at Stellenbosch University in the last years of the war. P. J. van der Merwe, who lectured there from 1938 until his death in 1977, had made the history of the trekboer his own field. His trilogy – *Die Noordwaartse Beweging van die Boere voor die Groot Trek (1770–1842)*, *Die Trekboer in die Geskiedenis van die Kaapkolonie*, and *Trek*[31] – said little about the San, the Khoi or the Bantu-speakers with whom the trekboers interacted. But in the last years of the war he directed a master's student to a consideration of the history of the Khoi in the western Cape in the late seventeenth century. H. J. le Roux's 'Die Toestand, Verspreiding en Verbrokkeling van die Hottentotstamme in Suid-Afrika 1652–1713', which was completed in 1945, was a pioneering work on an important aspect of the history of the indigenous people of the country. Sadly, it remained an isolated venture, forgotten until attention was called to it by Richard Elphick, the historian of the Khoi, in the 1970s.[32]

Two leading academic psychologists made noteworthy contributions in the 1930s to historical scholarship on aspects of black–white relations. H. A. Reyburn, professor of psychology at Cape Town, became interested in the way in which historians used evidence, and himself turned his hand to writing history. In a series of articles entitled 'Studies in Cape Frontier History' in *The Critic*, a journal which he had founded in 1932, Reyburn treated white–black relations on the Cape frontier dispassionately, and showed a concern to understand black societies as well as white.[33] Far more influential was *Race Attitudes in South Africa* (1937) by I. D. Mac-Crone, professor of psychology at Wits. It examined both racial prejudice in the contemporary situation and its historical roots. In his first 136 pages, MacCrone found those roots to lie in white race attitudes at the Cape in 'the formative eighteenth century'. He did not need to continue with his historical investigation beyond the early nineteenth century, he remarked, because 'the attitudes themselves, as they existed towards the end of the eighteenth and at the beginning of the nineteenth centuries, are very similar to those which we find displayed on all sides at the present time'.[34]

MacCrone's work appeared to provide detailed empirical support for 'the frontier tradition' thesis which Walker had advanced in 1930. Racism was treated as a product of the period before the British arrived; the white frontiersmen were viewed in negative terms because they were the first to adopt the racism which lay at the root of contemporary South African ills. De Kiewiet, writing his *History* a few years later, regarded the white frontiersmen as isolated and backward,[35] but stressed too that the trekboers and trekkers had not entered an empty interior. With his focus on white race attitudes, MacCrone was not really interested in the process of interaction; Walker mostly wrote from a white perspective and Marais was more interested in what happened on the white side of the frontier than the black. Only de Kiewiet and Robertson, in general terms, and Van der Horst, looking in detail at labour, began to tease out the nature of the economic interaction that had occurred.[36]

For the study of interaction to be taken further it was necessary for historians to begin to analyse the nature of African societies. No professional historian did so before the 1960s. In the 1930s, as we have seen, the major focus of attention was, instead, white racism. De Kiewiet, in his chapter in the *Cambridge History of the British Empire* and then in *The Imperial Factor*, went as far as any towards considering the history of Africans, and he did that hesitantly and briefly, in part because his holistic approach led him to concentrate on the way in which blacks and whites increasingly came to work together. Neither the separate histories of African societies, nor the economic and social processes which bound South Africans together, were explored in depth in the academic history-writing of the 1940s and 1950s.

12 Historians of the 1940s and 1950s

After Walker left for Cambridge in 1936, the King George V chair of history at the University of Cape Town went to the 45-year-old Harry Mandelbrote (1891–1971), who was very much a Walker protégé. Having, like Walker, received a first in modern history at Merton College, Oxford, he had joined the department as an acting lecturer in 1915, and developed an interest in constitutional and legal history. At Walker's request, he contributed two chapters to the South African volume in the *Cambridge History of the British Empire*, but otherwise he spent much of his time writing school histories. He was to remain head of the history department at Cape Town from 1937 until the end of 1958, and during that time produced nothing of scholarly significance.

Besides Mandelbrote and Marais, the other permanent member of the Cape Town department from 1938 was Jean van der Poel (1904–86). Though she and Marais exchanged correspondence in Afrikaans, she was, like him, thoroughly anglicised and a staunch liberal. She had been attracted to history by Walker's first-year survey course based on H. G. Wells's *Outline of History*. Walker, who was to describe her as 'the best student I ever had' at Cape Town,[1] suggested the topic of her master's thesis, on Basutoland as a factor in South African politics between 1852 and 1870, which she completed under his nominal supervision in 1925. De Kiewiet, who used her thesis for his own doctorate, rightly praised it as presenting 'a clear and well-told story'.[2] Walker also suggested the topic on which Van der Poel worked for her doctorate at the London School of Economics in the late 1920s: railway and customs policies in South Africa from 1885 to 1910. She clarified a complex story, and her dissertation was soon published in the Imperial Studies series of the Royal Empire Society. When she returned to Cape Town, Walker offered her a post in the department but she insisted on teaching at a girls' high school.

She showed a keen interest in African education – a lecture on *Education and the Native* was published in 1934 – but when she did move to the university she was led back to research in imperial and colonial history. The opportunity to consult the papers of James Rose Innes, the former chief justice of the Union, gave rise to her brilliant book on *The Jameson Raid*.[3] In 1951, the year that was published, she was asked to assemble the papers of General Smuts, who had died the previous year. They were to be used by W. K. Hancock, who was commissioned to write a biography for Cambridge University Press. Her commitment to the Smuts project, which included editing a series of volumes of selections from the papers, lasted for almost two decades, until after her retirement.[4] Throughout her university career she taught European history, and in retirement claimed never to have found South African history important or really interesting.[5]

From 1946 Leonard Thompson (born 1916) was Mandelbrote's senior colleague at Cape Town. Like Theal, Macmillan and de Kiewiet, he had not been born in South Africa, but was taken there when young by his parents. He attended Michaelhouse school in Natal, and then went to Rhodes University College in Grahamstown. At Rhodes he majored in history with distinction, and edited *The Rhodian*, a student journal. The acting head of the Rhodes history department – for John Ewing, who had been head, had died suddenly – when Thompson was an undergraduate was the eccentric I. J. (Pip) Rousseau, whose academic talents were modest – 'demoted' to senior lecturer in 1925, he made his students read his failed Oxford doctoral dissertation. But one of Thompson's fellow students was to recall that Rousseau 'certainly strengthened my growing belief that any attempt to see our past as providentially managed in the interests of one race alone was quite wrong.'[6]

Thompson remained at Rhodes to work on a master's thesis, and chose early Indian immigration into Natal as his topic. Then in 1937, having been awarded a Rhodes scholarship, he went to New College, Oxford, where he completed the thesis and read for the undergraduate honours history degree. In the summer of 1939, after writing the final exams, he and two friends travelled to central Europe and were canoeing down the Danube when Hitler marched into Poland. Fortunate to have got back to England, Thompson volunteered and became a probationary second lieutenant in the Royal Navy. He was trained as a navigator, and spent much of the war on escort duty in the North Atlantic. At the end of the war he returned to South Africa – after an absence of almost eight years – and was about to take employment with the Johannesburg City Council's Native Affairs Department when offered the post of senior lecturer in history at the University of Cape Town, where he would teach for fourteen years.[7]

In the late 1940s and the 1950s Thompson's research did not take an Africanist direction. Like other liberals of the time, he was concerned with the constitutional struggle over the removal of Coloureds from the common voters' roll, and with issues of civil liberty and academic freedom. Not surprisingly, therefore, his academic interests lay mainly in political and constitutional history. His first two publications were pamphlets in the New Africa series issued by the South African Institute of Race Relations, of which he was an active member. One, based on a talk given to an Institute Council meeting in January 1949, was entitled *Democracy in Multi-Racial Societies*. As the Westminster system had permitted the disastrous victory, as he saw it, of the National Party in 1948, with its republican and apartheid philosophy, constitutional reform was needed. The choice before the country was 'last ditch white supremacy ... the surest way to suicide for "white South Africa"', or 'civilised democracy', which was still possible if the National Party could be ousted and constitutional reform be achieved.[8]

His second pamphlet, on *The Cape Coloured Franchise*, discussed the history of that franchise and the threat to remove the Coloureds from the common electoral roll, and it was clearly designed to influence readers to resist any such action. Thompson later admitted, without apology, that this work had 'some of the characteristics of propaganda'.[9] By the early 1950s he had decided that his major academic work would deal with the political unification of the country.[10] This splendid theme was hardly touched by scholars, and a mass of relevant papers had recently become available. It was a large topic, which took him much of the decade to complete. He was offered a year at the Institute of Commonwealth Studies in London in 1953, but Mandelbrote would not let him go for more than six months, and once back at Cape Town he had a relatively heavy teaching load. He was active off campus as well: he was one of the founding members of the Civil Rights League, and was involved in the Liberal Party, established after the National Party won the 1953 election. When the government began threatening to segregate the universities, he served on the editorial committee which produced a booklet entitled *The Open Universities in South Africa* in 1957, in a vain bid to prevent the passage of legislation which two years later imposed a legalised colour bar on the English-speaking universities. In 1957 he became chairman of the Students' Health and Welfare Organisation at the university, which he helped set on a new and more productive footing.[11] He was active, too, in writing for local newspapers and giving extra-mural lectures. All this delayed the completion of his large book on unification, but it was ready for publication early in 1960, the fiftieth anniversary of Union. His work did not consider in depth black responses to unification. Over two decades later, André Odendaal's study of early black protest politics, which used archival records not available to Thompson as well as African newspapers, showed how much could be added to Thompson's account.[12]

* * *

Leo Fouché, Macmillan's successor at Wits, wrote little after taking up the chair there in 1934. His interests were not all Eurocentric: while at Pretoria he became involved in studying what became the archaeological site of Mapungubwe, south of the Limpopo River, the thirteenth-century date of which suggested early African occupation of the Transvaal lowveld. He edited a volume entitled *Mapungubwe: Ancient Bantu Civilization on the Limpopo* in which he wrote: 'A deeper knowledge of Native achievements, successes and failures of the past may aid us to appreciate their capacities and their needs of the present.'[13] He was, nevertheless, opposed to the Macmillan tradition, which he regarded as 'negrophile', and was not displeased when Margaret Hodgson, so closely associated with that tradition, married William Ballinger and had to leave the department.[14] Fouché had been Smuts's private secretary during the First World War, and thereafter an ardent supporter of the South African Party. He had written most of the report of a government commission of enquiry into the date of the discovery of gold on the Witwatersrand. When war came again in September 1939, and Smuts returned to the premiership, he was soon called upon to help the new government. He took indefinite leave from Wits while acting as chairman of the South African Broadcasting Service and as an adviser on internal security. He was not to return to academic life, and finally resigned his chair at the end of 1942.[15]

In the year his *Maynier* book was published, Marais succeeded

Fouché at Wits. He soon planned a Transvaal-centred topic, for which he would use the newly-opened records in the Public Record Office in London. The result was his finest work, *The Fall of Kruger's Republic*, eventually published in 1961.[16] Marais remained an outspoken liberal, who was seen in the streets of Cape Town, at the time of the constitutional crisis over the removal of the Coloured voters from the common voters' roll in the early 1950s, wearing a placard on which was written 'Defend the Constitution'.[17] In the sixties he began pioneering work on African squatters on white-owned farms, but wrote only one seminar paper on the subject before his death in 1969.[18]

Arthur Keppel-Jones (born 1902), like Jean van der Poel before him, was led to a career in history by the enthusiasm of Walker's teaching.[19] Born in Cape Town and educated at the South African College School and the University of Cape Town, he went to New College, Oxford – Marais's old college – in 1929 on a Rhodes scholarship. After three years at Oxford, he began teaching at Wits in March 1933 in Macmillan's place. When Macmillan resigned six months later, he stayed on. Keppel-Jones moved to Natal University College in 1935, but returned to Wits when offered a permanent post there in that year, to take the place of Margaret Hodgson (Ballinger).[20] The thesis which he began under Richard Pares at Oxford he continued to work on while at Wits, against the advice of Fouché, who urged him to take up research on South Africa.[21] Entitled 'The Public Schools and the English Governing Class 1815–1867', it was not completed until 1943, when it was submitted for a doctorate at the University of Cape Town.

Keppel-Jones's pessimism can be seen in an article he contributed to the liberal journal *Race Relations* at the time of the centenary of the Great Trek: he called the Trek a confession of failure, a divorce, and he feared another, greater trek in the future, 'in ships not wagons, and too precipitate to be a matter of pride'.[22] In 1946, alarmed by the prospect of Malan's National Party coming to power, he wrote an account of the history of the country from 1952 to 2010, entitled *When Smuts Goes*, which de Kiewiet described as 'a study in historical extrapolation'.[23] Given his view of the future course of South African history – his book ended with South Africa returning to 'barbarism' – it is not surprising that Keppel-Jones left for England on leave in 1947, expecting to remain there. He was unable to find an academic post, however, and Reginald Coupland, Professor of Imperial History at Oxford, who was editing a series of histories for Hutchinson, asked him to write the South African volume. Keppel-Jones believed that he was handicapped in the job market because he had not published a work of history, and so accepted the commission, but that meant returning to South Africa at the end of his leave.

Challenged by various people to present a constructive alternative for the country, he followed his 'future history' with *Friends or Foes?* – written in late 1948, but not published until 1950 – which proposed a federal solution for South Africa. Throughout these years, he wrote prolifically on political affairs for *The Forum*, a liberal fortnightly. His *South Africa A Short History*, published in 1949 – one review was headed 'Before Smuts Went' – helped make his reputation abroad. A competently and clearly written survey, it went through five editions between 1949 and 1975, it made no conceptual breakthrough and it still spoke of Africans arriving in the lands east of the Fish at the same time as the whites arrived to the west of that river, despite the evidence to the contrary which Marais had advanced in his book on Maynier.

With his *Short History* completed, Keppel-Jones in 1949 began a major historical project on the history of central Africa. But that did not reflect an Africanist concern; rather, his antipathy to South African politics was too great for him to write of its history.[24] From the late 1930s he had been a strong critic of communists and fellow-travellers, and that the early attempts at an Africanist history of South Africa came from radicals – as we shall see below – led him to dismiss it as mere polemic. When he went to Queen's University in 1953 on sabbatical leave, he was again planning to emigrate, but he was then offered the chair of history at Pietermaritzburg and decided to remain in South Africa a while longer. His understanding of the wider Africa grew from a visit to the newly independent Ghana in 1957, but it was not until after he finally did emigrate to Canada in 1959[25] – he was offered a full professorship at Queen's – that he began to see the need to incorporate an Africanist perspective into his work. The large project he began in 1949 was gradually narrowed down until it focused on the early colonisation of Zimbabwe. His emigration and his change of emphasis in mid-stream both helped delay the completion of the manuscript until the late 1970s, and his long book was not published until 1983.[26]

As he left South Africa, Keppel-Jones wrote an article which encapsulated much liberal thought in its title. 'Where Did We Take the Wrong Turning?' asked where, given that South Africa was 'on the wrong road', things had begun to 'go wrong'. Keppel-Jones disagreed with a remark Walker had made in his *History*: that the decision of the Dutch East India Company in 1717 to restrict European immigration was a crucial turning-point. Nor did he believe that enough whites could have been attracted to the country in the nineteenth century to have made South Africa another Canada. He argued instead that the wrong turning had been taken in 1854. His argument was that had the Orange River Sovereignty been annexed to the Cape in that year, and not been surrendered, the Cape system – with its non-racial franchise – would have been extended over half the country, well before the discovery of gold in the Transvaal. But he clearly had doubts about his own thesis, for he concluded: 'The fates conspired against us from the beginning.'[27]

* * *

Until 1954, when Keppel-Jones became professor at Pietermaritzburg, the heads of history at Natal and Rhodes were men of conservative views. Alan Frederick Hattersley (1893–1976), an Englishman educated at Cambridge, had begun the department in Pietermaritzburg, and was for long its only member. He did not confine his writing to South African topics,[28] and he wrote an important article on slavery at the Cape for the *Cambridge History of the British Empire*, but his major South African interest was the British colonists of Natal, on whose activities he published *The British Settlement of Natal*, *More Annals of Natal*, *Later Annals of Natal*, *Portrait of a Colony*, and *The Natalians*.[29]

Michael Roberts, his colleague at Rhodes, was an Englishman who, after getting the best first-class pass in modern history at Oxford in 1930, went on to complete a doctorate on the Whig Party in the early nineteenth century. At about the time he was appointed to the chair at Rhodes in 1935, he decided to make his name as the world authority in an unusual field of history, and chose that of Sweden, especially in the seventeenth century.[30] His Swedish work was only once interrupted by a venture into South African contemporary history, which he undertook at the request of Smuts. Drawing on information supplied by A. E. G. Trollip, the deputy speaker of the House of Assembly, he wrote a brilliant account of Afrikaner politics in the war years, published under the title *The South African Opposition 1939-45* in 1947. After visiting the South African universities at the end of 1947, de Kiewiet called Roberts 'the most intelligent man in the history field in the country',[31] but Roberts from then on devoted himself exclusively to research on Swedish history, from 1954 at Queen's University, Belfast, where he remained until his retirement in 1973.

When Roberts moved to Northern Ireland, he was succeeded in the Rhodes chair by the medievalist Winifred Maxwell, who had studied under V. Galbraith at Oxford.[32] She was an inspiring teacher, and a number of her students went on to become leading professional historians.[33] A remark of hers suggested to one of her students the idea of writing a positive study of the Mfecane.[34] But though she was a fund of mostly antiquarian information on the Cape eastern frontier, she published little beyond her inaugural lecture on *Random Reflections on the Study of History in South Africa* and in the 1950s she was no more in touch with new developments in the history of tropical Africa than other historians at South African universities.

Among Afrikaner historians, most of whom were concerned exclusively with Afrikaner history, narrowly conceived, the person most ready to think in terms of 'crossing the frontier' was the young T. S. van Rooyen (1922-67), whose doctorate from the University of Pretoria – where he lectured from 1961 – was on relations between Boers, British and blacks in the eastern Transvaal to 1882. Though interested in what had been written about blacks, his interest was a paternalistic one; he claimed the apparent lack of writing by blacks themselves was the result of their limited historical consciousness.[35]

* * *

By the early 1960s, then, the insights developed by Macmillan and de Kiewiet in the 1920s and the 1930s, had not been taken further by professional historians. Of Macmillan's students, de Kiewiet settled abroad, as did Lucy Sutherland, who made the eighteenth-century history of England her special field. Herbert Frankel, who remained close to Macmillan, as professor of economics at Wits worked for Lord Hailey and that led to his classic *Capital Investment in Africa*, published in 1938. At the end of the war Unilever funded a chair for him in development economics at Nuffield College, Oxford.[36]

A number of those appointed to posts in the history depart-

ments of South African universities in these years had done theses
abroad under scholars whose main interests did not lie in South
Africa – Marais at Oxford, Van der Poel at London, for example – or, like Keppel-Jones, they wrote theses in South Africa on
topics far removed from Macmillan's concerns. Walker's *History*,
not de Kiewiet's, was the major textbook at the English-medium
universities in the 1930s, 1940s and 1950s. The small history departments at those universities were always short of funds, teaching loads were heavy, there was no society to bring professional
historians together,[37] and there were few outlets for scholarly articles in South Africa. The Second World War handicapped research in a number of ways: some of those who would presumably
otherwise have worked on South African history instead served in
the forces;[38] of those who remained in South Africa, some were,
like Marais, to spend much time on garrison duty. The writing of
the Union War Histories, which continued for years after the end
of the war, absorbed the energies of J. A. I. Agar-Hamilton,
H. M. Robertson, Eric Axelson, whose field was the history of Por-
tugal in Africa, and others. Considerable research and writing was
done in these decades, then, but there was no methodological or
conceptual breakthrough.

The war gave liberals hope, for the Smuts government showed
signs of being ready to move away from some aspects of segregation, and it seemed possible that when fighting was over, the
values for which the war was being fought might triumph in South
Africa as elsewhere. But even before the fighting drew to a close,
segregation was again tightened, and as Afrikaner ranks closed the
prospect grew that a more reactionary government would come to
power. The victory of the National Party in 1948 was, nevertheless, a great shock for liberals. Some continued to hope that the
National Party could be ousted at the next election, until in the
1953 election it was returned with a larger majority. As apartheid
began to be implemented in its various forms, liberal historians
began a new search for the causes of their present woes. A
number went back to the period between the Jameson Raid and
Union, for which new evidence had recently become available.
Marais followed Van der Poel in showing how the imperialism of
Chamberlain and Milner had been largely responsible for bringing
about the South African War, which had served to promote an exclusive Afrikaner nationalism. Thompson examined the making of
the Union, the constitution of which made it possible for an Afri-

kaner nationalist party eventually to capture the South African state. Liberals now argued that the constitution of 1909 had failed and that there should be a new national convention to undo the mistake of the one that had met in 1908–9, and to adopt a federal constitution appropriate for South Africa's plural society. Liberal concerns were primarily constitutional, political. At the same time, also in response to the victory of the National Party, the African National Congress was further radicalised, and its leadership began to collaborate more closely with the Communist Party. That collaboration alienated liberals, most of whom remained distant from African politics. On the left there was a long tradition of radical writing, some of which concerned the past. But this tradition, which in the 1940s became quite strongly Africanist, was almost entirely ignored by liberal historians, who were not sympathetic to its political orientation. They remained largely Eurocentric and political in their approach; it was not until the 1960s that that began to change.

13 Early radical writing

In his concern for all the people of the country and his belief in the importance of economics in explaining South African history, Macmillan was a radical historian, for all that he was dismissed by some on the left as a reformist. The roots of a radical interpretation of South African history lie partly with him, but also elsewhere, in forays into history by men who were not professional historians. J. A. Hobson, who visited South Africa in 1899 to report on the country for the *Manchester Guardian*, wrote a book on his return to England to make the case that war had broken out in October 1899 because the mining capitalists wanted to overturn the Kruger state. *The War in South Africa* (1900) was a polemic, not a work of history, but in its pages on the Boer republics and on the policy of the capitalists Hobson began to develop the idea – common among Afrikaner notables in the Transvaal at that time – that Britain's role in South Africa in the nineteenth century was to be explained in economic terms.[1] Hobson in turn influenced later radicals: Macmillan perhaps, and certainly Sydney Olivier, Fabian socialist and one-time governor of Jamaica, though his *The Anatomy of African Misery* (1927) pointed to the legacy of slavery as a key to explaining segregationism, as well as more narrowly economic influences.

Macmillan and Olivier wrote of Africans in South Africa primarily as a rural peasantry. Leonard Barnes (1895–1977) was one of the first to recognise the significance of the new emerging urban petty-bourgeoisie and working class.[2] After resigning from the Colonial Office in 1925, Barnes farmed in Zululand until the local chief asked him why he had come from England 'to seize the land of the Bantu'. That question led him to investigate the history of forced relocation in the area. What he discovered caused him to quit farming, in order to expose the inequities of the racial system. While working as a journalist on various South African newspapers, he wrote *Caliban in Africa: An Impression of Colour Madness* (1930). This polemic condemned Afrikaners – Barnes acknowledged that the English in South Africa held similar racial ideas – as anti-humanitarian and explained their 'madness' chiefly in terms of their isolation from trends in European thought. A second book, *The New Boer War* (1932), described the evil effects of labour migration on Africans in the Protectorates (Basutoland, Bechuanaland and Swaziland). After his return to England, Barnes became a historian of the wider empire,[3] but in 1936 he wrote the most critical of all the reviews of the South African volume in the *Cambridge History of the British Empire*. He made the perceptive point that it gave the idea that blacks remained an essentially rural and pastoral people, and ignored the history of black protest and of proletarianisation.[4] He was one of the first to suggest a perspective on South Africa's past that was both radical and Africanist, but because he was not a professional historian he did not further extend his insights into the course of South African development.

In the 1920s and 1930s, intellectuals in the Communist Party of South Africa began to grapple with the problem of how to conceptualise the South African struggle. In pamphlets and in articles in the party newspaper *Umsebenzi* (Worker), later *Inkululeko* (Freedom),[5] they advanced a class interpretation of South Africa. Thomas Mbeki, who was prominent both in the Industrial and Commercial Workers' Union and in the Communist Party, wrote in *The Workers' Herald*, the newspaper of the ICU, of how whites had imposed a new form of slavery on Africans.[6] A. T. Nzula, the general secretary of the party in 1930–1, wrote articles for *The Negro Worker* and contributed a section on South Africa to a book on forced labour in Africa which was published in Russian in 1933, but the historical content in these was slight.[7] The polemical pamphlet which John Gomas, a member of the Cape Town branch of the Communist Party, wrote in 1934, entitled *100 Years. 'Emancipation of Slaves.' Smash the Chains of Slavery!*, argued that chattel slavery had been abolished in 1834 for economic reasons, and had merely been replaced by 'capitalistic wage slavery'. 'Theal, the S. African Historian' was quoted in a section headed 'Hottentots, Bantu and Bushmen Robbed of Land and Freedom!'[8] There were occasional references to history in the ephemeral left-wing pamphlets written by members of the communist Party and by, say, those who wrote for *The Spark*, organ of the Spartacists, a Trotskyite discussion group in Cape Town in the late 1930s. The two lectures which the communist trade-unionist W. H. Andrews delivered in Cape Town in October 1941 on the class struggle of white and black trade unions against their 'industrial capitalist oppressors' were printed, but like so much of this material received very limited circulation; a biography of Andrews published two years later was probably much more widely read.[9]

Slightly less ephemeral than such more-or-less obscure publications was *The Black Man's Burden* by 'John Burger', a pseudonym for Leo Marquard (1897–1974). Marquard came from a conservative Afrikaner background, read history at Oxford in the early 1920s, on his return to South Africa played a leading role in the founding of the National Union of South African Students, and taught at Grey College, Bloemfontein, from 1923 to 1940. In 1938 he wrote to Victor Gollancz suggesting he publish in the Left Book Club series a work on

the political, social and economic relations between Europeans and Natives ... an essay in imperialism and capitalism as it is working in a British dominion that produces gold. There is plenty of material to expose the particularly unpleasant features of the system of exploitation by the farmers, mine owners and industrialists, with the liberal use of British capital.... [I] have both the knowledge and the necessary Socialistic approach.[10]

Marquard sent Gollancz his typescript soon after war began, but it went to Harold Laski for review and was lost.[11] Another copy was assembled in 1942, and *The Black Man's Burden* was published in 1943. He used a pseudonym to avoid what he described as 'awkward consequences' for someone then employed in wartime army education. The historical sections of his book were brief, but Jean van der Poel noted in a review that Marquard's book showed 'our pitiless exploitation of the African people.... One motive above all is seen to dominate our Native policy – the maintenance of that cheap labour supply on which the profits of mine-owners, industrialists and farmers depend'.[12] Racial policies were, Marquard argued, firmly tied to economic interests.[13]

The Black Man's Burden was essentially a book on the present rather than the past. A history written by Hyman Basner, a Johannesburg lawyer who left the Communist Party over the Soviet invasion of Finland, remained unpublished. Entitled 'The Black Price of Gold in South Africa', it was mainly concerned with the exploitation of black labour after 1886.[14] By far the most important work of history from a radical perspective in these years was *Time*

Longer Than Rope by Eddie Roux (1903–66). A botanist by profession, who rose to become professor and head of the botany department at the University of the Witwatersrand, Roux joined the Communist Party in 1923, edited its newspaper in the early 1930s, and left the party in 1936 for a mixture of ideological and personal reasons. In 1934 African students at a Cape Town night school asked him for material on their past. In August that year he began publishing in *Umsebenzi* a series of articles under the title 'A Black Man's History of South Africa'. The first began by saying that the history of the country had 'never been written from the point of view of the people'. Histories 'written by the imperialist rulers' did not tell 'the true story of this country from the point of view of the people'. The central fact of that history was that '"civilisation" has been a continual process of land-grabbing and plunder'.[15] By 1939 Roux had a book in draft. During the war sections appeared in the journal *Trek* and in the biography Roux wrote of S. P. Bunting, who had been a leading figure in the Communist Party until expelled from it.[16] After the war, Gollancz agreed to publish his historical book, and Roux added some additional chapters before it appeared in print in 1948.[17]

The title, *Time Longer Than Rope*, was taken from a proverb by a West Indian slave which Olivier had quoted in his *Anatomy of African Misery* as 'the motto of Africanism'; it suggested that the African struggle was a just one and would eventually triumph: for demographic reasons, time was 'on the side of the Bantu' and time was longer than any rope.[18] As Roux remarked in the Foreword, there had been 'no general account of the political history of the black man in South Africa, the battles he has waged, the organisations he has built and the personalities that have taken part in the struggle'.[19] His book traced that story from 'The Coming of the Bantu' and the Xhosa prophet Makana in the early nineteenth century to Roux's own time, at which point his account became largely a history of left politics. The first major Africanist history to emerge from South Africa, *Time Longer Than Rope* treated blacks, in the words of one reviewer, 'as active self-conscious protagonists in ... South African affairs rather than as a dark acquiescent host before which the really important story of South Africa unfolds'.[20]

Though it made a considerable impact in radical circles in the country when it appeared,[21] Roux's book received no serious attention from professional historians there. If they knew of it, they presumably dismissed it because of Roux's former Communist Party connections and the book's obvious left-wing commitment, and also because it was the work of an amateur. Roux read some eastern Cape newspapers of the 1850s for his chapter on the Xhosa cattle-killing, and he tried to locate other relevant source material, but his early chapters drew heavily on Theal – evidence of the attention Theal himself had given blacks in his *History* – and the latter chapters drew on his own personal experiences, so that his book in part resembled a political memoir.[22] The result was a largely descriptive work, but one that rescued from obscurity many events in the black experience – such as the Bulhoek massacre of 1921, the rise and fall of the ICU in the 1920s, the Africanisation of the Communist Party, the anti-pass campaigns and the bus boycotts. Such events received at most a few lines in the second edition of Walker's *History*, which appeared in 1940,[23] and had otherwise been ignored by professional historians. When Walker, in retirement in Cambridge, came to revise his *History* for a third edition in the 1950s, Roux's book became an important source for the new material he incorporated on black and left-wing politics, as his footnotes make clear,[24] but more detailed work on such topics, by graduate students and professional historians, only began to be undertaken in the late 1960s. Brought out in a second, extended edition by the University of Wisconsin Press in 1964, Roux's book exerted a strong influence on American students entering the field of southern African studies in the late 1960s.[25] In South Africa itself, it only slowly gained a wide readership because, with Roux a 'listed' person in terms of the Suppression of Communism Act, the book was banned, and it remained banned after his death in 1966, though by an anomaly the paperback edition came to be freely available in bookshops in Cape Town and Johannesburg in the 1970s.[26]

* * *

The early 1940s were a time of ferment in radical politics in Cape Town. Hosea Jaffe, then a student at the University of Cape Town, began working on a history of South Africa from a radical perspective as early as 1942, the year before the establishment of the Non-European Unity Movement (NEUM), in which he was to be active. In the decade before he completed his historical project, he also wrote much else, on a variety of non-historical topics. He received help with the history from B. M. Kies, the leading intellectual in the NEUM, and from Dr A. C. Jordan, a Xhosa-speaker who taught African languages at the University of Cape Town and was a member of the Cape African Teachers' Association, an affiliate of the NEUM. Lecturing in Cape Town in 1951 on 'Wars of Dispossession', Jordan stressed, as professional historians were not to begin to do until the mid-1960s, the positive consequences of the Mfecane. He argued, for instance, that Dingiswayo of the Mthethwa had transformed the socio-political system in Natal–Zululand, and explained that transformation in terms of the growing importance of trade with the Portuguese.[27] In the same year, a series of articles in *The Torch*, newspaper of the Unity Movement, by 'Nxele' – meaning 'the left-handed', it was the nickname given Makana, who had led anti-white resistance in the second decade of the nineteenth century – had as their subject-matter 'A History of Despotism'. Also in the early 1950s, in the pages of *Discussion*, an intellectual journal published by the Forum Club of Cape Town, Ben Kies, Willem van Schoor and Kenneth Jordaan discussed the role of Van Riebeeck, the origins of segregation and other historical issues.[28] In the eastern Cape, W. M. Tsotsi, a Fort Hare graduate and lawyer who was linked to the Unity Movement, began to advance a radical view of South African history at this time;[29] it was to be over thirty years before he published a general history, entitled *From Chattel to Wage Slavery*, which then had nothing new to say.[30] Jaffe's history was published in 1952 under the title *Three Hundred Years* by the New Era Fellowship, the debating group which had helped give birth to the NEUM. Publication of the book was designed to counter the view of South Africa propagated by those who in April 1952 organised a massive festival in Cape Town to commemorate the tercentenary of the arrival of Jan van Riebeeck. Jaffe might have called his book *Three Centuries of Wrong* had not Patrick Duncan, son of a former Governor-General and staunch critic of apartheid, used that title for a pamphlet he brought out early in 1952, which compared the Afrikaners' struggle against the British – the subject of the polemic by J. C. Smuts and J. de V. Roos entitled *A Century of Wrong*, published on the eve of the South African War[31] – with the blacks' struggle against tyranny and oppression.[32] *Three Hundred Years* concluded that the history of South Africa was one of '300 years of struggle between oppressors and oppressed', the oppression of people of colour by whites. Resistance had been Roux's main thread, but Jaffe's story highlighted conquest, slavery, dispossession, and what the third part of his work termed 'colonial fascism'.

The title *Three Hundred Years* was chosen in view of the tercentenary and also to suggest three centuries of oppression, but the book began its narrative before 1652. Its first sections were on the San (the !Ke, Jaffe preferred to call them), the Khoi-Khoin and the Bantu-speakers. One of the first works of history to move away from the conventional and derogatory terms 'Bushmen' and 'Hottentot', it attempted to interpret South African history from the point of view of the indigenous people. The Great Trek, for instance, was not a central event in the history of European settlement – as it was for Walker – but an episode in the history of colonial conquest and dispossession.[33]

At the end of 1952 – its last chapter was dated November that year – another radical work appeared. *The Role of the Missionaries in Conquest* was published in Alexandra, an African suburb of Johannesburg, by the Society of Young Africa, an Africanist gingergroup linked to the Unity Movement. Again a pseudonym was used, so the author could escape possible retribution, and to depersonalise authorship.[34] 'Nosipho Majeke' was in fact Dora Taylor, wife of a psychology lecturer at the University of Cape Town. Like Jaffe, she had long been active in Trotskyite politics in Cape Town. They frequently visited each other while they were working on their projects.[35] Their works together embodied an Africanist interpretation of South African history more radical than Roux's. Whereas Roux, drawing heavily on Macmillan's books, depicted Philip and other Cape liberals as 'friends of the natives', 'Majeke' and 'Mnguni' regarded Philip as one of the prime agents of conquest. Both books were based on considerable original research – *Three Hundred Years* had more than twelve hundred footnotes – and though clearly written as polemics, they claimed to present a more accurate version of South African history than the one available in the writings of the professional historians. 'For a people engaged in a liberatory stuggle', wrote Taylor, 'it is necessary to rewrite the history of the past.'

The story, if truly told, is one of continuous plunder of land and cattle by the European invaders, of the devastation and decimation of people, followed by their economic enslavement.[36]

Both works briefly emphasised the importance of capitalism,[37] but neither used class analysis at all systematically. Many of the points they made for the first time in works of South African history would later be accepted by professional historians. Missionaries were shown to have been active agents in colonisation, for example, and Britain was revealed to have played a major role in the conquest of African societies in the nineteenth century.[38]

Few professional historians read the works by 'Mnguni' and 'Majeke' when they appeared. Leonard Thompson of the University of Cape Town, who did read *Three Hundred Years* when it was published in September 1952, informed W. M. Macmillan of

what purports to be a history of South Africa which a Cape Town group of non-whites have recently published surreptitiously: a large proportion of the work is devoted to convincing the reader that the white liberal has always 'ratted', and has been, indeed, used by the main body of whites to bluff the non-white and soothe them. Throughout the work the hero of the story is the Native or Indian or Coloured man who resisted the blandishments of the liberals; the others are 'collaborators', 'fascists', 'quislings'.[39]

As a liberal, Thompson was antagonised by such an approach. That the first beginnings of an Africanist perspective were incorporated in writing that was polemical and anti-liberal, probably served to alienate professional historians who might otherwise have been sympathetic to the approach. Various individuals of liberal views – among them Mr Justice Tindall and the economist Hobart Houghton – suggested to Macmillan that he was the best person to write a rebuttal of *The Role of the Missionaries in Conquest*, but he chose not to: he was by then out of touch, and Tindall had to admit 'that it would not be easy to deal with some of the points made in the book'.[40]

* * *

While Roux achieved a fundamental breakthrough by writing a history firmly focused on South Africa's majority, he was still largely concerned with political leaders, whereas 'Mnguni' and 'Majeke' stressed the processes of conquest and dispossession. In the late 1950s Lionel Forman (1928–59), lawyer, editor of the left-wing newspaper *New Age* and treason-trialist,[41] was inspired by *The People's History of England* (1938) written by A. L. Morton, a Marxist, to research and write a 'systematic history of the liberatory movement', or 'a people's history' of South Africa. His first attempts were published in *New Age* and subsequently as a short booklet entitled *Chapters in the History of the March to Freedom* (Cape Town, n.d.). After his death at the age of 31, Ray Alexander, a trade unionist and prominent member of the Communist Party, selected some essays from his notebooks, which appeared as another *New Age* pamphlet entitled *Black and White in S.A. History*. Though *Chapters* shows his interest in the inter-relationship between national oppression and class oppression, both pamphlets reveal him chiefly concerned to uncover examples of popular resistance and to trace the history of organised extra-parliamentary politics in the early twentieth century. His purpose was clearly apparent in his bringing *Chapters* to a close with what he portrayed as 'the first bonds of unity between democrats of all races'. Because he sought to inspire people in the present, he wrote simply, to reach a mass audience. After his death, Alexander and her husband, who taught at the University of Cape Town, drew on Forman's work in writing their massive and more scholarly radical history.[42]

* * *

Before the 1960s such amateur work as was done, either on black history or on the history of the underclasses in general, was not taken seriously by professional historians. The latter continued to believe that history depended entirely on written sources, and that sources did not exist that would permit the reconstruction of the history of African societies. In the Introduction to the general history called *Five Hundred Years*, published in 1969, Muller added that even were there evidence for pre-conquest societies, there would be no purpose in studying them, for they were of no real significance.[43]

By the time Muller wrote, however, another group of scholars had begun to recover the role of Africans in South African history. These early 'liberal Africanists' – the subject of the next chapter – had no sympathy for a radical perspective. But very soon after the Africanist breakthrough, another, more fundamental one was made. Those responsible for that 'radical challenge' were to develop – though often in ignorance of the earlier work – some of the ideas advanced by the polemicists and amateur scholars discussed above.

PART 4
The liberal Africanists

14 The beginnings of liberal Africanism

Those who in the 1960s and 1970s carried further the liberal tradition of South African historical writing initiated by Macmillan and continued by de Kiewiet have sometimes been called 'later liberals' or 'neo-liberals'. But as their chief contribution lay in their Africanist perspective, 'liberal Africanist', which is the label some of them have used for themselves,[1] would indeed seem the most appropriate term. They were Africanists in that they sought to show that Africans had played an important role in South African history. They endeavoured to recover the history of the black experience in the South African past. In advancing the liberal tradition to this position no one individual played as pioneering a role as Macmillan had in establishing the tradition in the 1920s, but Leonard Thompson was the single most important of the 'liberal Africanists' in the 1960s.

* * *

The reorientation in South African history which took place in the 1960s followed upon, and was prompted by, the revolution that occurred in the history of tropical Africa in the 1950s and early 1960s. That revolution in turn reflected changes in the relationship between the West and Africa, and the coming to independence of new African states. Before the 1950s it was generally accepted that there was no such thing as African history, only the history of Europeans in Africa, for history depended on writing, and writing only came with the advent of Europeans.[2] But after the Second World War the decolonisation process was set in motion in British tropical Africa. In 1948 Roland Oliver was appointed lecturer in African history at the School of Oriental and African Studies, University of London, the first such appointment anywhere in the English-speaking world. Together with Gerald Graham, Professor of Imperial History at the University of

144 THE LIBERAL AFRICANISTS

London, Oliver in the 1950s began to train historians from African countries. The first to obtain his doctorate in London was Kenneth Dike of Nigeria, whose *Trade and Politics in the Niger Delta 1830–1885* was published in 1956. Conferences on African history were held at the School of Oriental and African Studies, and history posts opened up at the new universities founded in tropical Africa. John Fage, another of the pioneers, took up an appointment at the University College in the Gold Coast, and there wrote the first history of West Africa, published in 1955.[3] He then combined with Oliver to produce the first *Short History of Africa* from a scholarly Afrocentric perspective.[4] By 1960, the year of independence for much of tropical Africa, and the year which saw the launching of the *Journal of African History*, Oliver, Fage, Dike and others had demonstrated the scholarly value of African history other than that of Europeans in Africa. There were still those who refused to accept this: as late as 1965 Hugh Trevor-Roper, Regius Professor of Modern History at Oxford University, dismissed 'the history of black Africa' as 'the unrewarding gyrations of barbarous tribes in picturesque but irrelevant corners of the globe'[5] – but by then it was clear to most that a revolution in African history was well under way.

As African countries gained their independence, and Africa seemed to assume a new importance on the world stage, so more posts in African history became available, not only in Britain and at the new African universities, but also in America. Some were given to South Africanists, who found themselves teaching with Africanist colleagues, among whom were anthropologists, linguists or historians working on tropical Africa. Contact with these colleagues helped widen their horizons and encouraged them to bring the writing of South African history more in line with that of tropical Africa, which now seemed much further advanced. Regarding South Africa as an essentially African country, they sought to set it within its African context in a way not achieved before. Because South Africa was in many ways different from the rest of Africa – there was to be no transfer of power as in tropical Africa – the attempt to Africanise South African history bore its own special character. Elsewhere, the new African history was written in part to give the new countries a past to look back to with pride, and to help legitimise African nationalist movements and the new independent nation-states. Much of the work written in the 1960s and early 1970s stressed the integrity of the new nation, or sought

to link primary resistance with modern mass nationalism, to demonstrate a long tradition of resistance, or else it treated of African
initiative and achievement. For South Africa, there was a world of
African achievement, and resistance, to recover. But the Africanist
historians of the 1960s did not entirely avoid the pitfalls of the
new approach. It was easy to overstress the glories of African
states and their rulers, or the vitality and continuity of resistance.
Early Africanist work often glossed over conflicts and divisions
among Africans, and presented an 'African point of view', as if
there was a single African point of view. That was to offer a mere
counter to the racist paradigm that was the target; it challenged
the old racist history by providing a history of 'the other side', assuming a separate identity for that 'other side'.[6] In South Africa
some early Africanists fell into that trap, writing as Africans were
a united, classless whole.

* * *

Leonard Thompson was the first professional historian of South
Africa to become aware of the need to accomplish for South African history what was being done for the history of tropical
Africa: to decolonise it. In June–July 1957 he visited the newly independent state of Ghana with Arthur Keppel-Jones and other
university colleagues. Then in 1960 he was invited to give a paper
at a conference, funded by the Leverhulme trust, held in Salisbury, at the University College of Rhodesia. His own paper on
'Afrikaner Nationalist Historiography and the Policy of Apartheid'
spoke of Afrikaner historiography perpetuating a mythology of
'bitter grievances and solemn heroics'.[7] Other papers at the conference, delivered by historians working on other countries in
Africa, were written from the new Africanist perspective, and
when Thompson returned to Cape Town, he reported as follows:

> The proceedings of the conference have left me in no doubt that archaeo
> logists, anthropologists and historians must co-operate if the history of
> this continent is to be adequately revealed. If, for example, the last cen
> tury is to be properly understood, the written evidence must be sup
> plemented from oral tradition, expertly recorded and critically handled.

He went on to warn that the universities of South Africa might
be surpassed as the principal institutions of scholarship on the
continent, and to express the hope that means might be found to
enable the University of Cape Town to convene a similar confer-

ence on African history, or African studies, in 1962 or 1963.[8] But
no such conference was held. The fiftieth anniversary of Union
was also the year of the Sharpeville massacre. Soon after his
return from the Salisbury conference, Thompson left to become
Visiting Professor in Commonwealth History at Duke University,
North Carolina. While there he was invited by Professor John
Galbraith to present a lecture at the University of California, Los
Angeles, and was offered a professorship in African history in the
newly established African Studies Center at that university, at a
time when the only other professors in African history in North
America were Philip Curtin and Jan Vansina. Thompson's decision to leave South Africa was not altogether sudden; he had told
Macmillan in 1952 that South Africa might 'become intolerable
fairly soon'.[9] He had now completed his large project on unification[10] and California seemed to offer limitless possibilities. He returned to Cape Town only to tell a farewell audience that
circumstances in the country in the aftermath of Sharpeville 'make
it difficult, if not impossible, for me to continue my work properly'.[11]

On his sabbatical in the USA Thompson was invited to Cambridge, Massachusetts, for a conference organised by Louis Hartz,
one of America's leading political scientists, on 'the founding of
new societies'. His paper, which became the South African chapter
in the book Hartz published under that title in 1964, demonstrated Thompson's ability to range over the whole of South African history, and to relate a general argument – about fragment
societies – to the particular case of South Africa. There was
nothing distinctively Africanist about his contribution, but at
UCLA Thompson found his interests moving more and more in
an Africanist direction. He worked with anthropologists, linguists
and other specialists on tropical Africa in an African Studies
Center, and his postgraduate students had to complete courses in
these other disciplines. He himself began research on a biography
of Moshoeshoe of Lesotho, which would use oral as well as
written sources. Its completion was to be very long delayed, for he
undertook other assignments – including an historiographical
survey which deplored the absence of research on Africans in
South African history [12] and a book on the politics of South Africa
published in 1966.[13] His other main preoccupation in these highly
prolific years was a new general history of South Africa.

* * *

From the mid-1950s it was widely known among professional historians of South Africa that Eric Walker, in retirement at Cambridge, had undertaken to be general editor of a new edition of the volume on South Africa in the *Cambridge History of the British Empire*. After numerous delays, the volume finally appeared in 1963. It came as a great disappointment to those hoping for new insights and perspectives. Walker himself was out of touch with new developments in the discipline and most of the key historical chapters – notably those by Macmillan and de Kiewiet – were reprinted without change in the new edition. Eric Axelson, who had succeeded to the King George V chair at the University of Cape Town in 1962, at once decided to plan a new history to replace the Cambridge volume, and in May 1964 he asked J. S. Marais, his opposite number at Wits, to act as co-editor. But the following month Axelson was told, both by the local branch of Oxford University Press, which had initially expressed interest in publishing such a work, and by Marais, who was then in England, that Thompson had approached the Clarendon Press in Oxford with the idea of a two volume history of South Africa, and that that Press, which had recently published the first volume of a *History of East Africa* edited by Roland Oliver and Gervase Mathew, had agreed to publish. That scuppered the Cape Town project.[14]

Thompson's co-editors were John Galbraith, Professor of Imperial and Commonwealth History at UCLA, who soon withdrew when he took up a full-time administrative post,[15] and Monica Wilson of the University of Cape Town. She brought to the project the Africanist scholarship of the anthropologists, but also a keen desire to see a new general history written from an Africanist perspective. Born at Lovedale in the eastern Cape, the daughter of a missionary and teacher at the famous school there, Monica Hunter (1908–82) was educated, first at Lovedale itself – in a class most members of which were Africans – then at the Port Elizabeth Collegiate School for Girls, and finally at Girton College, Cambridge, where she read history.[16] For a graduate degree in anthropology she chose to do her field-work in an area close to her home. In 1931–2 and again in 1934 she worked in Pondoland and in the Ciskei, and she received her doctorate for the classic work published in 1936 as *Reaction to Conquest*. That title was misleading inasmuch as it suggested a study of response over time. More than most members of Malinowski's famous seminar, which she attended in London, Monica Hunter had a keen interest in social change, but the bulk of her book was cast in the synchronic, struc-tural-functionalist mould then fashionable. With Godfrey Wilson, her husband and a fellow anthropologist from Cambridge who was appointed to the Rhodes–Livingstone Institute in Northern Rho-desia,[17] she worked among the Nyakyusa and the Ngonde of eastern Zambia and Nyasaland in 1935–8. Their concern with the impact of migrant labour on these people led the Wilsons during the early years of the war to write a seminal book on the analysis of social change. Its theme was the increase in social change that accompanied economic growth: they argued that enlargement of scale was an inevitable development of the modern world; with economic change came greater social interaction and the emer-gence of wider loyalties. These were seen as positive devel-opments.[18]

After her husband's death in 1944, Monica Wilson took up a lecturing post in social anthropology at Fort Hare University Col-lege, and from 1947 held the chair at Rhodes, where she carried out field-work in nearby Keiskammahoek. In 1952 she succeeded the eminent Isaac Schapera at Cape Town. Three years later she obtained a Carnegie Corporation grant to return to work among the Nyakyusa, afterwards producing a number of monographs based on the field-work she and her late husband had done in central Africa.[19] But in the 1950s she became increasingly con-cerned with contemporary events in South Africa, in particular the Nationalist government's assault on the 'open universities' and its propagation of myths about the South African past in the service of apartheid.

There were many such myths. One was that 'mixing' between different 'ethnic groups' had necessarily led to conflict, a myth much used in defence of the Group Areas Act of 1950.[20] Another was that Africans had in the past been divided into discrete ethnic units. And the old myth of the 'empty land' was refurbished as part of apartheid ideology in the age of Verwoerdian 'separate de-velopment'. A new paternalistic concern in official circles for 'the Bantu' as a distinct people created a revived interest in 'Bantu history'. In 1958 Dr de Wet Nel, Minister of Bantu Administration and Development, spoke of the 'sad neglect' of such history:

A reliable and objective history of the Bantu peoples was of the utmost importance to the Bantu themselves and also for the good relations be-tween Bantu and Europeans. Special attention should also be given to the history of Black–White relations in the country since the first contact was made. It was a fallacy to regard the Bantu as one people. The Xhosa, the Zulu, the Sotho, and the Venda were separate ethnic groups whose characteristics and histories widely differed. Only if the history of every group was known would their attitudes to different things be appreciated.[21]

Monica Wilson's abhorrence of apartheid strengthened her resolve to accomplish for South Africa what was being done in tropical Africa: she, more than anyone else in Cape Town, knew of the new work on the history of Africans being written in tropical Africa, and wanted it emulated in South Africa.

Her first attempt to do this, a seminal article published in *African Studies* in 1959 on the early history of the Transkei and Ciskei, deliberately set out to refute one of the central historical myths being peddled in the official propaganda of the Verwoerd era. Her article began by citing a remark made by Eric Louw, South Africa's Foreign Minister, concerning the simultaneous arrival of black and white in the country. She then drew on the reports of shipwrecked European sailors, records that had been available since Theal first brought them together in his *Records of South East Africa*, to demonstrate that Africans had lived in the Transkei and Ciskei long before whites arrived there. Any idea of two streams of colonisers, black and white, meeting on the Fish River was a myth. That there had been a settled African population east of the Fish for many centuries before whites arrived has since been confirmed by much detailed scholarship.[22]

In the early 1960s, in collaboration with Archie Mafeje, her most brilliant postgraduate student, Monica Wilson studied the African township of Langa on the outskirts of Cape Town. With that book completed, she spent her sabbatical leave during the American winter of 1963–4 at the School of Behavioral Sciences at Stanford University, a Californian think-tank. In California she renewed contact with Leonard Thompson, and they agreed that the second edition of the *Cambridge History* was a disaster, and that a new history was needed, on Africanist lines. A few years later Monica Wilson told the president of the Carnegie Corporation how she and Thompson had

cooked up a plan for a somewhat unorthodox history of South Africa when I was last in the U.S. and I have since put a great deal of work into it. Our argument is that the nub of South African history is the interaction between peoples (as de Kiewiet said long ago) and we have tried to analyse it in these terms. There has been all sorts of difficulties – among

them the number of authors who cannot be quoted if the book is to circu-
late here. But I think we have got round most problems.[23]

The problems were various. Clement Goodfellow, head of the
history department at the Lesotho campus of the University of
Botswana, Lesotho and Swaziland, having completed a book on
Great Britain and South African confederation in the 1870s, in
which he acknowledged his debt to 'the fact of life itself', committed suicide.[24] Thompson had to step in to write the chapter
Goodfellow was to have contributed on the subjection of the African chiefdoms in the late nineteenth century. Other potential
contributors – among them de Kiewiet, Marais, and Marquard –
declined or withdrew from the project.[25] The chapter on African
nationalism in the second volume gave the editors most problems,
for it quoted and cited many authors and books banned under
South African law. At Monica Wilson's suggestion – for she was
determined that the volume be available in South Africa – the
Clarendon Press agreed to omit the chapter by Leo Kuper from a
separate South African edition. In its place there would be 53
blank pages, which Monica Wilson hoped would serve as a protest
against the censorship laws. Kuper was furious at what he termed
'surrogate censorship'[26] and a Cambridge don made a scathing
attack on Oxford University Press for doing the South African
government's dirty work for it and 'depriving Africans in the
Republic of their history....' 'The Government of the Republic of
South Africa', wrote Ronald Hyam, 'merely denies them their
present and their future. The Oxford University Press denies them
their past as well.'[27] Not long after the separate editions appeared,
it became clear that the one which included Kuper's chapter could
in fact be sold in South Africa after all.

* * *

Before we assess the significance of the *Oxford History* we must
return to 1966, the year of the publication of the first pathbreaking Africanist monograph on the South African past, *The Zulu
Aftermath* by John Omer-Cooper. Though a South African by upbringing, Omer-Cooper had settled abroad. He had grown up in
Grahamstown, where his father became professor of zoology at
Rhodes. His parents, who had come out from England, were alienated from the dominant culture and had encouraged their children
to associate with Africans. His father told him at an early age that
he hoped he would become an anthropologist, and on another oc-

casion said that he hoped that 'some day someone would write the real history of South Africa, about the majority of the people'. When he went to Rhodes as a student, Omer-Cooper majored in history rather than anthropology, and remembers how struck he had been when Winifred Maxwell, then senior lecturer in history, observed that Shaka, Moshoeshoe and Mzilikazi were as much nation-builders as Clovis and others in medieval Europe.[28]

After completing a second undergraduate history degree at Cambridge, Omer-Cooper did not return to South Africa, but instead applied for and was given a post as lecturer at Ibadan, the first university to be established in Nigeria. There he inevitably came into contact with the new work on the history of tropical Africa. His head of department was Kenneth Dike, whom he joined in pressing for a greater emphasis on the teaching of African history. When London University – whose syllabus Ibadan followed – agreed to include more African history, he was commissioned to write the southern African section of a general textbook to meet the requirements of the new syllabus. The textbook project fell through, but Omer-Cooper decided to build on what he had collected on the Mfecane and to write a monograph on that topic. He researched the book in England, and it was published in the new Ibadan History series in 1966 under the title *The Zulu Aftermath*. Colin Legum, an ex-South African who was Africa correspondent of the London *Observer*, had told Omer-Cooper that only with 'Zulu' in its title would the book sell.[29]

Instead of describing the Mfecane in negative terms, as a destructive movement that had caused massive depopulation, Omer-Cooper stressed its epic proportions, and that it was an entirely African event, not brought about by any European intervention. In discussing early nineteenth century black history, Theal had dwelt on destruction, depopulation and even cannibalism. Omer-Cooper interpreted the Mfecane as a positive movement, creating major new states, such as the Ndebele state of Mzilikazi and Moshoeshoe's Sotho kingdom. Mzilikazi and Moshoeshoe, even Shaka, became transformed into creative innovators. *The Zulu Aftermath* was a product of the age of modernisation theory, which assumed that increases in scale were necessarily beneficial, and also a product of African nationalism and decolonisation, for Omer-Cooper sought to underline the capacity of Africans to respond to challenges, and to create new nations just as people had elsewhere. He even suggested, very misleadingly, for the context was quite different, that the states created out of the Mfecane had faced the same nation-building problems as the modern African states. Clearly *The Zulu Aftermath* was a product of what Terence Ranger was to call 'the demonstrative age of African history', when it was thought necessary to demonstrate that Africans had a history of their own, apart from that of Europeans, and that it had indeed been significant.[30]

The year 1969 saw the publication not only of the much-delayed first volume of the *Oxford History*, but also of a seminal collection of essays edited by Thompson. The chapters in *African Societies in Southern Africa* were first presented as papers at a conference held in Lusaka, Zambia, in 1968. That conference formed a key moment in the history of historical writing on South Africa. Omer-Cooper, by then professor of history at the University of Zambia, was the local host, and Thompson the organiser and guiding spirit of the conference, which for the first time revealed the extent of the new internationalism of South African history writing. No longer were the professional historians of South Africa almost all based at South African universities; indeed, by 1968 the most challenging work was being carried on outside the country.

In California Thompson had attracted a number of postgraduate students to write dissertations on southern African topics. Those flown out to Zambia for the conference included William Lye, whose doctoral dissertation dealt with the Difaqane on the high-veld,[31] and Gerrit Harinck, whose paper on interaction between Xhosa and Khoi in the seventeenth and eighteenth centuries was to be his last contribution to South African historiography because he was inexplicably refused a visa to visit South Africa to do research.[32] Martin Legassick, the most radical of Thompson's students, did not attend the Lusaka conference, but wrote a major paper for it on the early history of the Sotho-Tswana. From England came Shula Marks and Anthony Atmore, both of whom had been taught by Thompson as undergraduates at the University of Cape Town. They had gone on to postgraduate work at the University of London in the early 1960s under Roland Oliver. Marks was in 1968 completing a dissertation on the Bambatha revolt in early twentieth century Natal, a topic to which she had been led by George Shepperson's *Independent African*, on Chilembwe's rebellion in Malawi, one of the early classics of the new African history.[33] Atmore had helped Oliver write a textbook on *Africa since 1800* (1967) and was in the late 1960s working for a

University of London doctorate – never completed – on the Sotho resistance to the Cape in the 1870s and early 1880s, the most successful African resistance to white overlordship anywhere in southern Africa, which resulted in the exchange of Cape for British rule. From South Africa went the historian Colin Webb from Natal, and the anthropologists Monica Wilson and David Hammond-Tooke.[34] The important role played by the anthropologists at Lusaka served to show, as would the first volume of the *Oxford History*, that South African history could no longer be conceived in narrow disciplinary terms. In Lusaka the South African scholars were able to meet academics pioneering the study of the history of tropical Africa, including Terence Ranger and Andrew Roberts, both then at the university in Dar-es-Salaam.

Most of the papers delivered at the Lusaka conference were specialised analyses which attempted to come to grips with the internal dynamics of particular African societies. For the first time these societies were treated as important in their own right. The South Africanists at Lusaka were very conscious of being pioneers, of opening a new window onto the South African past. They believed themselves to be liberating South Africa from an albocentric view of its history, and so contributing to the struggle for justice and equity in that country. In the Introduction to the book which emerged from the conference, Thompson described the history of African societies as 'the forgotten factor' in the country's past.[35] Africans had indeed been 'forgotten', and their history before white conquest, as well as after, demanded recovery. But to the extent that the new work suggested that Africans – as a blanket category – were merely the one additional factor that was required to produce a new and rounded South African history, it oversimplified. We shall note, in Part 5, how historians sought to transcend the limitations of the approach adopted by the early Africanists.

15 The Oxford History

In their Preface to the first volume of the *Oxford History* Wilson and Thompson set out their purpose: to overturn certain misleading assumptions commonly made about the South African past in the existing historiography. South African history did not begin with the arrival of the Portuguese around the coast in the fifteenth century, or with the establishment of the Dutch settlement. It was not until the reader reached page 187, almost halfway through their volume, that 1652 came into sight.[1] Precolonial African societies, the Preface continued, were not static and timeless. Physical type, language and economy were not necessarily related. Moreover, South Africa did not contain several pure, uncontaminated 'races'. In general Wilson and Thompson strove to move away from an ethnocentric focus, and to look at the history of all South Africa's people on an equal basis.

This they sought to do by drawing upon a wider range of evidence than previous historians had used, including oral tradition and the findings of other disciplines. In the absence of historians able to draw such evidence together, the first chapters were written by Ray Inskeep, an archaeologist, and Monica Wilson herself. In the second volume, Wilson and Thompson were joined, as contributors, by two economists, two political scientists and a newspaper editor. That so many non-historians were involved was in part a reflection of the editors' wish to be interdisciplinary in approach, but it was also a commentary on the state of history at that time. At the South African universities, as also at many universities in Britain, in the 1960s historians did not write about economic or social history. Not surprisingly, the non-historians who wrote on economic or social change in the *Oxford History* presented their material in a way that historians were to criticise as ahistorical; not even an anthropologist as sensitive to social change as Monica Wilson concerned herself with the sequence of events over time as historians did.[2]

The major contribution which the *Oxford History* and other Africanist work of the late 1960s made to South African historiography was later forgotten by some eager to give every credit for recent advance to radical historians. When the *Oxford History* appeared, even liberal historians devoted more space to comment on its weaknesses than to welcome its strengths.[3] An article published in 1983 begins as follows: 'Over the past fifteen years radical [*sic*] historiography has demolished the unstated presumption that South African history began in 1652.'[4] It was in fact liberal historiography, in its Africanist phase, that demolished that myth. The *Oxford History* did not so much mark the apogee of the liberal tradition – as some critics suggested[5] – as signal the firm establishment of a revived liberal tradition in South African historical writing, a liberal Africanist one. It was the first general text to provide a substantial body of information about the history of blacks in the country, using a broader range of sources than any previous history. The first volume devoted as much space to blacks as to whites, and in the second there was a constant awareness of the presence of a black majority.

As a survey of South African history, then, the *Oxford History* marked a great advance. At a time when Verwoerdian apartheid was being implemented in its most elaborate form, the *Oxford History* and other Africanist work of the late 1960s regarded blacks as historical actors who were as important as whites, their initiatives and responses as significant in shaping events as white actions. If blacks had played a vital role in the past, by implication they should be able to play such a role in the present. If Africans had their own past, they might make their own future. With Africans recognised as the majority of South Africa's people, the country's past for the first time began to be seen by professional historians – as it had been earlier by the amateurs Roux and 'Mnguni'[6] – as predominantly a black past, at the very time when the government was moving towards stripping all blacks of their citizenship and, through the Bantustan policy, trying to make a truncated South Africa a 'white man's country'. The evidence from history meant recognising – as the novelist Anthony Trollope had, on his visit to the country in the 1870s – that South Africa was one country, and that that country was more black than white. Some members of the white community could indeed trace their roots in African soil over three hundred years, but this community as a whole was relatively small and predominantly of relatively recent immigrants. On the other hand, South Africa was not just another African country, and the Sharpeville massacre of March 1960 was not the prelude to the end of white supremacy which some at the time predicted it would be. In what became known as the 'silent sixties', white power was entrenched more strongly than ever, and Africans appeared powerless. Historians began to show that there had been a long and significant history of resistance and struggle,[7] but it had not led to liberation. Blacks had resisted and struggled, but had failed to secure their objectives. Historians might accord blacks a major role in the past, but white domination of the present was all too apparent.

* * *

Many of the limitations of the *Oxford History*, the single most important Africanist work on South Africa, flowed from the fact that it was a pioneering venture, written when little or no detailed research had been carried out on many of the topics it surveyed. Its authors did not draw on new material in the archives, or on newly collected oral traditions. Monica Wilson's chapters were based on her anthropological knowledge, and on missionary and travellers' accounts. It was only in the early 1970s that monographs began to appear on such topics as the history of the African National Congress and the Industrial and Commercial Workers' Union.[8] The first volume of the *Oxford History* was written before the Africanist doctoral dissertations supervised by Leonard Thompson at the University of California, Los Angeles, began to be completed,[9] before the papers in the *African Societies* volume were available, before Shula Marks began her seminar on the societies of southern Africa in the nineteenth and twentieth centuries at the University of London.[10]

The *Oxford History* was deliberately designed, as the Preface made clear, to counter a set of myths about the South African past. In its pages there was much explicit refutation of those myths. Monica Wilson included a detailed discussion of what shipwrecked sailors had sighted in the Ciskei and Transkei in order to refute Theal and prove that Bantu-speaking people lived there in the seventeenth century. In reaction to the stress Afrikaner nationalist historians placed on the Great Trek, Thompson split his discussion of it into two separate chapters, and altogether gave it less attention than the rise of the Zulu state. As the general theme of the work was interaction, however, and as the Great Trek vastly increased the area of interaction between white and black, downplaying its importance seemed inappropriate, and an example of anti-Afrikanerism. F. A. van Jaarsveld, the leading Afrikaner historian, could point out that while Monica Wilson remarked that the rule of law existed among the Xhosa, May Katzen in her chapter denied that there was a rule of law in Dutch society at the Cape in the eighteenth century. The English liberal historians were indeed hostile to an Afrikaner nationalism which had become intimately linked with apartheid, their main target. The use of phrases like 'ignorant complacency and insularity' for the eighteenth-century Dutch, and the marginalisation of the Trek, enabled Van Jaarsveld to dismiss the Africanist perspective as a new means by which English historians were trying to project their anti-Afrikaner prejudices on the past.[11]

Traces of the old approach remained in the *Oxford History*: slaves were called 'intractable', which was to reproduce the view of the slave-owner, and the way George Stow was cited on dispossession of the San by the Bantu-speakers seemed to suggest such dispossession paralleled that effected by whites.[12] But the work's Africanist sympathies were not disguised. Van Jaarsveld thought the first volume presented a 'pro-Bantu' attitude.[13] In later works, however, the Africanist perspective led to an even greater emphasis on the role of blacks, and diminution of the role of whites. Some of the chapters of the multi-volume *Cambridge History of Africa* written by Shula Marks in the late 1970s, in trying to set the early history of South Africa within that of Africa as a whole, reduced the role of the whites at the Cape to little account. And while the Africanist work of the 1970s showed without doubt the importance of oral tradition and anthropological insights for an understanding of precolonial African societies, hardly any work of a similar kind was carried out on Afrikaner social structure.[14]

To demonstrate the possibility of close working relations between black and white in the American South, the leading American historian C. Vann Woodward emphasised – overemphasised, according to critics – co-operation between black and white workers in the 1890s.[15] In a similar way, to combat the 'friction thesis' used by the apartheid regime to justify Group Areas and other segregationist measures – the idea that racial contact inevitably led to hostility – the authors of the *Oxford History* highlighted examples of co-operation across the colour line in the past.

Lovedale school became important just because it had taught both blacks and whites.[16] Out of a concern to stress interaction and interdependence, the separate histories of groups and 'traditional [ethnic] loyalties' tended to be ignored.[17] Violent conflict likewise tended to be downplayed, while trade and missionary work, and other examples of peaceful interaction, received major attention. Monica Wilson, in particular, did not hesitate to moralise and to make clear her political commitment. Fragmentation, she wrote, 'bedevils men', and she dwelt on the irony that the white settlers dismissed the conquered blacks as primitive and backward, yet expected them to learn their language, and cease 'squatting'.[18] She left no doubt which side was right in the conflict 'between isolation and wide-scale interaction; between a tribal outlook and a universal one; between an exclusive interpretation of "Who is My Neighbour?" and a Christian one'. At the end of another chapter she posed a series of rhetorical questions: 'Can close economic interdependence be combined with political independence? Can any country remain stable when the majority of its population ... are not citizens but foreigners...? Can any society built on the separation of families throughout a man's working life survive?'[19] Interaction was not merely the central theme; it was a 'Good Thing'.

Some of the problems with the first volume of the *History* were ironic in view of the stated aim of the editors to move away from a picture of a static, unchanging past. Monica Wilson's chapters in the first volume were much criticised for being too synchronic. She drew on anthropological evidence of, say, San marriage habits from recent field-work, when talking of the distant past. Such criticism extended beyond her chapters: Afrikaners too were largely seen in isolation, and their societies presented as virtually unchanging over a long period of time.[20] Though the authors of the *Oxford History* tried to break with the idea of discrete racial types – Bryant's use of 'purity' to refer to the Nguni, was said to stem 'from white South African traditions rather than black'[21] – physical type, language and economy still tended to be linked. Monica Wilson's hunters and herders were San and Khoi respectively. It was Shula Marks, whose review of the first volume of the *Oxford History* led her to a detailed examination of what happened to the Khoi in the eighteenth century, and Richard Elphick, who followed Thompson from UCLA to Yale and there completed a doctorate on the Khoi in the late seventeenth century, who first documented the complexities of the relations between hunters and herders, and showed how, say, herders had often become hunters.[22]

Rejecting racism, the liberal Africanists did on occasion admit that race had not always been the dominant cleavage in South African history.[23] Yet some critics charged that they in fact disseminated the very ideology they professed to condemn. Their use of racial categories did not challenge, but served to buttress, the racial system, for racial groups were seen as fundamental givens. South African history was interpreted in terms of race and of racism.[24] In dividing her material on African societies into 'Nguni' and 'Sotho' chapters, Monica Wilson suggested homogeneity among Sotho, on the one hand, and Nguni on the other, and separate histories for each. But those very categories were of relatively recent origin.[25] Ethnic categories were inappropriately read back into the past, as if they had some primordial existence. The development of ethnic consciousness over time, among Afrikaners and Africans, was ignored. The *Oxford History* devoted little explicit attention to the growth of white racism, which was mostly taken for granted, as something that had been present since the eighteenth century and therefore did not require historical explanation.

* * *

The dismissive criticism of the *Oxford History* that came from the right – from government officials as well as Van Jaarsveld and other conservative historians – was not unexpected. The editors and authors did not, however, anticipate the even stronger criticism which came from the left. By the time the *Oxford History* was published, recent Africanist historical writing on tropical Africa was already beginning to be viewed more critically. In the introduction to a collection of papers published under the title *Emerging Themes of African History* in 1968, Terence Ranger predicted, correctly, that 'radical pessimists', critical of the new governments in tropical Africa and the neo-nationalist historiography that buttressed them, would soon be in the ascendant.

The first volume of the *Oxford History*, like all early liberal Africanist work, tended to emphasise the political. The contributors did not follow Macmillan and de Kiewiet in stressing the importance of economics, and the interrelatedness of politics and economics. That non-economists should have steered clear of economics has, in part, an institutional explanation. Economic history was not taught in the history departments at Wits and

Cape Town, but in departments of economics or economic history. Most liberals of the 1950s and early 1960s were, moreover, concerned with problems of political power and constitutionalism. Liberals tended not to be critical of the record of capitalist development, which historians did not investigate, as outside their concerns. 'Business' – historically dominated by English-speakers – was conceived of as something separate from 'government', the records of which formed the basis for most work by liberal historians.

The relevance, let alone the dominance, of economic factors, then, was by and large ignored by the early liberal Africanists. Their explanations were idealist ones. Economic pressures – making, say, for the conquest of the African chiefdoms – received little attention. The South African War was explained in terms of a conflict between British supremacy and Transvaal nationalism[26] and was not related directly to the gold-mining industry or the supply of gold from the Witwatersrand. The system of racial discrimination was not linked to the economy, and the impact of the spread of capitalism was neglected because the study of economic change was largely left to economists. It was only the 'second wave' of Africanists – part of a radical school, to be discussed in the next chapter – who linked the political and the economic in the concept of political economy. Those who wrote in the 1960s and early 1970s not only tended to write political history – Thompson's biography of Moshoeshoe, begun in the early 1960s but not published until 1975,[27] was essentially political, for example – but also to adopt a top-down perspective. This was something Africanist historians of the later 1970s deliberately sought to correct.[28]

Critics on the left argued that the liberal authors of the *Oxford History* had not examined social inequalities of wealth and poverty. Though in apartheid South Africa race seemed all-important, the critics claimed that race 'mystified' the real nature of exploitation in the society. Class categories, they said, were in reality more salient than racial ones. Not all the writers in the *Oxford History* were blind to class and stratification – Monica Wilson, for example, stressed the importance of clientage[29] – but some of the contributors did indeed explicitly deny the importance of class: May Katzen, for example, remarked: 'Class distinctions, in the European sense, did not apply within the white community' at the Cape in the eighteenth century.[30]

In his chapter on African nationalism, Leo Kuper – though in- volved in the writing of a major study of *An African Bourgeoisie*[31] – tended to write as if that nationalism was relatively homogeneous, and as if Africans were divided mainly by attitudes towards whites.[32] The class bases of African nationalism – on which de- tailed work has now been done by Tom Lodge[33] – remained almost entirely unexplored in his chapter. The contributors to the *Oxford History* were methodologically conservative in their empiri- cism and in their unwillingness to use theory. In the critical re- views of the *Oxford History* that began to apppear in the scholarly journals in the early 1970s there could be found a new challenge to the then dominant liberal historiography, from historians who laid great stress on the importance of concepts of class, exploita- tion and political economy.

Some of the revisionists were to claim that their use of theory and concepts set South African history on an entirely new path, that they offered a totally new paradigm.[34] Liberal Africanist his- tory was seen to belong to a liberal tradition then in disrepute. These radical revisionists did not challenge the liberal Africanists for including blacks within their view of the South African past: that was now taken for granted. What they did not accept was that blacks should be treated as a general, undifferentiated cat- egory. The liberal Africanists, it was said, like their predecessors, were blind to the importance of material factors, to the role of class. The 'radical challenge' called for a further, even more fun- damental rewriting of the South African past.

PART 5
The radical challenge

16 The challenge begins

From about 1970 a concerted challenge was mounted to the prevailing liberal view of South Africa's historical evolution by scholars who, to a greater or lesser degree, adhered to a materialist view of the past. These revisionists were centrally concerned to explain the nature of South Africa's political structures in terms of its economic development. They rejected any idea that the political could be separated from the economic and focused on the inter-relationship between the two. Beyond a general commitment to a materialist approach, however, these revisionists were far from united, and there was soon a more vigorous debate amongst them than between them and those they criticised, for few liberals, and none of them historians, chose to respond directly to the new challenge. As in previous chapters, the new work will be considered through an examination of the careers and work of some of the principal scholars involved.

* * *

The intellectual origins of the new radicalism lie more in new currents in Western historical scholarship generally, and in African history specifically, than in earlier radical writing on South African history. Of the professional historians, Macmillan was the one who – correctly – was most frequently seen as a pioneer, for he had called for the writing of social history, had investigated social conditions through field-work, had begun the study of rural stratification, and had stressed the importance of economics.[1] His insights, and more specifically his work on the Herschel district in the 1920s, were to be used by Colin Bundy in the 1970s in his work on the African peasantry.[2] But many of the early revisionist writers tended to be dismissive of all previous writing, including that of Macmillan. In its hostility to liberalism, the new writing belonged to a radical tradition with deep roots, some of which we surveyed in Chapter 13, though it is difficult to trace direct links with the earlier writing. The proposition that segregation was integrally connected with the capitalist system – a key argument in the early 1970s – was asserted, for instance, in the work of Hosea Jaffe in the early 1940s,[3] but the revisionist scholars of the early 1970s did not explicitly draw upon such earlier radical writing. Most of the writings of the intellectuals associated with the small Communist Party or Trotskyite movements were unknown to the young revisionist scholars of the early 1970s. They saw themselves as academics, not polemicists, even if they hoped that their writing would serve a political as well as an academic purpose.

One work that was widely read by the new generation was *Class and Colour in South Africa 1850–1950* by Jack and Ray Simons, which appeared in a large Penguin paperback in 1969 and formed something of a bridge from the earlier, polemical and often recondite radical writing to the scholarly work of the 1970s. Jack Simons (born 1907) obtained degrees in law and politics while working in the civil service in Pretoria. He then went to the London School of Economics to study for his doctorate, returning in 1938 to head a sub-department of Native law and administration – the name was changed in 1960 to comparative African government and law – at the University of Cape Town. He wrote on legal and political topics, and was active as a leading member of the Communist Party of South Africa. In December 1964 he was barred from teaching in terms of the Suppression of Communism Act. Ray Alexander, born in Latvia, had joined the communist movement before she emigrated to South Africa in 1929. In the 1930s and 1940s she worked tirelessly as a trade-union organiser in Cape Town and surrounding areas. In 1954 she was elected to parliament by African voters but was prevented from taking her seat because she was 'listed' as a communist. She and her husband left the country in May 1965, and Jack Simons took up a research fellowship at Manchester University for a year. In Britain they completed their detailed history of radicalism in South Africa, for which they had collected material over many years.

They called their book, not a history, but 'an exercise in political sociology on a time scale',[4] and they made it clear that their purpose was not merely to recover the history of left-wing political activity, but to move beyond description to an analysis of the interaction between class interests and racial interests, between radical politics and the 'national movement', by which was meant the opposition of blacks to their oppression as blacks. They wrote, for example, of how in the first decade of the twentieth century members of the Social Democratic Federation, and later other socialists, insisted that class, not race, was 'the basic cause of conflict' in the society. To such people – and the Simonses did not hide their own sympathy for this position – colour consciousness was something 'artificially stimulated', whereas class consciousness was 'natural'.[5] Yet the attempts by radicals to forge a nonracial labour movement failed; the radical vision of a single society without class or colour distinctions did not materialise. Colour, not class, triumphed. Working-class solidarity had decreased, not grown, over the years; white working-class racism had been a powerful force. The Simonses explained all this by saying that white workers had traded their socialism for a share in white power. Also, the white minority regime had used fascist means to perpetuate a racial order in a country with an advanced industrial economy. In their concluding chapter, the Simonses explicitly challenged the liberal view that the industrial colour bar was incompatible with economic expansion. In reality, they pointed out, racial discrimination had intensified as the economy had grown.[6]

Class and Colour included much more detail – from left-wing newspapers and journals in large part – on the history of the radical left than had Roux's *Time Longer Than Rope*, and was altogether a more scholarly work. But its chief importance lay in the way it grappled, over more than 600 pages, with the interrelationship of class and race in South African history. It was less successful in analysing class formation, or showing how the class structure had been transformed over time.[7]

* * *

The Simonses, who settled in Lusaka, Zambia, did not make further interventions in the historiographical debate. Because they were 'listed' people in terms of South Africa's Suppression of Communism Act (from 1982 the Internal Security Act), their book was banned for possession as well as distribution in South Africa; though soon read clandestinely by people on the left in that country, it remained largely unknown to professional historians there, most of whom would anyway have dismissed it as the work of non-historians. But it helped shape the ideas of those who led the radical challenge.

Most of these were young emigrés from South Africa who were

studying in Britain for doctorates in the late 1960s and early 1970s. That a number of individuals were involved reflected the new opportunities offered thanks to the economic and population boom of the 1960s: universities expanded, new jobs became available, and there was more money for research. Some of the white exiles or emigrés had been active in South African student politics, but could find no political role abroad and so turned to historical research. They had been radicalised by the Sharpeville massacre of 1960 and by what had followed: the banning of the African National Congress and the Pan-Africanist Congress in April 1960, the decision by the nationalist movements the following year to turn to armed struggle, and the progressive dismantling of most of what remained of the rule of law by John Vorster, Minister of Justice from 1962. Any prospect of peaceful reform or opportunity for extra-parliamentary protest seemed to disappear, and liberalism increasingly appeared to have no further role to play as South African society polarised, with blacks within the country preferring to work on their own in the black consciousness movement. The emigrés no longer believed in the possibility of evolutionary change and instead hoped for a rapid, revolutionary transformation.

The radical challenge developed in large part as a response to the publication of the two volumes of the *Oxford History*. The first volume appeared only months before Shula Marks and Anthony Atmore began their seminar on the societies of southern Africa at the Institute of Commonwealth Studies, University of London. Both Marks and Atmore wrote critical reviews of the first volume, as did Stanley Trapido, who had taught briefly in Jack Simons's department at the University of Cape Town in the early 1960s before moving to Britain, where in 1970 he completed his doctorate on Cape liberalism in the nineteenth century at the University of London.[8] In these reviews a new revisionist perspective on South African history began to emerge.[9] That the *Oxford History* presented an Africanist interpretation, in which the history of South Africa was equally that of blacks and whites, was welcomed, but the revisionists concentrated on the failure of the volumes to explain central processes in South African society.

In his chapter in the second volume of the *Oxford History* the economist Hobart Houghton suggested that the history of industrialisation in South Africa was much the same as that in Britain. In an earlier unpublished but widely circulated paper, a young executive at the Anglo American Corporation, Michael O'Dowd, had predicted that just as industrialisation in Britain had led to greater democracy, so South Africa would follow a similar path.[10] Trapido now argued that whereas Britain had been the first country to industrialise, South Africa, like other late industrialising countries, had taken 'the Prussian road', an autocratic route to modernisation, with the state intervening massively to impose discipline and to mobilise labour.[11] State intervention had not hindered economic growth, but had been designed deliberately to promote the industrialisation process. Developing capitalism had not merely adapted itself to the racial system; it had played a major role in the creation of segregation and apartheid, the latter-day manifestations of that system. Segregationist racial policy had indeed served capitalist interests.

Those revisionists whom David Yudelman in 1983 christened the 'elder statesmen' of 'the new school'[12] – Frederick Johnstone, Harold Wolpe and Martin Legassick – were not old in the early 1970s: the two trained as historians were under 30 when they began to pioneer the new approach. Frederick Johnstone was a Canadian with a cosmopolitan background, who had received some of his education in Geneva, Switzerland. As a graduate student at Queen's University, Kingston, Ontario, in the mid-1960s, he was drawn to work on a South African topic under Arthur Keppel-Jones. His master's dissertation at Queen's was a largely empirical and descriptive study of the 1922 Rand Revolt. He then went to St Antony's College, Oxford, on a Canada Council scholarship in 1967, and there both expanded his master's thesis into a doctorate, and adopted class analysis, for which his subject was eminently suited. The May 1968 student revolt in Paris and the anti-Vietnam war protests in America were radicalising influences, and a new, more flexible Marxism was taking the place of the old Stalinist dogmatism in British intellectual circles. Edward Thompson's classic account of *The Making of the English Working Class*, first published in 1963, became available in a Penguin paperback in 1968, and made a profound impression on Johnstone and others, with its stress on the importance of class as a relationship, and therefore as an historical phenomenon.[13] Barrington Moore's *Social Origins of Dictatorship and Democracy: Lord and Peasant in the Making of the Modern World* (1967) was almost as influential. By the late 1960s Marxist scholars – Edward Thompson, Eric Hobsbawm and Christopher Hill in Britain, Eugene Genovese in the United

States – were producing exciting historical work, which grappled with great themes of social and economic change.

When Johnstone visited South Africa in 1968–9 to undertake research in the Pretoria archives and in Cape Town, he was not only horrified by the inequalities in South African society; he was struck by the prosperity of most whites. Economic growth was said to be second only to that of Japan, and the average white standard of living to be comparable to that of Californians. Yet this was accompanied by ever more rigid apartheid policies. Liberal scholars seemed unable to explain this. Historians offered no answer, and economists assumed that the demands of a modern economy were at odds with an archaic, racist political system. Economic growth would bring about the elimination of racial discrimination. On his return to Oxford, Johnstone published in *African Affairs* an article which sought to explain how segregationist policies were compatible with economic growth. In 'White Prosperity and White Supremacy in South Africa Today', he did not confront explicitly liberal interpretations of the course of South African history, but his challenge had implications for the way the past as well as the present was viewed.

Johnstone first outlined what he called 'the conventional wisdom': that there was an essential contradiction between racism and capitalism; that racial discrimination was dysfunctional to the rational development of an industrial economy; that restrictions on the mobility of black labour – influx control – and the reservation of jobs for whites made no economic sense. Liberals had tended to see industrialisation as a progressive, modernising process that required new social relations in which race would be excluded as a determining factor. If left unimpeded, they had implied, industrialisation would establish a rational, free social order. In his *Anatomy of South African Misery* de Kiewiet had spoken of the laws of the country frustrating economic growth. Other liberals had argued that greater foreign investment would promote economic growth and so help break down the racial order. Johnstone argued instead that the system of racial discrimination had aided economic growth. The liberal view of an incompatibility between state policies and economic interests was wrong; it 'mystified' the true relationship between capitalism and apartheid: apartheid had been functional for capitalism and aided its development.

Walker, de Kiewiet and other English-speaking liberal historians had indeed traced the origins of segregation to an Afrikaner, frontier tradition of racism. A younger liberal, David Welsh, who succeeded Jack Simons as head of the department of comparative African government at the University of Cape Town, suggested in a book published in 1969 that 'The Roots of Segregation' lay instead in Shepstone's policy in pre-industrial Natal.[14] Johnstone advanced a different argument: that industrial capitalism had been responsible for many of the key elements of the system of segregation. The liberal historians had failed to link the development of the economy to the evolution of the system of racial domination, or to explore the history of industrialisation. That was a task the revisionists began to take up.

After his visit to South Africa, Johnstone spent some further years at Oxford, completing his doctorate and then turning it into the book eventually published as *Class, Race and Gold* in 1976, the first full-length scholarly monograph on a South African topic from a radical perspective. For Johnstone the gold-mining industry was 'the play within the play', which revealed what the struggle in South Africa was all about: a struggle not of white against black but one in which a capitalist class sought to exploit two different groups of workers, the one white, the other black. Johnstone set out to explain the actions of the white mineworkers in 1922, not by their race, but in terms of their structural, class position.

Harold Wolpe, another influential figure among the early revisionists, had been a member of the central committee of the underground South African Communist Party while working as a lawyer in Johannesburg in the 1950s. A member of Umkhonto we Sizwe, the organisation set up by the African National Congress in 1961 to plan sabotage, he was among those arrested in the police raid on the Umkhonto headquarters in the Rivonia suburb of Johannesburg in 1963. Together with another Rivonia detainee, he bribed a warder, escaped from jail and fled overseas. He became a lecturer in sociology at the new University of Essex and there began writing influential theoretical articles on South Africa from a Marxist perspective. They were not based on documentary research – he was not trained as an historian – but they threw up questions that directly challenged the liberal view of South African history. In his much-cited 'Capitalism and Cheap Labour Power: From Segregation to Apartheid', which appeared in *Economy and Society* in 1972, Wolpe argued that the reserves, a central element in the whole system of segregation, had served the interests of mining capital by subsidising labour costs. Migrant labour was highly exploitative because the mineowners paid a minimal wage, on the grounds that the families of the migrant workers could support themselves in the reserves and that the migrants themselves would, after their period on the mines, resume subsistence farming in the rural areas. This was not a new idea – it could be found in Leo Marquard's *Black Man's Burden*, for example[15] – but Wolpe elaborated it within a sophisticated Marxist framework which spoke of the articulation of pre-capitalist and capitalist modes of production.

* * *

The single most important figure in the radical challenge of the early 1970s was Martin Legassick. Born in Scotland, but educated in Cape Town, where he attended the Diocesan College, he began studying science at the University of Cape Town in 1959, where he was soon active in student politics (he later wrote the history of the National Union of South African Students).[16] Before completing his degree at Cape Town, he went on a Rhodes scholarship to Oxford. He was radicalised by Sharpeville and the repression that followed, while the dismissal of his father as head of the General Botha naval academy by the Nationalist government because he was English-speaking increased Legassick's hostility to the regime. After gaining a first class for physics at Balliol in 1963, he switched fields. He first went to study at the Institute of African Studies at the University of Ghana for a year, there working with Thomas Hodgkin, a British Marxist then pioneering the study of the politics of tropical Africa. From Accra Legassick moved in 1964 to the University of California, Los Angeles, to work under Leonard Thompson, the leading South African historian of the day, who had served under Legassick's father on a Royal Navy ship in the North Atlantic during the Second World War.

In California Legassick chose to research the Cape northern frontier in the early nineteenth century. He could not return to South Africa to consult the archives, for the government had barred his return after he had urged the executive of NUSAS to adopt a more radical stance, but he went to London to use the extensive mission records there. The result was an outstanding thesis, which was never to be published because he was soon unhappy with it, and his interests moved to other fields.[17] In over

700 pages, Legassick examined what he called the politics of a
'frontier zone', a concept derived in part from the insights of Jan
Vansina's work on the kingdoms of the savanna region of tropical
Africa.[18] Legassick focused on relations between the Griqua, the
Sotho-Tswana and the missionaries along, and to the north of, the
Orange River from 1780 to 1840. He was later critical of the limitations of his analysis, arguing that the very concept of frontier
was descriptive rather than explanatory, but many other scholars
found most fruitful the way he developed the idea of a 'frontier
zone', in which there was no single legitimate authority, yet in
which acculturation took place.[19] Legassick wrote his dissertation
as an Africanist, wanting to understand the dynamics of African
society, and arguing that the establishment of white supremacy
had been no easy, straightforward process. He stressed, too, the
long history of autonomy for black societies, and criticised the
failure of white-supremacist historians to recognise this.[20] Like the
liberals, Legassick was concerned to ask whether South Africa
could have taken 'a different path'. He suggested that had the
Griqua states survived, they might have 'provided the nucleus for
a South Africa less dichotomized along "racial" lines'; the growth
of a class of freed slaves and persons of mixed descent at the
Cape might have provided the social base for 'a society whose divisions were not based on colour'.[21] But even in his dissertation, Legassick began to move away from a liberal Africanist approach: his
introduction noted that two major themes dominate the history of
nineteenth-century South Africa: the extension of white colonial
control *and* the integration of the peoples of the region into a capitalist system which had its ultimate centre in industrialising
Europe.[22] He was soon to believe that the second theme – not
tackled in his thesis – was the determining one.

In California in the late 1960s various personal, intellectual and
political influences further radicalised Legassick. While completing his dissertation, he taught South African history at the
University of California, Santa Barbara, from 1967 to 1969, years
of much turmoil and ideological flux: of black power, the Berkeley
free speech movement and the protests against the Vietnam war.
Among American historians, a 'New Left' began to demand a relevant and usable past.[23] Some of these historians criticised their
predecessors for assuming that white racism had always existed
and had not undergone change over time, and that it could be explained adequately in psychological terms. They started to explore

the ways in which it had served capitalist interests, securing privilege and dividing the working class. Vulgar Marxists reduced racism to a class phenomenon, but Legassick was influenced by the much more sophisticated work of Eugene Genovese, of the University of Rochester, on slavery and racism in the American South.[24] Genovese denied a simple relationship between the development of American capitalism and the growth of racism, pointing to the precapitalist roots of racism, and observing that, in the aftermath of the First World War, American capitalism had no longer needed racial discrimination and had sought to remove it. Genovese concluded that racism in America grew out of a complex conjunction of historical forces, and that, while it could only be adequately explained in class terms, it could not be reduced to a question of class.[25]

His dissertation completed, Legassick settled in Britain, where Marks, Atmore, Trapido, Johnstone and others were developing their criticisms of the *Oxford History* and other liberal work. A Ford Foundation grant enabled Legassick to research the development of segregation in South Africa, its intellectual roots and material underpinnings. He now argued that the essential features of segregation dated, not from the seventeenth- or eighteenth-century frontier, but from the early twentieth century, and that they were intimately related to the development of the modern economy. The larger work he planned was never completed, but in London in the early 1970s Legassick produced a number of preliminary papers – some not published, and only circulated in cyclostyled form – of seminal importance to the development of the new radical perspective. The most famous of these developed what he had sketched in the first pages of his dissertation: a critique of the frontier thesis advanced by Eric Walker in his Oxford lecture of 1930 and then by other liberal historians. Legassick knew that Frederick Jackson Turner's thesis on the significance of the frontier in American history, which had so influenced Walker, had come under heavy fire from American historians. Presented to Shula Marks's London seminar in 1970, Legassick's critique of 'the frontier tradition in South African historiography' questioned the use to which the notion of frontier had been put by liberal historians, and suggested that racism could not simply be explained on its own terms, as something carried intact from the eighteenth-century frontier into the twentieth century, but had to be related to the changing material base of society.[26] That mature racism was intimately related to capitalism in its mining phase was a theme he explored further in other papers.

One of the most important of these, entitled 'South Africa: Forced Labour, Industrialization, and Racial Differentiation', was completed in 1971 and circulated in mimeographed form, but not published until 1975 in a volume of case-studies written, according to its editor, 'as a protest and hopefully as an alternative to the conventional Western social science literature on Africa'.[27] In it Legassick rejected the idea that 'modernization' would necessarily have led to a reduction in racial inequality, had it not been for white racism and the existence of a separate African 'subsistence economy'. He cited Barrington Moore's *Social Origins of Dictatorship and Democracy* to make the point that 'modernization' had taken different forms in different countries, depending on pre-existing social relationships. In South Africa no 'dual economy' had developed, but rather one 'forced labour economy of gold and maize'. Economic growth had not taken place despite white racism but as a result of a variety of forms of non-economic coercion, created through conquest and justified by an ideology of white racism. In a dazzling 30-page outline of South African history, Legassick sketched how economic changes had produced new classes, how racial segregation had emerged, and how what he termed 'the development of underdevelopment' had taken place in South Africa.

Like both Wolpe and Johnstone, who joined the staff at Memorial University, Newfoundland, in the mid-1970s, Legassick became a lecturer in sociology when he took a teaching post. That Johnstone and Legassick should, despite their historical training, have become sociologists was a reflection of the way their political-economy approach drew them from detailed empirically based research to more theoretical, conceptual work. After the publication of *Class, Race and Gold*, not having access to original sources in South Africa, Johnstone turned to writing general historiographical articles on the 'new school'.[28] At the University of Warwick Legassick became increasingly involved with trade-union activity related to South Africa and exile politics, and his academic writing virtually ceased. Suspended, and then expelled, from the African National Congress because he and others criticised the organisation for laying too much stress on armed struggle and not enough on mobilising workers, he resigned his lectureship to devote himself full-time to political and propaganda activity, and then worked in the East End of London for the Southern African Labour Education Project, formed in 1980 to provide materials for workers' education to trade union movements in southern Africa. He spent much of his time producing the journal of the Marxist Workers' Tendency of the African National Congress, *Inqaba ya Basebenzi.*

In the early 1970s Johnstone, Wolpe, and Legassick by no means always agreed with each other's work. Legassick's 'Forced Labour' paper was criticised in print by Wolpe, as well as by non-Marxists, before it was published.[29] That the radical revisionists criticised each other's work helped keep the flood of papers appearing in the early 1970s, as did a sense of intellectual excitement similar to that among the Africanists at the time of the Lusaka conference. They were developing what seemed to them a quite different interpretation of South Africa's past, one which they believed had important political implications and would influence the course of the struggle in that country. If the system of racial segregation was indeed intimately connected with the form of the capitalist economy that had evolved in South Africa, then it could be argued that both should be eliminated together. Many of the new revisionists believed that the power of black labour would grow and the capitalist order eventually be swept away in a revolutionary transformation. A number, after writing of the past, ended with some such prognostication for the future.[30]

17 Class and race, structure and process

For liberal historians, race was the dominant social reality in South Africa, and therefore the key element in any explanation of the overall course of South African development, though, as we saw, Macmillan in particular had not been unconcerned with social class. In emphasising class rather than race, the revisionists of the early 1970s were reacting especially against the emphasis given race in writing of the 1950s and 1960s, which had largely, if not completely, ignored or rejected class. In the mid-1960s Pierre van den Berghe, an American-based sociologist who had done field-work in South Africa, went so far as to state explicitly that 'social classes in the Marxian sense of relationship to the means of production ... are not meaningful social realities in South Africa'.[1] And there were various reasons why professional historians at that time paid no attention to class.

Though Anglophone liberal historians were shocked when an Afrikaner nationalist government came to power in 1948 committed to the implementation of a thorough-going policy of racial separation, they did not respond to the advent of apartheid by rejecting the importance of race in the country's history. Monica Wilson, seeking in the *Oxford History* to counter the apartheid myth that people were happiest when separated racially, did cite examples of individuals co-operating across 'the colour line' in the pre-industrial past.[2] But liberals continued to conceive of South Africa essentially in terms of the interaction of 'racial groups'. None of the contributors to the *Oxford History* spent time tracing the emergence of classes; the reader of those volumes gathered that race had been the dominant cleavage in the country's past. The liberal historians of the 1950s and 1960s abhorred racism, but the obsession with race in the politics of the day made them focus on – and exaggerate – the importance of race in the past. In a somewhat similar way, in Guyana the racial tensions which erupted on the

eve of independence encouraged historians of that country to analyse its past in terms of racial animosities and divisions, and to
ignore the fact that historically other divisions had been as, if not
more, important.[3]

Most professional historians of the 1950s and 1960s, whether in
Britain, America or South Africa, worked within an empirical tradition in which concepts such as class were distrusted for their
imprecision. The Marxist definition linked class to the means of
production, and few historians of this era attempted to integrate
economics into their analyses.[4] While the Cold War was at its
height, any economic interpretation ran the risk of being branded
Marxist, and Marxism was associated with communist politics. In
South Africa, ideological divisions ran particularly deep. Heavy
penalties were prescribed by law for what the Suppression of
Communism Act of 1950 defined, very vaguely, as 'communism'.
Professional historians had no time for ideas thrown up on the
radical left. Under the influence of neo-capitalist economics, they
took capitalism as given, something outside of and seemingly unrelated to the racial order.

For de Kiewiet, going to London in the 1920s had meant expo-
sure to new ideas, where race seemed so much less relevant than
it had in South Africa. Young South Africans who went abroad to
study in the 1960s not only found in Britain and America a strong
anti-racist climate, but also a new freedom to consider ideas taboo
in their repressive country. When South Africa was viewed from a
distance, race seemed to diminish in importance. How indeed
could something as irrational as race prejudice explain the course
of South African development? By the late 1960s, as we have
noted, a new, more flexible Marxism, given intellectual respect-
ability by the work of such eminent historians as Edward
Thompson, Eric Hobsbawm and Christopher Hill, was gaining
ground at British universities. Marxism, as a coherent body of
theory, attracted emigré intellectuals searching for a way to understand South Africa. Many historians, not on the far left politically,
nevertheless began to be influenced by a Marxist approach to history. It gave them, if nothing more, a materialist perspective and a
conviction that class, and class struggle, were the key to unlock
the past.

In reaction to the liberal neglect of class, some of the radical revisionists played down, and others entirely denied, the significance of race in the country's past. Legassick accepted the

importance of racist ideology,[5] but others more crudely stood Van den Berghe on his head, claiming that class explained all, and dismissing racism as mere false consciousness. While the fact of racial discrimination could not be denied, revisionists could, and did, argue that it was merely a cloak, a mask for class exploitation, and that the significant cleavages in South African society were, and always had been, those of class rather than of race, though they acknowledged that the two had often coincided. Some argued that the very concept of race was itself a myth, inasmuch as there existed no such groups as 'whites' and 'blacks'; by emphasising ethnic and racial cleavages, the liberal historians had accepted racial categories that had no existence outside segregationist ideology. Did not physical anthropologists agree that it was impossible to divide the human species into 'whites' and 'blacks'?[6] By concerning themselves exclusively with 'race', liberal historians had obscured or ignored the fundamental transformation that flowed from the spread of capitalist social relations.[7]

Whereas for liberal historians irrational race prejudice, explained in mere psychological terms, was often cited as the reason for segregation and apartheid, for the revisionists racism itself – even the very racial categories historians used – had to be explained, and understood in its historical context. Racism had performed different functions over time: in the nineteenth century, it had helped justify white dispossession of blacks; in the twentieth it had served to divide the working class. It was not the frontier tradition of racism – the 'no equality in church or state' of the trekker republics – that had spawned twentieth-century segregation, as Walker and de Kiewiet had suggested, but the mining houses and other capitalist interests. Legassick found the origins of white racism to lie in the slave society of the south-western Cape rather than on the frontier,[8] but he did not trace the origins of segregation to early white racism or to the spread of mercantile capitalism in the early nineteenth century Cape. Instead, for him the early years of the twentieth century were the crucial seedplot for segregation, as South Africa's industrial revolution got under way.[9] The racial policies then implemented, far from handicapping capitalist development, promoted it. These policies had been designed to keep blacks poor, and give the mines and farms the plentiful supply of labour required. Segregation had propped up precapitalist societies and functioned to coerce a black labour force and restrict its bargaining power. The migrant labour system, linking the reserves and the more developed areas, had subsidised labour-costs. State and capital had worked together, the state intervening to create a hierarchical division of labour based on race, in capitalist interests. Segregation had not conflicted with those interests, but had served them, whatever the individual motivation of the policy-makers and legislators.

For the revisionists, then, class analysis offered an exciting new tool to be used to reinterpret the South African past. In *The Making of the English Working Class* Edward Thompson had used class not as a fixed category, but one that was defined in struggle. So attention swung to class formation and class struggle, whether in precapitalist African societies or the very recent past. Trapido pointed out, for example, that late nineteenth century Boer society on the highveld had not been monolithic and homogeneous, but highly stratified.[10] Others spoke of how the mineral revolution had created a totally new class structure, with a vast African workforce of 100 000 on the Witwatersrand goldmines by the end of the century. For them the South African War had been fought over access to a valuable material resource – gold – and not mainly for reasons of British imperial supremacy in the sub-continent. Afrikaner nationalism was no longer understood as a movement of ethnic mobilisation, but as a class-based phenomenon. Throughout, South African history was seen to have been shaped by material forces.[11]

In South Africa, as elsewhere, arguments about the past have often reflected hopes for the future. Radical revisionists hoped that black and white workers would combine in a 'non-racial mass movement for democracy'.[12] They were concerned, then, to argue that racial divisions were artificial, and had been exploited, if not created, by segregationists to buttress their minority power. Claiming that there had been a much greater degree of class solidarity than previously admitted, and that it had often transcended racial and cultural divisions, they hoped to promote the cause of a non-racial class alliance. Others redefined the white workers as a 'new petty bourgeoisie', which enabled them to interpret conflicts between white labour and black workers as class struggles.[13]

* * *

In the late 1960s and early 1970s, as the *Oxford History of South Africa* was published, a more critical attitude to the Africanist history of tropical Africa gained ground. By the end of the 1960s it was clear that independence was not going to solve the problems of African development, as many naïvely had hoped. Those who became disillusioned with the governments of the new states often also grew critical of the historical writing which had accompanied the rise of African nationalism. Walter Rodney, a West Indian whose doctoral dissertation at the University of London was on the history of the upper Guinea Coast and who taught at the University of Dar-es-Salaam, now argued, together with other 'radical pessimists', that much of the Africanist history of the 1960s had served to legitimise the national bourgeoisie, the new ruling class. It had not explained Africa's poverty. Rodney explained that poverty by using a concept borrowed from a debate on Latin America:[14] in a classic polemic he surveyed the way Africa had been 'underdeveloped' by Europe.[15] More detailed, scholarly application of underdevelopment theory was undertaken by others, most notably on East[16] and South Africa. Colin Bundy, a South African who wrote his doctorate at St Antony's College, Oxford, described how a group of Africans had responded to new market opportunities and become successful 'peasants', producing for exchange, and how the state had then acted to cut off this development.[17] Bundy and other revisionists rejected the idea of two quite separate economies, one modern and white-run, the other backward and African. For them, as for Macmillan fifty years before, South Africa's history was the story of the development of a single economy. To this the historians of the early 1970s added that the other side of the coin to the emergence of the highly developed 'metropoles' had been the underdevelopment of the 'peripheries'. It was not African backwardness that had made the rural reserves such backwaters, but their structural relationship with the more developed regions. Underdevelopment seemed to explain the stark inequalities that had arisen in South Africa, where most whites were affluent, almost all blacks poor.

By the time Johnstone's *Class, Race and Gold* appeared in 1976, revisionist writing – a stream of articles, reviews and unpublished seminar papers – had become richly varied.[18] Beyond a basic commitment to materialism, there was no unanimity among the new revisionists. Those who in the early 1970s adopted a highly structuralist approach to the South African past were not specifically trained as historians, and their writing was heavily sociological. Robert Davies, Dave Kaplan, Mike Morris and Dan O'Meara – whom a critic labelled the 'gang of four', after Madame Mao and the Chinese 'hard-liners'[19] – worked together as graduate students at Sussex University in the early-to-mid-1970s, and were influenced by the structural Marxism of Poulantzas. They focused their work on the twentieth-century state, and sought to show its functionality for capital accumulation, especially in mining and agriculture, and demonstrate how different capitalist interests – fractions of capital – had shaped state policies.[20] Belinda Bozzoli, another doctoral student at Sussex, investigated the ideology of the manufacturing class, relating that ideology to the changing material base.[21] Davies and his colleagues were more concerned with capital than labour, and with white workers rather than black. O'Meara did write about the African mineworkers' strike of 1946, but he set the strike in a broad political economy context.[22] It may be that the relative lack of attention these scholars paid Africans reflected the fact that they had been undergraduates in South Africa at a time when blacks had either been 'silent' or had taken a black consciousness position and rejected whites.[23] In the early 1970s, state and capital seemed all-powerful, and able to determine state policy without any consideration for African responses. These young South Africans were already abroad when the Durban strikes of 1973 ushered in a new phase of struggle in South Africa. They began their dissertations before 1976, after which black resistance was indelibly associated with the name Soweto. In turning away from the study of African societies, the use of oral tradition, and the concern of Leonard Thompson and others to write an Afrocentric history, they rejected the Africanism as well as the liberalism of the historians of the 1960s.

Other revisionists had kept the Africanist perspective alive, and after Soweto the link between radical work and an Africanist perspective was strengthened. This was in part a result of the influence on South African scholars of the work of French Marxist anthropologists on precapitalist societies, the revival of peasant studies, and the social history – 'history from below' or 'history from the bottom up' – approach of the British Marxist historians and the History Workshop movement. Shula Marks, in London, was well placed to learn of the new developments in historical writing, and she exploited that opportunity to the full. Students who worked on doctorates under her supervision – most notably Jeff Guy and Philip Bonner – led the way in the exploration of the nature of precapitalist African societies, and the transition to capitalism. In July 1976 the first of two workshops on precapitalist societies and colonial penetration in southern Africa was held in Lesotho, where Guy was teaching. Those who attended were interested in the way precapitalist societies worked, the forms of stratification and exploitation which had existed in them, and how precapitalist modes of production were transformed, first by merchant capital and then by industrialisation. Whereas underdevelopment theory focused on exchange relations – the capitalist core was seen essentially to control the dependent periphery through the market – the historians of precapitalist societies wrote of systems of production and how they had changed over time.[24] The development of new ways of approaching the precolonial past did, however, come at a price – the doctorates written by Guy on the Zulu and Bonner on the Swazi took a decade to bring to completion.[25]

Others followed Guy and Bonner in writing the history of a nineteenth-century African state or 'ethnic group': Jeffrey Peires, for example, wrote on the history of the Xhosa of the eastern Cape, for a doctorate at the University of Wisconsin, Peter Delius went to London to work on his doctorate on the Pedi of the eastern Transvaal under Shula Marks.[26] Conservative historians who were apologists for the apartheid regime attempted to appropriate the new work on precolonial societies for an ethnic interpretation of South African history which might fit the government's Bantustan ideology. A conference on 'African History' organised by the Rand Afrikaans University in 1974 implicitly attempted just that.[27] A leading Afrikaner historian, Professor F. A. van Jaarsveld, found in Omer-Cooper's *Zulu Aftermath* what he regarded as historical justification for the Bantustan policy; for him the African states which Omer-Cooper had depicted emerging from the Mfecane were the precursors of the Bantustans being led to 'independence' in the 1970s.[28] What Omer-Cooper had conceived of as an anti-apartheid project – one aiming to give Africans back their past, and so to promote their cause in the present – was used in support of Bantustan nationalism.[29] The marrying of an Africanist and a materialist approach was one response to the 'ethnic trap'.[30]

The early work of the liberal Africanists tended to present African societies as classless and undifferentiated. Now an attempt was made to understand the divide between rulers and ruled, chiefs and commoners, as the major cleavage or 'contradiction' in precolonial African societies. Peires argued this in the Xhosa case at a workshop he organised in 1979 on Nguni history at Rhodes University, Grahamstown.[31] When it came to explaining why these societies were destroyed, Guy, Delius and others emphasised – as Atmore and Marks had in their seminal article on the role of the imperial factor[32] – the importance of the British army, but they also sought to show that the British intervention in the 1870s was a response to the new era of capitalist development ushered in by the discovery of diamonds.

Whereas the structuralists depicted Africans as victims of the overwhelming power of a new capitalist order which made them helots, those revisionists who studied African societies showed, through detailed empirical work, that Africans had shaped their own history. Migrant labour, for example, did not originate with the new needs of mining capital, but had an earlier history, and was to be explained in part in terms of inter-generational struggles within black societies themselves, as a response to ecological disasters, and as a means of acquiring guns for defensive purposes.[33]

* * *

Other revisionists turned to the writing of South Africa's more recent social history, and in doing so adopted an empirical approach. Much influenced by the work of Edward Thompson, they distrusted theoretical abstractions, stressed the importance of human agency, and believed in bringing history to life by dealing with the activities of 'ordinary people' in the past.[34] Though Macmillan had recognised the importance of the productive and other activities of such people half a century earlier, by the beginning of the 1970s no professional historian had successfully rescued the lives of the underclasses from what Thompson, in a much-quoted phrase in *The Making of the English Working Class*, called 'the enormous condescension of posterity'.[35] A highly structuralist approach could so emphasise the collective that the individual seemed to play no role. Those who allowed room for human agency and did not see state policies as only impositions from above – the mere *diktat* of capital – were able to point to how whites had often been divided, and how Africans had helped determine the way they were ruled. Consciousness became an important theme, to explain, say, why some blacks had worked with whites in the elaboration of the system of segregation. After the revival of worker action in the early 1970s – the Durban strikes of 1972–73 ushered in a new phase of militancy – historians turned from the institutional and organisational history of working-class action to worker experience. The doctorate which Charles van Onselen wrote at St Antony's College, Oxford, on labour in the gold-mining industry in Rhodesia led him to study worker consciousness, and then the lives of ordinary people, black and white, criminals, cab-drivers and liquor-merchants, in the early years of Johannesburg.[36] The best of such work always related individual lives to broader social processes, so opening new perspectives on the changing experience of the majority.[37] Van Onselen explicitly styled his volumes on Johannesburg an 'exercise in historical materialism', but though he analysed how the exploitation of the gold deposits on the Rand had social consequences for individuals and classes, he also showed how 'ordinary people', black and white, had to some extent made their own lives.[38] As first director of the African Studies Institute at Wits, Van Onselen was a key figure in helping to set the agenda for work on both urban and rural social history, as was Belinda Bozzoli, his wife, a lecturer in sociology at Wits, who took the lead in organising in 1978 what became the first of a series of Wits history workshops, held at three-yearly intervals. They were a leading forum for the presentation of work in the new social history.[39]

18 Changing perspectives

Historical truth is often arrived at by what C. Vann Woodward has termed the 'adversary procedure'.[1] A challenge to an existing historiography initially passes too far in the opposite direction. It is, after all, easier to speak in either-or terms than with due concern for complexity, and those who see the error in another's position are tempted to stress, and overstress, the new truth and deny any truth in what is being attacked. But, as Vann Woodward points out, the pendulum usually soon swings back, as it becomes generally recognised that truth lies somewhere between the new position and the old. This happened in the case of the radical challenge of the 1970s to the prevailing historiography of South Africa. From an almost exclusive focus on 'race' the pendulum swung sharply to the opposite extreme of an almost exclusive focus on 'class', then returned to a more subtle and complex position in-between.

* * *

For many years leading professional historians of a liberal persuasion conspicuously refrained from responding in print to the radical challenge. There were various reasons for this. Much of the new work did not appear in the established journals, but as unpublished seminar papers or in sociological journals which liberal historians did not read in the ordinary course of events. As the new work was often written by sociologists, or historians becoming sociologists, rather than historians 'proper', and as much of it was highly theoretical and abstract, and almost all of it jargon-ridden, historians, if they knew of it at all, dismissed it as unscholarly. That a number of its leading practitioners adopted an aggressive and dismissive tone towards liberal historians – not hiding their contempt for 'the conventional wisdom' – did not help to induce liberal historians to read the new work, much of which was inward-looking, written for fellow radicals, and not easily accessible to 'outsiders'. Liberal historians were put off, too, by the fact that some of the charges levelled against them were misplaced. Few professional historians had in fact addressed themselves explicitly to the relationship between economic growth and segregation, or believed that racism was the sole explanation for segregationist policies. David Welsh had suggested that segregation emerged, not only from the racist legacy of the pre-nineteenth-century frontier, but also from the numerical superiority of Africans in nineteenth-century Natal, and Van der Horst and others had pointed to the importance of the new labour demands from the mines in the late nineteenth century. It was not correct to say that the work of the liberal historians had been dominated by the belief, held by some economists, that the capitalist economy as it had developed in South Africa was rational, efficient and beneficial to all.

That many liberal historians only gradually began to realise the nature of the challenge was also in part due to the fact that, as empiricists, they were unaccustomed to think conceptually. When they did learn of the new arguments, they accepted many of them, realising the value of a political economy approach, that class was important, and that economic factors had been more significant than historians had allowed.

The main critics of Johnstone, Wolpe and Legassick in the early 1970s were not professional historians, though a number of them had worked under Leonard Thompson. Norman Bromberger, a history undergraduate at the University of Cape Town, had gone on to become an economist, first in Britain and then back in South Africa.[2] David Yudelman, a political scientist who completed a dissertation at Yale, worked in Johannesburg as a financial journalist and then an academic, and later emigrated to Kingston, Canada. [3] He did not accept that class was as important as most radicals claimed, though followed Trapido in arguing that South Africa's path to industrialisation was not set apart from that of other countries because of the racial factor.[4] Merle Lipton (Babrow), who challenged Legassick and other radicals in a number of articles before writing a major monograph on the relationship between capitalism and apartheid, had read history as an undergraduate at the University of Cape Town in the late 1950s. After completing a master's thesis on Theal, she settled in Britain, where she was for a time Director of Studies at Chatham

House, headquarters of the Royal Institute of International Affairs. In the early 1970s she investigated white farming in South Africa, and later wrote a commissioned report for the Anglo American Corporation on labour migrancy to the Witwatersrand goldfields. Her monograph, finally published in 1985, showed how crude much of the early radical writing had been, and how there was in fact no simple relationship between capitalism and apartheid.[5]

Some of the limitations of the new work of the early 1970s were all too apparent. Many of the central concepts the revisionists employed – such as 'exploitation', or 'class' itself – were as problematic as 'race'. Much of the new work crudely reduced everything to the economic. O'Meara's work on Afrikaner nationalism, for example, usefully corrected the fallacy that Afrikaner nationalism was monolithic and static, but fell into an opposite error: for O'Meara economic interests alone were significant and class became the sole category of analysis, all-important and determinant.[6] Johnstone soon realised that the revolution he had helped begin could be taken too far. Of O'Meara's work, he wrote, in a lecture delivered in 1979: 'The historical role and sociological significance of Afrikaner nationalism cannot be entirely grasped in these new and important terms of its class instrumentality ... we are faced with a situation in which the salient role of ethnic factors, while not understandable without class analysis, is not fully understandable through class analysis alone.'[7] For Johnstone class analysis remained essential, but it was not sufficient. Liberal pluralists, for their part, came to accept that class had been an important factor, along with race. After the work of O'Meara and Lodge appeared in the early 1980s no-one could deny the importance of class in understanding Afrikaner and African nationalism respectively.[8] So the issue became the relative importance of, and the inter-relationship between, race and class, both fluid categories which changed over time. To assert the primacy of either race or class on *a priori* grounds was to be ahistorical; the nature of the relationship could only be determined by examining the evidence. There might be different interpretations of the evidence, but sometimes it could be shown, say, that the evidence cited by those attempting to argue the primacy of class pointed the other way.[9]

Much of the new work of the early 1970s made the error of assuming that the function of something explained its existence. In arguing that the reserves were functional to capital, Wolpe and

Legassick implied that they had been created to serve capitalist interests. But though the reserves did eventually come to subsidise capital, they had not come into existence for that purpose: in the early twentieth century many capitalists had seen them as a problem, not a solution, for they locked up labour away from the mines. Their extent was determined in part by the nature of African resistance to white penetration in the nineteenth century. The Wolpe–Legassick argument was ahistorical inasmuch as it suggested a functional relationship had always existed, when in fact that relationship was the product of a particular set of circumstances. To explain the reserves, many different factors had to be taken into account.

* * *

It was a short monograph by Harrison Wright which first brought the issues involved to the attention of a wider public. An American who taught history at Swarthmore College, Pennsylvania, Wright had written on the early history of New Zealand and then the Gold Coast before turning to the Cape in the late nineteenth and early twentieth centuries.[10] His book on the 'liberal–radical debate' was dismissed by some radical revisionists as 'a scurrilous and politically motivated attack' on them – as if their work was not as 'politically motivated'[11] – while others more subtly criticised Wright by expressing their view that the task of relating past and present was a challenge rather than a burden.[12] *The Burden of the Present* was written in 1975, before Johnstone's *Class, Race and Gold* was published. It was more concerned with the use of evidence and methodology than with substantive issues, though Wright argued that the two were linked, and it wrongly suggested a rigid divide between 'liberals' and 'radicals'.[13] The implication that historians were unchanging in their views – that liberals, in particular, would not take over ideas from revisionists – was soon shown to be incorrect.

By the time Wright's book appeared, indeed, it was becoming clear that the deepest divide in fact lay between those who were intellectual pluralists – as liberals were, and radicals could be – and Marxist dogmatists, who assumed, *a priori*, that class was determinant and selected evidence to fit what they knew before they began: that class struggle was the motive force in history. Liberal pluralists had come to recognise the importance of class and material forces generally, though they continued to insist on the importance of race. Van Onselen's evidence for common working-class action in early Johannesburg, for example, when race seemed of little or no consequence in the brothels or on the brickfields, could not be denied, but it had to be weighed alongside other evidence suggesting instead strongly held racial attitudes and a deep cleavage between white and black. Many revisionists came to accept that the racial 'faultline'[14] was no mere creation of capitalist interests, that racism was not merely functional to capital but an independent variable, and that the link between race and class was not necessarily straightforward. White racism prevented the mineowners employing more black workers at lower wages; segregation brought the mining companies the benefits of cheap labour and state intervention to secure it, but restricted their using blacks in skilled jobs. In the early 1980s, with a measure of deracialisation occurring in the social and labour fields in South Africa, and with much big business now critical of at least some social and economic aspects of apartheid, revisionists conceded that not all forms of racism always benefited all branches of capitalism, and even that a non-racial capitalist future for South Africa might be possible.[15]

For some radical revisionists both racial and gender divisions were aspects of false consciousness, without objective significance. But from the late 1970s historians began to add to the dialectic of race and class that of gender. As the early liberal Africanists set out to document an African role, so the task began of making visible the role of women in history. Wishing to lay emphasis on the idea that women's experience was qualitatively different from that of men, historians at first tended to write as if women were a monolithic category. As liberal Africanists had rejected the idea that Africans had been passive, so now historians sought evidence on ways in which women had helped shape their history. But feminist historians soon grew sensitive to differentiation in race, class and age, and began to analyse how the subordination of women had taken specific forms in different circumstances, with Marxist feminists concerned especially to show the role of capitalism in that subordination.[16]

* * *

The radical challenge of the early 1970s was successful in the sense that once it was made no serious historian could ignore class or a political-economy approach. By the late 1970s, as liberal pluralists realised this, and materialists became more flexible, there was a movement towards common ground, though pluralists could not accept historical materialism because of its deterministic implications. Some liberals still argued that the growth of the economy demanded changes in the racial order – and in the mid-1980s there seemed evidence that this was happening, as some aspects of the racial system were dismantled; others argued that the economy was neutral, adjusting to changes that occurred for other reasons. Many radical revisionists, for their part, accepted that the unique should be taken into account as well as the structural, that human agency, ideology and consciousness were important, and that the material base was not always determinant.

In the mid-1980s the cutting edge of South African historiography remained the relative importance of class and race and gender. History advances by argument, but is, as the eminent Dutch historian Pieter Geyl so aptly put it, an argument without end. While some of the new work took up concerns expressed by Macmillan more than fifty years before, far more was now known about all aspects of the South African past than in Macmillan's day, and the discussion of it was far more sophisticated. What is certain is that the South African past will continue to be 'made' in new ways, as new sources and theoretical concepts are employed, and as new perspectives on what has been are derived from the ever-changing present.

Conclusion

In the United States, Canada, Australia and New Zealand, the indigenous people largely disappeared – sometimes dying as a result of disease, sometimes shot – in the face of white conquest and dispossession. They largely disappeared, too, from the historiographies of those countries. 'During the first half of the 20th century', writes an Australian historian, 'the Aborigines were dispersed from the pages of Australian history as effectively as the frontier squatters who had dispersed them from the inland plains a century before.'[1] In the past two decades efforts have been made by some historians in those countries to 'break the silence' about the indigenous peoples, and to consider 'the other side of the frontier'.[2] Yet the history of the indigenous peoples and of their interaction with the intrusive Europeans remains a relatively minor sub-theme in the historiography of those countries as a whole. The history of white settlement was still seen to involve the conquest of a hostile environment rather than the dispossession of indigenous people. This was partly because the indigenous people were so few in number, partly because that history of dispossession was an embarrassment, partly because so much history writing was nationalistic. In the historical writing of Canada, for instance, nation-building has been the central theme.[3]

In South Africa the white invaders faced a large indigenous population, and as white power triumphed and was consolidated the indigenous people did not 'disappear', but remained the overwhelming majority. Many whites tried to evade this reality and thought of South Africa as a 'white man's country'; historians played an important role in that evasion, by ignoring the majority in their accounts of white settlement. But such an evasion could not be sustained. Theal, as we saw, did not ignore the black majority, but for him they remained 'barbarous', inferior. Gradually professional historians came to take seriously the history of the majority, and began to see Africans not merely as an obstacle in the way of white settlement and nation-building, but as worthy of historical investigation in their own right, and as active participants in South African history.

Theal, the immigrant, became a colonial nationalist historian, his nation a white South African nation-in-being. Though interested in blacks, he was an out-and-out racist, whose writings are littered with what we recognise today as absurd prejudices and stereotyping. Until relatively recently, the majority of South African historians, whether Afrikaner or English-speaking, followed in that tradition. Most Afrikaner historians directed their attention to topics, such as the Great Trek or resistance to the British, in the history of the Afrikaner people.[4] If the indigenous peoples were allowed onto the historical stage at all, it was only as subordinates. Theal, writing in the late nineteenth century as white supremacy was being established, took it upon himself to justify their subordination. Later historians in the tradition he established wrote when white supremacy was firmly in place, and accepted it as given.

It was among English-speaking historians who rejected major aspects of the socio-political system, and who unlike Afrikaners had no interest in helping to create a 'nation', that there first emerged another tradition, critical of Theal and his Eurocentricity and racism. The liberal historians debunked myths about the past in the work of Theal and his successors, and stressed what brought people together rather than what set them apart. For them South Africa was a unity, with all its people part of a vaguely conceived 'common society'. Interaction became the main theme in their writing. Nevertheless, in the 1920s and 1930s, as we have seen, their break with Eurocentricity was limited. Though poor whites and poor blacks were treated together in de Kiewiet's *History*, African societies were not examined in the same detail as white communities, nor were the same questions asked about them.

While Theal and other 'settler' historians buttressed the racial order through their writings, those in the tradition inaugurated by Macmillan sought instead to present a picture of the past deliberately designed to undermine that order, and to help shape an alternative future. More than in most countries, historical writing in South Africa has had a political purpose. Because of the harsh political climate in which they worked, many of South Africa's leading historians in the critical tradition looked to a personal future in England or America, and many did settle abroad. The result – before it was possible to go abroad and then return for research visits – was that they stopped making original contributions to South African history. De Kiewiet made extremely good use of the Public Record Office in London, and by using printed government reports and assimilating secondary work on social and economic themes he was able to write his masterly *History*, but even he was limited by what he could do abroad. He recognised that the very existence of the black majority, coupled with the establishment and maintenance of white supremacy through a system of legalised and institutionalised racial discrimination, gave the country's history a special fascination, but he did not tease out that special significance which, he said, South African history owed to the black man[5] or write at any length on the black experience. From Australia and Canada far fewer leading historians settled abroad and were lost to historical writing on their country of origin. South Africa was no Australia or Canada, and it may be that de Kiewiet would have written less had he not settled abroad. Both the liberal Africanist and radical revisionist advances were made in fact by historians who had left the country. The best people went, and outside they found new freedom, and were exposed to new ideas. As we have seen, South African history has been as much influenced by general trends in historical scholarship – most notably in recent decades the broadening of the discipline to include the social and the economic – as by events in South Africa itself.

In the United States, writes one of that country's leading historians, 'in almost every generation one or more historians have been among the leading lights of American culture'.[6] Afrikaners have placed a high value on history: a vision of history – largely a series of myths – underpinned their struggle against the British, and later their drive for domination.[7] English-speaking South Africans have not looked to history to give them an identity, or to guide them in the present. Yet the 1970s saw a renaissance in historical studies in South Africa, with large numbers of exciting works appearing from the English-medium universities, some by scholars who had decided to return after periods abroad. That it was history that was pre-eminent in the formulation of a new perspective on South Africa may partly be explained by the fact that political studies was handicapped by an arid interest-group approach, derived from America, and sociology by the limitations of the old survey techniques. Difficulties in studying the contemporary scene in South Africa led some sociologists into a sterile theoreticism, involving the use of often impenetrable jargon, but encouraged others to explore the past. History offered scope for theorising, constrained – and the more constrained it was, the better the history – by attention to rich empirical detail. Mere empiricism – and much of the history written in South Africa did not rise far above that – verged on antiquarianism, but theory so abstract that it lost touch with the empirical was even less useful. The best history was always well grounded in close attention to the sources. The historian's commitment was, above all, to the evidence: when polemicists moved away from the evidence – exaggerating, say, in the interests of 'working-class solidarity', interracial unity among workers – historians had a duty to point out what the evidence revealed.[8]

It took time for the new insights of the 1970s to penetrate beyond a very narrow circle. The establishment of new publishing houses prepared to publish the new work – David Philip in 1971, Ravan Press the following year – helped its dissemination. The New History of Southern Africa Series which Ravan Press published in the 1980s in attractively packaged paperbacks, was of special importance. Yet such titles often sold at most a few thousand copies. Belinda Bozzoli, who did as much as anyone to stimulate and popularise the new history, spoke of the dominant South African culture as anti-historical.[9] But history was also a vital terrain of struggle: white supremacists continued to peddle old racial and ethnic myths, while others, who knew how Afrikaners had used history in their struggle for liberation, sought to employ it as a weapon against apartheid ideology and for a democratic South Africa. Some saw only a history of separate peoples, hostile to each other, while for others South African history, despite the cleavages of race and class, was essentially integrative. Revisionists won most of the historical arguments, for their work reflected realities: the importance of the black majority, of class, or the fact that ethnicity was often a recent construct. There could be little doubt that eventually their views would become a new orthodoxy. But there was also a sense in which South Africa's future would determine its past. Professional historians had at best a small role to play in shaping that future.

* * *

This study has concerned itself both with what certain key historians have known about the past, and with their attitudes to people of colour and their relationship to whites. We have traced the progression in historical thought from the full-blown racism of Theal, who believed in superior and inferior races, and justified conquest and dispossession, to the liberalism of Macmillan and de Kiewiet, who believed that blacks should be considered with sympathy, but who paid little attention to African societies, to the later liberal Africanists who accorded blacks equal attention, and finally to the radical revisionists who argued that racial categories themselves were wrong, and that class was the prism through which the country's past should be viewed. As Macmillan reacted against the 'conventional wisdom' of his day, so the revisionists of the 1970s reacted against the liberalism that dominated Anglophone historical writing. We have noted that in the study of African societies and in consideration of the economic dimension of South Africa's history, amateur scholars led the way, and how professional historians for long did not take up their ideas. In the 1970s, many of those who took the lead in the reinterpretation of the South African past were not historians, either by training or by profession. Professional historians were, on the whole, slow to change their view of the past. But today most of those writing in English accept the importance of class, while believing that race cannot simply be reduced to class, and that, while it would be ideal to dispense with racial categories altogether – for they reject racism – in practice that cannot be done. Though race has no objective validity, it has been a key – if not the key – determinant of behaviour in our past, and not a mere tool used in the interest of something else. How new ethnic identities were constructed over time has become a major subject of study,[10] but historians have not yet found a way to avoid using racial categories in their writing.

One theme of this study has been the way in which historians have over time acquired greater knowledge of blacks and of black–white relations in South Africa's past. Historically, historians played a major role in the making of myths and in the denial of equality to blacks, and they encouraged racial thinking; much of South African historical writing has been saturated with racist ideas and assumptions. But in the accumulation of knowledge there has been great progress, and historians have gradually moved away from racism in their own writing, and broadened and refined the ways they have approached the study of race and class. No survey of that aspect of their writing can have a neat conclusion, for even a survey is part of that ongoing dialogue between the living and the dead which takes place as historians seek to establish the meaning of the present by relating it to what has gone before.

References

Introduction

[1] I borrow the phrase from L. Stone, *The Past and the Present* (London, 1981).

[2] E. H. Carr, *What is History?* (Harmondsworth, 1964), p. 44.

[3] C. Becker,'What is Historiography?', *American Historical Review*, 43 (1938), 1.

[4] C. Berger, *The Writing of Canadian History* (Toronto, 1976), p. 2.

[5] Esp. F. A. van Jaarsveld, *Wie en Wat Is die Afrikaner?* (Cape Town, 1981); *Die Afrikaners se Groot Trek na die Stede* (Johannesburg, 1982).

[6] In recent years a major contribution to the understanding of race and class has been made by Hermann Giliomee, who regards himself as an Afrikaner historian though his most important contributions were written in English.

[7] W. M. Macmillan, *My South African Years* (Cape Town, 1975). George Cory's unpublished autobiography is in the Cory Library; Edgar Brookes's *A South African Pilgrimage* (Johannesburg, 1977) says very little of history as a discipline.

[8] Contrast the position in Canada, where there are numerous collections of such papers; see Berger, *The Writing of Canadian History*, Note on Sources.

[9] The lecture was printed in F. A. van Jaarsveld, *The Afrikaner's Interpretation of South African History* (Cape Town, 1964) and in revised form in his *Geskiedkundige Verkenninge* (Pretoria, 1974).

[10] F. A. van Jaarsveld, *Omstrede Suid-Afrikaanse Verlede* (Johannesburg, 1984).

[11] H. M. Wright, *The Burden of the Present* (Cape Town, 1977); M. Cornevin, *Apartheid. Power and Historical Falsification* (Paris, 1980).

[12] Cornevin, *Apartheid*, pp. 84-85, 103.

[13] K. Hughes, 'Challenges from the Past', *Social Dynamics*, 3 (1977), 50.

[14] R. Hofstadter, *The Progressive Historians* (New York, 1969), p. 3.

[15] Recent contributions of note include B. Bozzoli, *The Political Nature of a Ruling Class* (London, 1981) and P. Rich, *White Power and the Liberal Conscience* (Manchester, 1984).

1. A Canadian becomes South African

[1] *The Prominent Men of Cape Colony, South Africa* (Portland, Oregon, 1902), p. 198.

[2] I. D. Bosman, *Dr George McCall Theal as die Geskiedskrywer van Suid Afrika* (Amsterdam, n.d.[?1932]).

[3] M. Babrow, 'A Critical Assessment of the Work of George McCall Theal'; D. Schreuder, 'The Imperial Historian as Colonial Nationalist' in G. Martel (ed.), *Studies in Imperial History* (London, 1986).

[4] Cf. the bibliography below. The Theal papers at Stellenbosch, the largest body of private papers, are disappointing on the private man.

[5] G. Theal, *Notes on Canada and South Africa* (Cape Town, n.d.), quoted in C. Saun-

ders, 'The Making of an Historian: the Early Years of George McCall Theal', *South African Historical Journal*, 13 (1981).

⁶ *Dictionary of South African Biography* 4 (Durban, 1981), p. 645.

⁷ For publication details of the works mentioned in this paragraph see the bibliography below.

⁸ C. Saunders, 'George McCall Theal and Lovedale', *History in Africa*, 8 (1981).

⁹ R. Thornton, 'Wilhelm Hendrik Immanuel Bleek's Discovery of Southern African Literatures', University of Cape Town seminar paper, 1983.

¹⁰ C. Saunders, 'The Missing Link in Theal's Career: The Historian as Labour Agent', *History in Africa*, 7 (1980).

¹¹ Theal, *History of South Africa* (11 vols., reprint, Cape Town, 1964), 10, pp. 124-5.

¹² Cf. below, p. 19 for Donald Moodie's use of them.

¹³ *Cape Parliamentary Paper* C1-1895, p. 16.

¹⁴ Cape Archives, CO 4218: memo. by Theal.

¹⁵ *Cape Argus*, 13 January 1881. His nephew was John Noble, Sprigg's brother-in-law.

¹⁶ *Cape Argus*, 11 May 1881.

¹⁷ Cape Archives, NA 185: Theal to Secretary for Native Affairs, 5 April 1881.

¹⁸ The fourth volume is in the Cape Archives.

¹⁹ F. Brownlee (ed.), *The Transkeian Territories: Historical Records* (Lovedale, 1923).

²⁰ Theal, *History*, 3, p. 140.

²¹ Cape Archives, NA 407: Theal to Under-Secretary for Native Affairs, 9 April 1892.

²² *Cape Times*, 19 December 1905: letter by Theal.

²³ South African Library: Stow Papers.

²⁴ *South African News*, 21 September 1905.

²⁵ South African Library, Odd Accessions: Theal to Sauer, 17 April 1909; *South African News*, 14 December 1905.

²⁶ Cf. his introduction to W. Bleek and L. Lloyd, *Specimens of Bushmen Folklore* (London, 1911).

²⁷ Cory Library: memoir by G. Cory, 'Reminiscences of the Past'.

²⁸ *Cape Times*, 7 May 1919; *Cape Argus*, 30 March 1925.

2. The making of a settler historian

¹ G. M. Theal, *Progress of South Africa in the Century*, (Toronto and Philadelphia, 1902), p. vi.

² G. M. Theal, *History of South Africa under the Administration of the Dutch East India Company* (London, 1897), 1, pp. xv-xvi.

³ Merriman to Scully, n.d., quoted in J. Marquard, 'W. C. Scully', Ph.D. thesis, University of the Witwatersrand, 1984, p. 26. Scully had published an abridged edition of Theal.

⁴ Theal, *Progress*, p. 501.

⁵ John Edgar was professor from 1903 until 1911, when he resigned to become editor of the *Transvaal Leader;* on Marais and Van der Merwe see below, chapter 11.

⁶ J. S. Marais, *Maynier and the First Boer Republic* (Cape Town, 1944), p. vi.

⁷ D. Moodie (comp.), *The Record* (Cape Town, 1838-41, reprinted Cape Town, 1960).

⁸ See esp. 'A Member of the Late Committee', *Remarks Upon Some of the Results Depicted by the Publication of a Portion of the Cape Records* (Cape Town, 1841).

⁹ R. Godlonton, *Narrative of the Irruption of the Kaffir Hordes into the Eastern Province of*

the Cape of Good Hope (Grahamstown, 1835-6).

[10] I. Schapera (ed.), *David Livingstone. South African Papers* (Cape Town, 1974).

[11] A. Wilmot, *The History of Our Own Times in South Africa* (2 vols., London, 1897), 1, p. 242.

[12] Cory MS. 7359: Theal to Noble, 1 February 1877.

[13] G. M. Theal, *Compendium of South African History and Geography* (2nd ed., Lovedale, 1876), Preface.

[14] 'J' in *Cape Monthly Magazine* (1873), 127. Cf. Theal, *Compendium* (3rd ed, Lovedale, 1877), esp. p. 116.

[15] *The Telegraph and Standard* (Port Elizabeth), August 1873: letter by Theal to Editor.

[16] G. M. Theal, *History of the Boers in South Africa* (2nd. ed., London, 1888), p. 357.

[17] *Ibid.*

[18] Theal, *History of the Boers* (London, 1887), pp. xii-xiii.

[19] Theal, *Dutch East India Company*, 1, p. xv.

[20] Theal, *Progress*, p. vi.

[21] G. M. Theal, *Willem Adriaan van der Stel* (Cape Town, 1913), p. 254.

[22] Theal, *History*, 5, p. vi.

[23] *Cape Argus Weekly*, 9 April 1902.

[24] Theal in *The Globe* (Toronto), 24 August 1901.

[25] Cf. esp. Theal in *The Globe* (Toronto), 24 August 1901.

[26] G. M. Theal, *History of South Africa since 1795*, 4, p. 179.

[27] Theal, *History since 1795*, 4., pp. 265-6.

[28] E.g. Theal, *Korte Geschiedenis van Zuid-Afrika 1486-1835* (Cape Town, 1891).

[29] *Queen's University Journal*, 22 (1895), 189.

[30] Interview with the *Manchester Guardian*, reprinted as *The Prospect in South Africa* (London, n.d.), p. 6.

[31] *De Goede Hoop*, 1919.

[32] E.g.Theal, *Progress*, p. 510; G. M. Theal, *South Africa* (London, 1894), p. 387.

[33] *Cape Argus*, 24 July 1889.

[34] J. Cappon, *Britain's Title in South Africa* (London, 1901).

[35] Theal, *Dutch East India Company*, 1, p. 70.

[36] Theal, *Dutch East India Company*, 1, p. 254.

[37] Theal, *History*, 6, p. 359.

[38] Theal, *History*, 4, p. 170.

[39] Theal, *History of South Africa from 1828 to 1846* (London, 1904), p. 143.

[40] Theal, *History*, 6, p. 475.

[41] Theal, *South Africa* (6th ed., 1899), p. 181.

[42] *Saint Andrew*, 26 October 1899.

[43] Cappon, *Britain's Title*, p. 263, quoting Theal, *History*, 3, p. 342.

[44] Theal, *Progress*, pp. 190-91; Theal, *History of South Africa from 1828 to 1846* (London, 1904), p. 79.

[45] Theal, *Progress*, p. 183.

[46] Theal, *History*, 6, p. 394; and cf. J. Bird (ed.), *Annals of Natal* (2 vols, Pietermaritzburg, 1888) 1, pp. 568-71.

[47] Theal, *Progress*, p. 506.

[48] Theal, *History*, 10, pp. 299-300, 305.

[49] Theal, *History*, 10, p. 28.

[50] Theal, *History*, 10, p. 1.

51 Theal, *South Africa* (3rd ed., 1897), p. 386.

52 Theal, *History*, 10, pp. 28-9.

53 Theal, *History*, 10, pp. 96, 172; 3, p. 482.

54 Theal, *Progress*, p. 226.

55 Theal, *History*, 6, p. 4.

56 Theal in *The Globe* (Toronto), 24 August 1901.

57 Theal, *Progress*, p. 510.

3. Race and class

1 Theal, *Progress*, p. 9; *South Africa* (8th ed., London, 1916), p. 3.

2 Theal, *History*, 1, p. 123.

3 G. M. Theal, *The Beginning of South African History* (London, 1902), p. 27.

4 Theal, *History*, 1, p. 209.

5 Theal, *History*, 1, p. 273.

6 Theal, *History*, 4, pp. 393-94.

7 Theal, *History*, 4, p. 393.

8 Theal, *History*, 1, pp. 292-3, 253-4.

9 Theal, *The Beginning*, pp. 94-95.

10 Theal, *History*, p. 293n.

11 Theal, *History*, 1, p. 203; *Progress*, p. 180; *History*, 9, pp. 58-60.

12 Theal, *History*, 10, p. 87.

13 Theal, *History*, 1, pp. 310-11.

14 Theal, *Progress*, p. 469.

15 Theal, *History*, 10, p. 218.

16 G. M. Theal, *Kaffir Folk-lore* (London, 1882), p. 2.

17 Theal, *History*, 5, p. 332n.

18 Theal, *History*, 3, p. 464.

19 Theal, *History*, 5, pp. 344, 491.

20 E.g. Theal, *History* 2, pp. 238-9; *Notes*, p. 3.

21 Theal, *History*, 4, p. 118.

22 Theal, *History*, 5, p. 481.

23 Theal, *History*, 2, p. 80.

24 R. J. Mann in *Transactions of the Ethnological Society* (1867), cited in R. Martin, 'British Images of the Zulu', Ph.D. thesis, University of Cambridge, 1982, p. 136.

25 Theal, *History*, 10, p. 28. Cf. also p. 175.

26 Theal, *History*, 3, pp. 416-17.

27 Theal, *Progress*, p. 443.

28 Theal, *Notes*, pp. 10, 22, 36.

4. Racial myths and Theal's legacy

1 Theal, *The Beginning*, p. 29.

2 Theal, *History*, 1, p. 420.

3 Theal, *History*, 2, p. 228.

4 Theal, *History*, 5, ch. 19 and p. 485; 6, p. 121.

5 Theal, *The Beginning*, p. 29.

6 Theal, *History*, 1, p. 422n.

7 Theal, *Compendium*, p. 55.

8 Theal, *The Beginning*, p. 99.

9 Quoted in J. S. Galbraith, *Reluctant Empire* (Berkeley and Los Angeles, 1963),

pp. 257-58.

[10] Theal, *Progress*, p. 341.

[11] Theal, *Notes*, p. 31.

[12] Theal, *Progress*, p. 501.

[13] Theal, *Notes*, p. 31; *South Africa* (8th ed., 1916), p. 423.

[14] *Cape Parliamentary Paper* G58-1895, p. 5.

[15] *Cape Parliamentary Paper* A22-1906, p. 18.

[16] Theal in *The Globe* (Toronto), 24 August 1901.

[17] *Cape Times*, 18 September 1909.

[18] Theal in *South African News*, 5 March 1909.

[19] Theal, *History*, 1, p. 87; M. Wilson and L. Thompson (eds.), *The Oxford History of South Africa* (2 vols., Oxford, 1969, 1971), 1, p. 78.

[20] Theal, *History*, 1, p. 192.

[21] M. Wilson, 'The Early History of the Transkei and Ciskei', *African Studies*, 18 (1959).

[22] R. Derricourt, 'Early European Travellers in the Transkei and Ciskei', *African Studies*, 35 (1976).

[23] Theal, *History*, 1, p. 183.

[24] E.g. Theal, *The Beginning*, p. 5.

[25] That was the theme of G. W. Stow's *The Native Races of South Africa*, which Theal edited for publication in 1905.

[26] The maps are reproduced in T. R. H. Davenport and K. Hunt, *The Right to the Land* (Cape Town, 1974), pp. 16-17.

[27] G. Cory, *The Rise of South Africa* (6 vols. Cape Town, 1965), 4, pp. vii-viii.

[28] As a result, Cory joined D. F. Malan on the platform as a speaker at the Dingaan's Day celebrations in the 1920s.

[29] Cf. review of Cory, *Rise*, 1, in *Times Literary Supplement*, 14 April 1910.

[30] S. Olivier, *White Capital and Coloured Labour* (London, 1929), pp. 5l, 47-8.

[31] E.g. G. Preller, *Day Dawn in South Africa* (Pretoria, 1938), pp. 150-1.

[32] *The Bantu World*, 10 September 1932 and subsequent issues. The author 'Veritas' was a white person.

[33] E. Walker, *A History of South Africa* (rev. ed., 1935), pp. 210, 183.

[34] *The Times*, 21 January 1902.

[35] M. Seton in *The Spectator*, 15 February 1902.

[36] See below Chapter 14.

[37] T. Cameron and B. Spies (eds.), *An Illustrated History of South Africa* (Johannesburg, 1986), esp. map on p. 137.

[38] F. A. van Jaarsveld, *From Van Riebeeck to Vorster, 1652–1974* (Pretoria, 1975).

[39] Van Jaarsveld, *From Van Riebeeck*, pp. 16, 18, 54 and note 1, 59, 62, 107, 112, 115, 127, 143.

5. Macmillan: The South African years, and after

[1] The tapes were transcribed and edited by his wife Mona, and the narrative condensed and reshaped by Martin Legassick.

[2] They can be read in what was his study, in his home close to the Thames, south of Oxford.

[3] M. Macmillan, *Champion of Africa* (Long Wittenham, 1985).

[4] J. Naidoo, 'W. M. Macmillan', M.A. thesis, University of South Africa, 1983.

[5] Macmillan, *South African Years*, p. 2.

⁶ Cf. also his *Democratize the Empire!* (London, 1941), p. 9.

⁷ At Stellenbosch he had three coloured schoolmates: see his *South African Years*, p. 22.

⁸ Macmillan, *South African Years*, pp. 36, 46, 48.

⁹ Macmillan, *South African Years*, p. 61.

¹⁰ Macmillan, *South African Years*, p. 36.

¹¹ Macmillan, *South African Years*, pp. 48-49, 70, 22, 26.

¹² My thanks to Jeremy Krikler for this information.

¹³ Macmillan, *South African Years*, p. 76.

¹⁴ Mona Macmillan to the author, 26 February 1985.

¹⁵ Macmillan, *South African Years*, p.2.

¹⁶ Macmillan, *South African Years*, p. 90.

¹⁷ Macmillan, *South African Years*, p. 92.

¹⁸ Macmillan, *South African Years*, p. 78. On Schmoller (1838-1917) see e.g. M. J. Bonn, *Wandering Scholar* (New York, 1948), p. 51.

¹⁹ Macmillan, *South African Years*, p. 114.

²⁰ Macmillan, *South African Years*, pp. 124, 195.

²¹ R. H. Tawney (1880–1962), who received a personal chair in economic history at the London School of Economics in 1931, wrote of *The Agrarian Problem of the Sixteenth Century* and probably inspired Macmillan's own *Agrarian Problem*.

²² Macmillan, *South African Years*, p. 126.

²³ W. M. Macmillan, *The South African Agrarian Problem* (Johannesburg, 1919), p. 7.

²⁴ Cf. P. Rich, *White Power and the Liberal Conscience*.

²⁵ On which now see C. van Onselen, *Studies in the Social and Economic History of the Witwatersrand* (2 vols., London, 1982).

²⁶ Macmillan, *Agrarian Problem*, p. 49.

²⁷ L. Fouché, *Die Evolutie van die Trekboer* (Pretoria, 1909). Fouché taught at the University College in Pretoria from 1910 to 1933.

²⁸ Macmillan, *South African Years*, p. 143.

²⁹ Report of the Transvaal Local Government (Stallard) Commission, 1922.

³⁰ Macmillan, 'Native Land and the Provision of the Natives Land Act of 1913', in *European and Bantu: Papers and Addresses Read at the Conference on Native Affairs 27 to 29 September 1923* (Cape Town, 1923).

³¹ Rhodes House Library, Oxford: Notes on the Philip papers: e.g. a note on a letter of 1821 on the back of Joint Council minutes of 1924.

³² Copy in Macmillan papers.

³³ He was later to recognise that he had done less than justice to Herschel's small African petty bourgeoisie and peasantry.

³⁴ De Kiewiet papers: Macmillan to de Kiewiet, 7 January 1927.

³⁵ De Kiewiet papers: Macmillan to de Kiewiet, 10 September 1929.

³⁶ De Kiewiet papers: Macmillan to de Kiewiet, 10 September 1929.

³⁷ Macmillan, *South African Years*, p. 217; University of the Witwatersrand Library: Pim papers: Macmillan to Pim, 12 October 1933.

³⁸ Macmillan, *South African Years*, p. 215.

³⁹ Macmillan, *Complex South Africa* (London, 1930), p. viii.

⁴⁰ Macmillan, *South African Years*, p. 216.

⁴¹ Macmillan, *South African Years*, p. 194.

⁴² Macmillan papers: Macmillan to Walker, 17 November 1954; cf. *South African Years*, p. 218.

[43] Cf. W. M. Macmillan, *Bantu, Boer, and Briton* (rev. ed., Oxford 1963), p. vii.

[44] Macmillan, *South African Years*, p. 219.

[45] B. Murray, *Wits. The Early Years* (Johannesburg, 1982), pp. 130-1; Macmillan papers.

[46] Macmillan, *South African Years*, p. 246.

[47] B. Murray, *Wits*, pp. 329-33.

[48] *American Historical Review*, 43 (1938); Naidoo letters: de Kiewiet to Naidoo, 1980.

[49] W. M. Macmillan, *Africa Emergent* (London, 1938), pp. 16-17, 186, 184.

[50] Macmillan, *Africa Emergent*, p. 31.

[51] Macmillan, *Champion of Africa*, chs. 7, 8, 9.

[52] Macmillan papers: Macmillan to Walker, 17 November 1954; Walker to Macmillan, 23 August 1957.

[53] University of Cape Town Library: Marquard papers: Macmillan to Marquard, 1 December 1957; Marquard to Faber, 14 October 1959. Cf. below, p. 133.

6. The revisionist historian

[1] Information from Mona Macmillan.

[2] It was reprinted in 1974. Cf. W. Beinart, P. Delius and S. Trapido (eds.), *Putting a Plough to the Ground* (Johannesburg, 1986).

[3] Macmillan, *Agrarian Problem*, p. 23.

[4] J. F. W. Grosskopf, *Rural Impoverishment and Rural Exodus* (Stellenbosch, 1932), p. 19.

[5] Cf. Macmillan, *South African Years*, p. 135.

[6] Macmillan, *South African Years*, p. 146.

[7] Cory, *Rise of South Africa*, 2, p. 426.

[8] Macmillan, *South African Years*, p. 162.

[9] Macmillan, *South African Years*, p. 167.

[10] W. M. Macmillan, *Bantu, Boer, and Briton* (London, 1929), Preface. References are to this edition unless otherwise indicated.

[11] Macmillan, *South African Years*, p. 169.

[12] W. M. Macmillan, *The Cape Colour Question* (London, 1927), p. viii.

[13] Macmillan, *Cape Colour Question*, p. 267. Cf. his review of J. S. Marais, *The Cape Coloured People* in *New Statesman*, 1939.

[14] Macmillan, *Cape Colour Question*, pp. 287-88.

[15] Macmillan, *Cape Colour Question*, p. 288.

[16] Macmillan, *South African Years*, p. 177.

[17] Macmillan, *Bantu, Boer, and Briton*, Preface.

[18] Macmillan, *South African Years*, p. 188.

[19] Macmillan, *Cape Colour Question*, p. 289.

[20] Cf. Macmillan, *South African Years*, p. 182.

[21] Macmillan, *Bantu, Boer, and Briton*, p. 288.

[22] Macmillan, *Bantu, Boer and Briton*, Preface.

[23] Macmillan, *Bantu, Boer, and Briton*, Preface.

[24] Macmillan, *Bantu, Boer, and Briton*, p. 317.

[25] Macmillan, *Bantu, Boer, and Briton*, p. 317.

[26] Rich, *White Power and the Liberal Conscience*.

[27] E. Walker, *The Frontier Tradition in South Africa* (Oxford, 1930); below, pp. 114 and 174.

28 Macmillan, *South African Years*, p. 167.
29 As pointed out by M. Legassick in R. Elphick and H. Giliomee (eds.), *The Shaping of South African Society* (Cape Town, 1979), p. 244.
30 Macmillan, *Cape Colour Question*, p. 11.
31 Macmillan, *Bantu, Boer, and Briton*, p. 317.
32 Macmillan, *Bantu, Boer, and Briton*, pp. 9, 12; rev ed., p. 28.
33 Macmillan, *Cape Colour Question*, p. 289; *Bantu, Boer, and Briton*, Preface.
34 Macmillan, *South African Years*, pp. 212, 160-61.
35 Macmillan, *South African Years*, p. 216.
36 Macmillan, *South African Years*, p.46.
37 Macmillan, *South African Years*, p. 234.
38 On Bryant see below, p. 105.
39 Macmillan, *Bantu, Boer, and Briton*, Preface.
40 W. M. Macmillan, *Warning from the West Indies* (London, 1938), p.53.
41 S. Newton-King in S. Marks and A. Atmore (eds.), *Economy and Society in Pre-Industrial South Africa* (London, 1980), ch. 7.
42 A. Atmore and S. Marks, 'The Imperial Factor in South Africa: Towards a Reassessment', *Journal of Imperial and Commonwealth History*, 3 (1974).
43 Galbraith, *Reluctant Empire*.
44 Atmore and Marks, 'Imperial Factor'.
45 'N. Majeke', *The Role of the Missionaries in Conquest* (Alexandra, 1952); H. Jaffe, *Storia del Sud Afrika* (Milan, 1980).
46 T. Keegan, 'Crisis and Catharsis in South African Agriculture', *African Affairs*, 84 (1985).
47 Foreword to 1968 reprint.
48 W. K. Hancock, *Country and Calling* (London, 1954), p. 245.

7. De Kiewiet: from Johannesburg to America

1 For fuller details on his life see my *C. W. de Kiewiet, Historian of South Africa* (Cape Town, 1986), ch. 1.
2 Naidoo letters: de Kiewiet to Naidoo, 17 August 1980.
3 Interview with C. W. de Kiewiet; Naidoo letters.
4 No copy is known to have survived; at least one was destroyed in the fire in the Wits University Library in 1931.
5 De Kiewiet papers (Cornell University Library, unless otherwise stated): Macmillan to de Kiewiet, 21 September 1924.
6 Macmillan papers: Walker to Macmillan, 28 August 1925.
7 Naidoo letters.
8 De Kiewiet papers: de Kiewiet to Frankel and Harvey, n.d.
9 De Kiewiet papers: Macmillan to de Kiewiet, 14 March 1925.
10 E. Brookes, *The History of Native Policy in South Africa from 1830 to the Present Day* (Cape Town, 1924). For Brookes's career see his *A South African Pilgrimage* (Johannesburg, 1977).
11 Brookes, *History*, p. 9.
12 De Kiewiet papers: Macmillan to de Kiewiet, 14 March 1925.
13 J. A. I. Agar-Hamilton, *The Native Policy of the Voortrekkers* (Cape Town, n.d.[1928].) Like Brookes, Agar-Hamilton taught at the Transvaal University College, Pretoria.
14 Macmillan papers: de Kiewiet to Macmillan, 19 July 1926.

[15] Interview with C. W. de Kiewiet.

[16] De Kiewiet papers: Macmillan to de Kiewiet, 10 September 1929.

[17] Macmillan papers: de Kiewiet to Macmillan, 1 March 1931.

[18] Cf. B. Murray, *Wits*, p. 269, and ch. 2 above.

[19] Macmillan papers: de Kiewiet to Macmillan, n.d.[1936].

[20] Cambridge University Library: Cambridge University Press Archives: Newton to Roberts, 11 October 1936, enclosing report.

[21] For details cf. Saunders, *C. W. de Kiewiet*, ch. 3.

[22] J. S. Marais, *The Fall of Kruger's Republic* (Oxford, 1961).

[23] Saunders, *C. W. de Kiewiet*, ch. 3.

8. The master historian

[1] Naidoo letters: de Kiewiet to Naidoo, 17 August 1980.

[2] De Kiewiet, *British Colonial Policy and the South African Republics* (London, 1929), pp. 308-9.

[3] Macmillan papers: de Kiewiet to Macmillan, 13 January 1935.

[4] De Kiewiet, *British Colonial Policy*, p. 1.

[5] A. P. Newton, 'Africa and Historical Research', *Journal of the Africa Society*, 22 (1922-3), 275-6.

[6] De Kiewiet, *British Colonial Policy*, pp. 311, 114.

[7] De Kiewiet, *British Colonial Policy*, p. 3.

[8] De Kiewiet, *British Colonial Policy*, pp. 1-3.

[9] De Kiewiet, *British Colonial Policy*, p. 116.

[10] De Kiewiet papers: undated cutting from *The Star*.

[11] *English Historical Review*, April 1930.

[12] De Kiewiet papers: Newton to de Kiewiet, 3 April 1931.

[13] A. P. Newton and E. Benians (eds.), *The Cambridge History of the British Empire*, 8 (Cambridge, 1936), p. 824.

[14] *Manchester Guardian*, 25 September 1936; *Spectator*, 20 November 1936. On Barnes see below, pp. 131-32.

[15] De Kiewiet, *The Imperial Factor in South Africa* (Cambridge, 1937), p. 117, n.2; p. 109, n.3.

[16] De Kiewiet, *Imperial Factor*, pp. 1-5.

[17] W. Hall in *American Historical Review* (April 1938).

[18] W. M. Macmillan, in *New Statesman and Nation*, 29 January 1938.

[19] Below, pp. 117-18.

[20] De Kiewiet, *Imperial Factor*, pp. 2-3, 14.

[21] De Kiewiet, *Imperial Factor*, p. 176; *New Statesman*, 29 January 1938.

[22] De Kiewiet, *Imperial Factor*, p. 231.

[23] E.g. N. Etherington, 'Labour Supplies and the Genesis of South African Confederation', *Journal of African History*, 20 (1979); R. Cope in *History in Africa*, 13 (1986).

[24] De Kiewiet, 'The Frontier and the Constitution' in C. Read (ed.), *The Constitution Reconsidered* (New York, 1938).

[25] Macmillan papers: de Kiewiet to Macmillan, 14 March 1938.

[26] De Kiewiet papers: de Kiewiet to Clarendon Press, 10 January 1939.

[27] Cf. University of Cape Town Library: de Kiewiet papers: manuscript of the 'History'.

[28] J. S. Galbraith, personal communication, 18 October 1983.

²⁹ His *Imperial Factor* was published by Frank Cass in a new impression in 1965, but was never available in paperback and did not sell widely.

³⁰ W. P. Morrell, *A Select List of Books Relating to the History of the British Commonwealth* (London, 1944), p. 10.

³¹ W. K. Hancock, *Australia* (London, 1930), ch. 1.

³² De Kiewiet, *History*, p. 79.

³³ Below, pp.119-20.

³⁴ De Kiewiet, *History*, pp. 150-51, 212 and cf. 56, 58, 71.

³⁵ De Kiewiet, *History*, pp. 182, 193.

³⁶ De Kiewiet, *History*, pp. 179, 276.

³⁷ De Kiewiet, *History*, pp. 20, 242-45 and cf. p. 56.

³⁸ De Kiewiet, *History*, pp. 176, 227-8, 248.

³⁹ Knaplund in *American Historical Review*, 48 (1942), 64.

⁴⁰ *Manchester Guardian*, May 1941.

⁴¹ B. A. le Cordeur, 'The Reconstruction of South African History', *South African Historical Journal*, 17 (1985).

⁴² Marks and Atmore, *Economy and Society*, p. 1.

9. Race, class and liberal history

¹ Cf. R. Hofstadter, *Progressive Historians*.

² H. Butterfield, *The Whig Interpretation of History* (London, 1931).

³ See, e.g., de Kiewiet, *Imperial Factor*, p. 1; *History*, p. 179.

⁴ Part 5 below.

⁵ Cf. R. Winks (ed.), *Historiography of the British Empire-Commonwealth* (Durham, North Carolina, 1966).

⁶ De Kiewiet, *History*, p. 286; cf. pp. 73, 81.

⁷ De Kiewiet, *Imperial Factor*, p. 150.

⁸ J. Lewis, 'The Rise and Fall of the South African Peasantry: A Critique and a Reassessment', *Journal of Southern African Studies*, 11 (1984).

⁹ De Kiewiet, *History*, p. 20.

¹⁰ De Kiewiet, *Imperial Factor*, p. 273.

¹¹ *Washington Post*, 25 April 1981: letter by de Kiewiet.

¹² Cf. p. 43 above.

¹³ De Kiewiet, *History*, p. 19.

¹⁴ C. Bundy, *The Rise and Fall of the South African Peasantry* (London, 1979), Preface, n.p.

¹⁵ Interview with C. W. de Kiewiet.

¹⁶ M. Legassick, 'The Making of South African "Native Policy" 1903-1923: The Origins of Segregation', unpublished seminar paper, University of London, 1972; J. Cell, *The Highest Stage of White Supremacy* (Cambridge, 1982).

¹⁷ De Kiewiet, *History* , pp. 242-3.

¹⁸ Naidoo letters: de Kiewiet to Naidoo, 31 August 1980; interview with de Kiewiet.

¹⁹ E. Walker, *A History of South Africa* (2nd ed.), p. 543, n.1. Cf. C. Bundy, 'Vagabond Hollanders and Runaway Englishmen' in Beinart, Delius and Trapido (eds.), *Putting a Plough to the Ground*.

²⁰ De Kiewiet, *History*, p. 197.

²¹ De Kiewiet, *History*, p. 111.

²² De Kiewiet, *Imperial Factor*, pp. 208, 220; cf. C. Webb in A. Duminy and C.

Ballard (eds.), *The Anglo-Zulu War: Towards a Reassessment* (Pietermaritzburg, 1979), esp. p. 11, n.1.

10. Early Africanist work

[1] These were eventually reprinted under the title *A History of the Zulu and Neighbouring Tribes* (Cape Town, 1964).

[2] *Rand Daily Mail*, 23 December 1922.

[3] *Rand Daily Mail*, 19 April and 25 May 1923.

[4] *Olden Times in Zululand and Natal, Containing the Earlier Political History of the Eastern-Nguni clans* (London, 1929), Preface.

[5] S. Marks, 'The Traditions of the Natal "Nguni": A Second Look at the Work of A. T. Bryant', in L. Thompson (ed.), *African Societies in Southern Africa* (London, 1969), p. 127.

[6] J. Stuart and D. Malcolm (eds.), *The Diary of Henry Francis Fynn* (Pietermaritzburg, 1950); Julian Cobbing in *The Weekly Mail*, 7-13 November 1986.

[7] *Daily News*, 2 June 1944.

[8] C. Webb and J. Wright (eds.), *The James Stuart Archive* (Pietermaritzburg, 1976—.)

[9] *Bantu Studies*, 5 (1931).

[10] J. K. Bokwe, *Ntsikana. The Story of an African Convert* (Lovedale, 1896).

[11] U. Barnett, *A Vision of Order. Black South African Literature in English 1914-80* (London, 1984) p. 10.

[12] The first such biography was of Tiyo Soga, published two decades earlier.

[13] Cf. C. Saunders, 'F. Z. S. Peregrino and *The South African Spectator*', *Quarterly Bulletin of the South African Library* (1978).

[14] *Izwi Labantu*, 30 October 1906. Keir Hardie had written an introduction for it. I thank Bob Edgar for the reference.

[15] T. D. Mweli Skota, *The African Yearly Register* (Johannesburg, 1930); cf. *Dictionary of South African Biography*, 2, p. 608.

[16] W. B. Rubusana, *Zemk'iinkomo Magwalandini* (London, 1906).

[17] S. Marks and R. Rathbone (eds.), *Industrialisation and Social Change*, p. 246.

[18] S. Plaatje, *Native Life in South Africa* (London, 1916; new ed. Johannesburg, n.d.[1982] with introduction by B. Willan).

[19] B. Willan, *Sol. T. Plaatje* (Johannesburg, 1984), p. 255, quoting Plaatje's notebook; Willan, personal communication.

[20] Review by 'Tau' in *The Torch*, 28 August 1951. 'Tau' was anti-A.N.C.

[21] S. M. Molema, *Chief Moroka* (Cape Town, 1951), p. 190.

[22] M. Fuze, *The Black People and Whence They Came* (Pietermaritzburg, 1979).

[23] Wilson and Thompson (eds.), *The Oxford History*, 1, pp. 85-86, n.9, citing R. T. Kawa, *I-Bali lama Mfengu* (Lovedale, 1929) and works by W. D. Cingo, V. P. Ndamase, and A. Z. Ngani.

[24] Cf. J. Peires, *The House of Phalo* (Johannesburg, 1981), p. 177.

[25] D. D. T. Jabavu, *The Black Problem* (Lovedale, 1920), Preface.

[26] Richard Tshabala, in *The Workers' Herald*, the newspaper of the Industrial and Commercial Workers' Union, 15 August 1927.

[27] J. Peires, 'Lovedale and Literature for the Bantu', *History in Africa*, 7 (1980).

[28] E.g. J. H. Soga, *The South-Eastern Bantu*, p. 58.

[29] J. H. Soga, *The Ama-Xosa, Life and Customs* (Lovedale, n.d.[1932]}.

[30] Edited by S. Trapido, it was eventually published in London in 1970. Other autobiographies, including one by R. Selope Thema, were never published.

[31] Skota hoped to bring out annual volumes but only one further volume appeared, in 1966, which was a pale shadow of the original.

[32] E.g. articles on Zulu history by Vilakazi in 1943.

[33] Newbolt in 1931 edition, p. xi.

[34] T. Couzens, *The New African. A Study of the Life and Work of H. I. E. Dhlomo* (Johannesburg, 1985), p. 139.

[35] Radcliffe-Brown's influence in South Africa derived partly from the fact that he was the first holder of the chair of social anthropology at Cape Town; he left for Australia in 1926.

[36] See below, ch. 14.

11. Walker and other historians of the 1930s and 1940s

[1] C. Saunders and B. le Cordeur, 'The South African Historical Society and Its Antecedents', *South African Historical Journal*, 18 (1986).

[2] Walker, *History* (1928), p. vi.

[3] E. Walker, *The Great Trek* (London, 1934).

[4] E. Walker, *The Cape Native Franchise* (Cape Town, 1936).

[5] E. Walker, 'Of Franchises', *The Critic*, 4 (1936), pp. 67, 71.

[6] J. Walker, *Skin Deep* (Kommetjie, 1977); Walker Papers, University of Cape Town: Reitz to Mrs Walker, 19 July 1944.

[7] Below, p. 147. A savage attack on his methodology came from B. Liebenberg in 'Eric Walker's Interpretation of Recent South African History', *Historia*, 11 (1966).

[8] E.g. H. M. Robertson, 'Some Trends in South African History Writing', p. 3.

[9] Macmillan, *Cape Colour Question*, p. 248. Cf. also pp. 20-1.

[10] Walker to Macmillan, 21 January. 1930, quoted in Legassick, 'The Frontier Tradition', p. 64 note.

[11] Walker, *History*, 2nd ed., p. 62.

[12] E. Walker, 'A Zulu Account of the Retief Massacre', *The Critic*, 3 (1935).

[13] K. Sinclair in Winks, *Historiography of the British Empire-Commonwealth*, p. 178.

[14] University of Cape Town Archives: applications for the chair of history, 1936.

[15] I. Schapera (ed.), *The Bantu-Speaking Tribes of South Africa* (London, 1934).

[16] J. S. Marais, *The Cape Coloured People*, pp. viii, x.

[17] Marais, *Cape Coloured People*, ch. 1 and pp. 284-5.

[18] Marais, *Cape Coloured People*, pp. 282, 283.

[19] The first work by a professional historian from a Xhosa perspective was Jeffrey Peires, *The House of Phalo* (1981).

[20] J. S. Marais, *Maynier and the First Boer Republic* (Cape Town, 1944), Preface.

[21] Marais was critical of an economic interpretation of racism: *Cape Coloured People*, p. 282 note.

[22] M. H. de Kock, *Selected Subjects in the Economic History of South Africa* (Cape Town, 1924). Chapter 17 was on African labour, however.

[23] D. M. Goodfellow, *Modern Economic History of South Africa* (London, 1931).

[24] *Report of the South African Association for the Advancement of Science*, 21 (1924). Cf. D. Scher, 'Margaret Ballinger', *Kleio*, 13 (1981).

[25] Robertson, 'Some Themes', p. 52.

[26] *South African Journal of Economics*, 2-3 (1934–35).

[27] Robertson, 'Some Themes', p. 56.

[28] P. Wickins, 'Hector Monteith Robertson', *CABO*, 3 (1985); J. de V. Graaff, 'H. M. Robertson 1905–1984', *South African Journal of Economics*, 52 (1983).

[29] Robertson, 'Some Themes', p. 56.

[30] S. van der Horst, *Native Labour in South Africa* (London, 1942), p. 325.

[31] Published in the Hague, 1937, Cape Town, 1938, and Cape Town, 1945 respectively.

[32] In his Yale dissertation (1972) and then in *Kraal and Castle* (New Haven, 1977), Introduction, n. 4.

[33] H. Reyburn, 'Studies in Cape Frontier History', *The Critic*, 3-4 (1934-36).

[34] I. D. MacCrone, *Race Attitudes in South Africa: Historical, Experimental and Psychological Studies* (London, 1937), pp. 135-6.

[35] De Kiewiet, *History*, p. 17.

[36] Robertson did not forget that interaction involved conflict as well: e.g. H. M. Robertson, *South Africa. Economic and Political Aspects* (Durham, 1957), p. 18.

12. Historians of the 1940s and 1950s

[1] Mandelbrote papers: Walker to Mandelbrote, 2 January 1938.

[2] De Kiewiet, *British Colonial Policy*, p. 310. It was published, much later, in the *Archives Yearbook for South African History*, 1949, 1.

[3] J. van der Poel, *The Jameson Raid* (London, 1951).

[4] For details see C. Saunders, 'Jean van der Poel, Historian', *Quarterly Bulletin of the South African Library*, 41 (1986).

[5] Interview with J. van der Poel, 1984.

[6] G. Butler, *Bursting World* (Cape Town, 1983), p. 83 and cf. pp. 45-46, 74.

[7] Information from L. M. Thompson, and from his 1958 application for the chair of history: University of Cape Town archives.

[8] L. M. Thompson, *Democracy in Multi-Racial Societies* (Johannesburg, 1949), *passim*.

[9] L. M. Thompson, 'Interest, Ideology and History: the South African Case', unpublished seminar paper, Yale University, c. 1978, note 86.

[10] For his other work of these years see C. Saunders, 'U.C.T Historians I: Leonard Thompson', *Janus* (1977).

[11] Cf. E. van Heyningen, *The History of Shawco* (Cape Town, 1975).

[12] A. Odendaal, *Vukani Bantu!* (Cape Town, 1984).

[13] L. Fouché, *Mapungubwe: Ancient Bantu Civilization on the Limpopo* (Cambridge, 1937), p. 178.

[14] Above, p. 58.

[15] 'Fouché' in *Standard Encyclopaedia of South Africa*; personal communication from Eric Axelson, 15 October 1984.

[16] J. S. Marais, *The Fall of Kruger's Republic* (Oxford, 1961).

[17] Information from L. M. Thompson.

[18] J. S. Marais, 'African Squatting on European Farms in South Africa, with Special Reference to the Cape Colony 1842-1913', University of London, AH 66/12.

[19] Interview with A. Keppel-Jones, 1986.

[20] In 1937 she was elected to parliament as a Natives Representative, and retained her seat until 1960, when the Natives Representatives were abolished: cf. her *From Union to Apartheid* (London, 1969).

[21] Personal communication from E. Axelson, 15 October 1984. Axelson was in the history department at Wits in 1940.

[22] *Race Relations*, 5 (1938).

[23] Carnegie Corporation Papers: de Kiewiet, confidential memorandum on visit to South Africa, 1947. Cf. C. Saunders, '*When Smuts Goes* Revisited', *Die Suid-Afri-*

kaan, Winter 1986.

[24] Keppel-Jones, personal communication, 27 February 1984, and interviews, 1983 and 1986.

[25] University of Cape Town archives B.C.631.A91.31: A. Keppel-Jones, 'Why We Went', *Sunday Times*, 26 July 1959.

[26] For more details see C. Saunders, review of A. Keppel-Jones, *Rhodes and Rhodesia* (Pietermaritzburg, 1983) in *Queen's Quarterly*, 92 (1985), pp. 224-26.

[27] A. Keppel-Jones, 'Where Did We Take the Wrong Turning?', *Race Relations Journal*, 26 (1959).

[28] He wrote a short history of western civilisation, and a book on *History Teaching at Schools* (London, 1933).

[29] Cf. E. Brookes, *A History of the University of Natal* (Pietermaritzburg, 1966).

[30] University of Cape Town archives: applications for the chair in history, 1936.

[31] Carnegie Corporation papers: de Kiewiet's confidential memorandum on his 1947 visit to South Africa, p. 39.

[32] Cf. the festschrift edited by J. Benyon *et al.*, *Essays in Local History* (Cape Town, 1975).

[33] They included B. le Cordeur, A. Duminy and D. Schreuder, who in 1987 headed the departments of history in Cape Town, Durban and Sydney.

[34] Below, p.150-51.

[35] T. S. van Rooyen, 'Die Bantoe in die Suid-Afrikaanse Historiografie', in G. Cronje (ed.), *Aspekte van die Suid-Afrikaanse Historiografie* (Pretoria, 1967), pp. 134-35. Cf. A. van Jaarsveld, 'T. S. van Rooyen', *Historia*, 30 (1985).

[36] F. Madden and D. Fieldhouse (eds.), *Oxford and the Idea of Commonwealth* (London, 1982), p. 16.

[37] Cf. Saunders and le Cordeur, 'The South African Historical Society'.

[38] Kenneth McIntyre (1917–77) was blinded, but nevertheless rose to become head of the history department at the University of Natal, Durban.

13. Early radical writing

[1] J. A. Hobson, *The War in South Africa* (London, 1900) and 'Capitalism and Imperialism in South Africa', *Contemporary Review*, 76 (1900). Cf. N. Etherington, *Theories of Imperialism* (London, 1984).

[2] Cf. P. Rich, *Race and Empire in British Politics* (Cambridge, 1986), p. 81.

[3] A. McAdam, 'Leonard Barnes and South Africa', *Social Dynamics*, 3 (1977).

[4] *Manchester Guardian*, 25 September 1936.

[5] E.g. S. P. Bunting, *Imperialism and South Africa* (Johannesburg, 1928); articles in *Umsebenzi* in the late 1920s.

[6] *The Workers' Herald*, 20 February 1926.

[7] Cf. R. Cohen (ed.), *Forced Labour in Colonial Africa* (London, 1979).

[8] J. Gomas, *100 Years. 'Emancipation of Slaves.'* (Cape Town, n.d.), p. 9.

[9] W. H. Andrews, *Class Struggles in South Africa* (Cape Town, 1941); R. K. Cope, *Comrade Bill: the Life and Times of W. H. Andrews* (Cape Town, 1943).

[10] University of Cape Town: Marquard papers: BC 587 F2.1.

[11] Marquard Papers: F2.21.

[12] Review in *Trek*, 30 July 1943.

[13] L. Marquard, *The Black Man's Burden* (London, 1943), p. 189. Marquard's later, much more historical *The Story of South Africa* (London, 1955) was, in contrast to *Black Man's Burden*, a strictly liberal work.

[14] University of the Witwatersrand Library: H. Basner, 'The Black Price of Gold in South Africa'.

[15] 'A Black Man's History of South Africa', *Umsebenzi*, 18 August 1934. Fourteen chapters of Roux's history had appeared in that newspaper by October 1935.

[16] E. Roux, *S. P. Bunting* (Cape Town, 1944).

[17] E. and W. Roux, *Rebel Pity* (London, 1970), p. 171.

[18] E. Roux, *Time Longer Than Rope* (London, 1948), p. 378.

[19] Roux, *Time Longer Than Rope*, p. 7.

[20] *The Historian*, quoted on the cover of the paperback edition of *Time Longer Than Rope*.

[21] Information from, e.g., Baruch Hirson.

[22] It would also seem that Roux had access to Kadalie's autobiography, not published until 1970.

[23] E. Walker, *A History of South Africa*, 2nd ed., pp. 582, 615-6.

[24] E. Walker, *A History of Southern Africa* (London, 1957).

[25] Information from, e.g., Robert Edgar, whose doctorate on the Bulhoek massacre was entitled 'The Fifth Seal', University of California, Los Angeles, 1977.

[26] Until 1987 undergraduates were unable to read it in the University of Cape Town Library because the librarians insisted on abiding by the provisions of the Internal Security Act of 1982.

[27] *The Torch*, 13 November 1951.

[28] Unfortunately, no full set of this journal appears to have survived.

[29] See, e.g. his comments on the Great Trek in *Eastern Province Herald*, 19 December 1949. His autobiography, entitled 'Out of Court', remained unpublished.

[30] W. M. Tsotsi, *From Chattel to Wage Slavery* (Maseru, 1981).

[31] F. J. le Roux and D. J. van Zyl (eds.), *'n Eeu van Onreg* (Cape Town, 1985).

[32] 'Melanchthon', *Three Centuries of Wrong* (Cape Town, 1952). Cf. C. J. Driver, *Patrick Duncan. South African and Pan African* (London, 1980), p. 83.

[33] An enlarged edition of *Three Hundred Years* was published under the title *Storia del Sudafrica* in Milan in 1980.

[34] Among those who may have helped Taylor was I. B. Tabata, author of a history of the All-African Convention published in 1950 under the title *The Awakening of a People*.

[35] For details see C. Saunders, '"Mnguni" and *Three Hundred Years* Revisited', *Kronos*, 11 (1986).

[36] 'Majeke', *The Role of the Missionaries in Conquest* (n.p., n.d.), Introduction.

[37] E.g. 'Majeke', *Missionaries in Conquest*, ch. 12.

[38] Cf. e.g. A. Dachs, 'Missionary Imperialism: The Case of Bechuanaland', *Journal of African History*, 13 (1972); A. Atmore and S. Marks, 'The Imperial Factor in South Africa'.

[39] Macmillan papers: Thompson to Macmillan, September 1952.

[40] Macmillan Papers: B. A. Tindall to Macmillan, 18 October 1955.

[41] Cf. the sketch of his life in R. Alexander (ed.), *Black and White in S.A. History* (n.p., n.d.[1960]), pp. 31-33.

[42] See below, Chapter 16.

[43] C. Muller (ed.), *Five Hundred Years* (Pretoria, 1969), Introduction.

14. The beginnings of liberal Africanism

[1] E.g. T. R. H. Davenport, *South Africa. A Modern History* (London, 1977), p. xiv.

[2] See, e.g., J. D. Fage in J. Ki-Zerbo (ed.), *General History of Africa*, 1 (London, 1980), esp. p. 32.

[3] J. Fage, *An Introduction to the History of West Africa* (Cambridge, 1955).

[4] R. Oliver and J. Fage, *A Short History of Africa* (Harmondsworth, 1962).

[5] H. Trevor-Roper, *The Rise of Christian Europe* (London, 1965), p. 9.

[6] C. Neale, *Writing 'Independent' History* (Westport, 1985); B. Jewsiewicki and D. Newbury (eds.), *African Historiographies* (Beverly Hills, 1986).

[7] L. M. Thompson, 'Afrikaner Nationalist Historiography and the Policy of Apartheid', *Journal of African History*, 3 (1962), 141.

[8] University of Cape Town archives: report by L. M. Thompson.

[9] Macmillan papers: Thompson to Macmillan, 26 August 1952.

[10] Above, p. 124.

[11] C. Saunders, 'U.C.T. Historians 1: Leonard Thompson', *Janus* (1977), 3.

[12] R. Winks (ed.), *Historiography of the British Empire-Commonwealth*.

[13] L. Thompson, *Politics in the Republic of South Africa* (Boston, 1966).

[14] E. Axelson, personal communication, 15 October 1984.

[15] J. S. Galbraith, personal communication, 18 October 1983.

[16] There was no undergraduate anthropology at Cambridge at that time. Cf. A. Richards in M. West and M. Whisson (eds.), *Religion and Social Change in Southern Africa* (Cape Town, 1975); C. Murray in *Journal of Southern African Studies*, 10 (1983).

[17] Cf. R. Brown on Godfrey Wilson in T. Asad (ed.), *Anthropology and the Colonial Encounter* (London, 1979).

[18] G. and M. Wilson, *The Analysis of Social Change* (Cambridge, 1945).

[19] *Good Company* (1951) was followed by *Rituals of Kingship* (1956), *Peoples of the Corridor* (1958) and *Communal Rituals* (1959).

[20] Cf. J. Western, *Outcast Cape Town* (Cape Town, 1981), ch. 3.

[21] *Cape Times*, 7 November 1958, reporting address to the Rapportryers.

[22] M. Wilson, 'The Early History of the Transkei and Ciskei', *African Studies*, 18 (1959). The most recent archaeological survey is M. Hall, *The Changing Past* (Cape Town, 1987).

[23] Carnegie Corporation archives, M. Wilson file: M. Wilson to A. Pifer, 26 June 1967.

[24] C. Goodfellow, *Great Britain and South African Confederation* (Cape Town, 1966), p. x. He threw himself off a cliff overlooking the university at Roma in 1966. Cf. A. Brink, *Rumours of Rain* (London, 1978), p. 102.

[25] E.g. Marquard papers: correspondence between Marquard and Thompson.

[26] L. Kuper, *Race, Class and Power* (London, 1977), Appendix 2: 'A Matter of Surrogate Censorship'.

[27] R. Hyam,'Are We Any Nearer an African History of South Africa?', *Historical Journal*, 16 (1973), 617.

[28] Omer-Cooper, personal communication, 30 November 1983.

[29] Omer-Cooper, personal communication, 30 November 1983.

[30] A similar, positive view of Shaka can be found in S. Marks, 'The Rise of the Zulu Kingdom' in R. Oliver (ed.), *The Middle Age of African History* (London, 1967).

[31] W. F. Lye, 'The Sotho Wars in the Interior of South Africa 1822–1837', Ph.D thesis, UCLA, 1969; for Legassick's thesis see below, ch. 16.

[32] Other American scholars refused visas in following years included Sheridan Johns and Hunt Davis.

[33] S. Marks, *Reluctant Rebellion* (Oxford, 1970), p. v. The earlier, semi-official ac-

count was J. Stuart, *A History of the Zulu Rebellion, 1906* (London, 1913).

[34] The present writer attended, by kind invitation of Leonard Thompson.

[35] L. Thompson (ed.), *African Societies in Southern Africa* (London, 1969).

15. The Oxford History

[1] The significance of 1652 was further reduced because May Katzen, the author of the chapter on the establishment of the Dutch settlement, chose to begin it in the late eighteenth century.

[2] Cf. esp. N. Garson, 'South African History: A New Look', *African Studies*, 29 (1970).

[3] Perhaps the most judicious assessment was the review article by P. Lewsen in *South African Historical Journal*, 5 (1973).

[4] R. Ross, 'The First Two Centuries of Colonial Agriculture in the Cape Colony', *Social Dynamics*, 9 (1983), 30.

[5] E.g. P. Kallaway, 'What Happened in South African History', *Concept*, 6 (1975).

[6] Above, p. 134-36.

[7] E.g. S. Marks, *Reluctant Rebellion* (Oxford, 1970).

[8] P. Walshe, *The Rise of African Nationalism in South Africa* (London, 1971); P. Wickins, *The Industrial and Commercial Workers' Union of Africa* (Cape Town, 1978)

[9] By William Lye on the Difaqane, Martin Legassick on the Cape northern frontier. Thompson moved to Yale in 1968.

[10] See below, p. 168.

[11] F. A. van Jaarsveld, 'Ons Verledebeeld: Geskonde Oue of Vertekende Nuwe?', *Standpunte* (1969), reprinted in his *Geskiedkundige Verkenninge* (Pretoria, 1974), esp. p. 179, citing Wilson and Thompson (eds.), *Oxford History*, 1, p. 232.

[12] Wilson and Thompson (eds.), *Oxford History*, 1, pp. 194, 253.

[13] Van Jaarsveld, *Geskiedkundige Verkenninge*, p. 177.

[14] On this see esp. A. Atmore and N. Westlake, 'A Liberal Dilemma: A Critique of the Oxford History of South Africa', *Race*, 14 (1973) and also the review by Richard Gray in *ibid.*, 14 (1972), 84.

[15] D. Potter, 'C. Vann Woodward and the Uses of History' in M. Cunliffe and R. Winks (eds.), *Pastmasters* (New York, 1969), p. 169.

[16] Wilson and Thompson (eds.), *Oxford History*, 1, p. 261.

[17] Cf. the reviews of the two volumes by R. Gray in *Race*, 11 (1969) and 14 (1972).

[18] Wilson and Thompson (eds.), *Oxford History*, 1, pp. 74, 73.

[19] Wilson and Thompson (eds.), *Oxford History*, 1, p. 271; 2, p. 103.

[20] Atmore and Westlake, 'A Liberal Dilemma', pp. 112 ff.

[21] Wilson and Thompson (eds.), *Oxford History*, 1, p. 105.

[22] S.Marks, 'African and Afrikaner History', *Journal of African History*, 11 (1970); 'Khoisan Resistance to the Dutch', *Journal of African History*, 13 (1972); R. Elphick's 1972 Yale dissertation was published as *Kraal and Castle* in 1977.

[23] E.g. Monica Wilson in *Oxford History*, 1, p. 271.

[24] See esp. D. O'Meara's review of T. R. H. Davenport, *South Africa: A Modern History*, in *Utafiti*, 4 (1979), 258-61.

[25] Cf. L. Thompson, *Survival in Two Worlds* (Oxford, 1975), pp. 332-3; J. Wright, 'Politics, Ideology and the Invention of the "Nguni"', in T. Lodge (ed.), *Resistance and Ideology in Settler Societies* (Johannesburg, 1986).

[26] Wilson and Thompson (eds.), *Oxford History*, 2, p. 324.

[27] L. Thompson, *Survival in Two Worlds* (Oxford, 1975).

[28] See below and, e.g., J. Peires (ed.), *Before and After Shaka* (Grahamstown, 1979).

[29] Wilson and Thompson (eds.), *Oxford History*, 1, p. 179.

[30] Wilson and Thompson (eds.), *Oxford History*, 1, p. 232.

[31] L. Kuper, *An African Bourgeoisie* (New Haven, 1965).

[32] M. Legassick, 'The Dynamics of Modernisation', *Journal of African History*, 13 (1972).

[33] E.g. T. Lodge, *Black Politics in South Africa* (Johannesburg, 1983).

[34] J. Wright,'Clash of Paradigms', *Reality*, 9 (1977), 14-17.

16. The challenge begins

[1] See e.g. F. R. Johnstone's tribute to the earlier work in *Class, Race and Gold* (Johannesburg, 1976), pp. 52-54.

[2] C. Bundy, 'Peasants in Herschel' in Marks and Atmore (eds.), *Economy and Society*; and C. Bundy, *The Rise and Fall of the South African Peasantry* (London, 1979).

[3] C. Saunders, '"Mnguni" and *Three Hundred Years* Revisited', *Kronos*, 11 (1986).

[4] H. J. and R. E. Simons, *Class and Colour in South Africa 1850-1950* (Harmondsworth, 1969), p. 9.

[5] Simons and Simons, *Class and Colour*, pp. 140, 144.

[6] Simons and Simons, *Class and Colour*, ch. 26.

[7] Cf. reviews in L. Kuper, *Race, Class, and Power* (London, 1974), Appendix I, and by I. Smith in *Third World Quarterly*, 7 (1985).

[8] S. Trapido, 'White Conflict and Non-White Participation in the Politics of the Cape of Good Hope, 1853-1910', Ph.D thesis, University of London, 1970.

[9] S. Marks, 'Afrikaner and African History', *Journal of African History*, 11 (1970); A. Atmore and N. Westlake, 'A Liberal Dilemma: A Critique of the Oxford History of South Africa', *Race*, 14 (1972); S. Trapido, 'South Africa and the Historians', *African Affairs*, 71 (1972).

[10] O'Dowd's thesis — sometimes dubbed the Oppenheimer thesis, after the chairman of Anglo American — was published in A. Leftwich (ed.), *South Africa. Economic Growth and Political Change* (London, 1974).

[11] S. Trapido, 'South Africa in a Comparative Study of Industrialisation', *Journal of Development Studies*, 7 (1971).

[12] D. Yudelman,'Dan O'Meara's Afrikaner Nationalism', *Social Dynamics*, 9 (1983), 102.

[13] E. Thompson, *The Making of the English Working Class*, Preface. Cf. H. Kaye, *The British Marxist Historians* (London, 1984).

[14] D. Welsh, *The Roots of Segregation* (Cape Town, 1969). Welsh did not develop the point in his book.

[15] Marquard, *The Black Man's Burden*, p. 251. Wolpe was much influenced by the French anthropologist Meillassoux.

[16] M. Legassick, *The National Union of South African Students: Ethnic Cleavage in the South African Universities* (Los Angeles, 1968).

[17] A small part of it, with autobiographical critique, appeared in Elphick and Giliomee (eds.), *The Shaping*, ch. 7.

[18] J. Vansina, *Kingdoms of the Savanna* (Madison, 1966).

[19] For his later critique see Elphick and Giliomee (eds.), *The Shaping*, pp. 243-5.

[20] M. Legassick, 'The Griqua, the Sotho-Tswana, and the Missionaries, 1780-1840: The Politics of a Frontier Zone', Ph.D. thesis, UCLA, 1969, pp. 4-5.

[21] Legassick, 'The Griqua', pp. 21, 77-78.

[22] Legassick, 'The Griqua', pp. 2-3.

[23] Cf. e.g. I. Unger, 'The "New Left" and American History', *American Historical Review*, 72 (1967); D. H. Donald, 'Radical History on the Move', *New York Times Book Review*, 19 July 1970.

[24] Note the citations to Genovese's work in Legassick, 'Frontier Tradition'.

[25] E. Genovese, 'Class and Nation in Black America' in *In Red and Black* (London, 1971), *passim*.

[26] Legassick, 'Frontier Tradition'.

[27] R. Harris (ed.), *The Political Economy of Africa* (New York, 1975), p. vii.

[28] E.g. F. R. Johnstone, 'The Labour History of the Witwatersrand', *Social Dynamics*, 4 (1978).

[29] Wolpe, 'Capitalism and Cheap Labour-Power'; N. Bromberger in Leftwich (ed.), *South Africa*; M. Lipton. 'White Farming', *Journal of Commonwealth and Comparative Politics*, 1 (1974).

[30] E.g. Legassick, 'Forced Labour', pp. 268-70.

17. Class and race, structure and process

[1] P. van den Berghe, *South Africa. A Study in Conflict* (Berkeley, 1967), p. 267.

[2] Cf. above, p.157.

[3] Cf. W. Rodney, *A History of the Guyanese Working People* (London, 1982).

[4] One South African agronomist, S. D. Neumark, did so in *Economic Influences on the South African Frontier* (Stanford, 1957); written in Johannesburg in the early 1940s, this book was 'rediscovered' by materialists in the 1970s.

[5] E.g. Legassick, 'Forced Labour', p. 232.

[6] E.g. R. Leakey and R. Lewin, *Origins* (London, 1977), p. 242.

[7] For sophisticated expositions of this view see, e.g., 'No Siswe' [pseud.], *One Azania, One Nation* (London, 1980) and N. Alexander, *Sow the Wind* (Johannesburg, 1985).

[8] Legassick, 'Frontier Tradition'.

[9] M. Legassick, 'The Making of South African "Native Policy"'.

[10] S. Trapido, 'Reflections on Land, Office, and Wealth in the South African Republic, 1850–1900' in Marks and Atmore (eds.), *Economy and Society in Pre-Industrial South Africa*.

[11] Cf. e.g. the essays in Marks and Rathbone (eds.), *Industrialisation and Social Change* for such arguments.

[12] M. Legassick, 'Apartheid and the Struggle for Workers' Democracy', *Die Suid-Afrikaan* (Winter 1985), 26.

[13] Cf. esp. R. Davies, *Capital, the State and White Labour in South Africa, 1900-1960* (Brighton, 1979).

[14] The key text was A. G. Frank, *Capitalism and Underdevelopment in Latin America* (New York, 1967).

[15] W. Rodney, *How Europe Underdeveloped Africa* (Dar-es-Salaam, 1972).

[16] In East Africa the key works were C. Leys, *Underdevelopment in Kenya: The Politics of Neo-Colonialism* (London, 1975) and E. Brett, *Colonialism and Underdevelopment in East Africa* (London, 1973).

[17] C. Bundy, 'The Emergence and Decline of a South African Peasantry', *African Affairs*, 71 (1972). Cf. also, e.g., Legassick's chapter in R. Palmer and R. Parsons (eds.), *The Roots of Rural Poverty* (London, 1977).

[18] This was seen, for example, by the papers presented to a workshop on the social and economic history of South Africa held at Oxford in September 1974.

[19] D. Yudelman, 'Dan O'Meara's Afrikaner Nationalism', *Social Dynamics*, 9 (1983), 102.

[20] On the 'fractionalists' see esp. S. Clarke, 'Capital, Fractions of Capital and the State', *Capital and Class*, 5 (1978).

[21] B. Bozzoli, *The Political Nature of a Ruling Class*.

[22] D. O'Meara, 'The 1946 African Mineworkers' Strike in the Political Economy of South Africa', *Journal of Commonwealth and Comparative Politics*, 13 (1975).

[23] S. Marks, 'The Historiography of South Africa: Recent Developments', in B. Jewsiewicki and D. Newbury (eds.), *African Historiographies* (Beverly Hills, 1986), p. 170.

[24] For Bonner's use of 'tributary mode' see his essay in Marks and Atmore (eds.), *Economy and Society in Pre-Industrial South Africa*; this was in fact as much concerned with distribution as production.

[25] J. Guy, *The Destruction of the Zulu Kingdom* (London, 1979); P. Bonner, *Kings, Commoners and Concessionaires* (Johannesburg, 1983).

[26] J. Peires, *House of Phalo*; P. Delius, *The Land Belongs to Us* (Johannesburg, 1983).

[27] The present writer attended.

[28] F. A. van Jaarsveld, *From Van Riebeeck to Vorster*.

[29] Omer-Cooper did not reply, but did attack apartheid apologists in 'South Africa's Bantustans the Embodiment of Separate Nations?', paper to African Studies Association of Australia and the Pacific conference, Sydney, August 1981.

[30] For how the 'ethnic trap' could be avoided see esp. C. Hamilton, 'The Study of Southern African Pre-Colonial History: Bantustan Propaganda?', *Reality*, 14 (1982).

[31] J. Peires (ed.), *Before and After Shaka*.

[32] Atmore and Marks, 'The Imperial Factor in the Nineteenth Century'.

[33] E.g. essays by P. Delius in Marks and Atmore (eds.), *Economy and Society in Pre-Industrial South Africa* and by P. Harries in Marks and Rathbone (eds.), *Industrialisation and Social Change in South Africa* (London, 1982).

[34] For a response to a critique of 'the poverty of theory' see esp. P. Anderson, *Arguments Within English Marxism* (London, 1980).

[35] Thompson, *The Making of the English Working Class* (1968 ed.), p. 13.

[36] C. van Onselen, *Chibaro: African Mine Labour in Southern Rhodesia, 1900–1933* (London, 1976) and *Studies*.

[37] Cf. generally, e.g., Marks and Rathbone (eds.), *Industrialisation and Social Change*, *passim*.

[38] C. van Onselen, *Studies*, esp. 1, p. xvi.

[39] Selections of papers presented were published in B. Bozzoli (ed.), *Labour, Townships and Protest* (Johannesburg, 1979) and Bozzoli (ed.), *Town and Countryside in the Transvaal*.

18. Changing perspectives

[1] C. Vann Woodward, *American Counterpoint. Slavery and Racism in the North-South Dialogue* (Oxford, 1964), p. 234.

[2] Esp. N. Bromberger in Leftwich (ed.), *South Africa. Economic Growth and Political Change*. Another response from economists was B. Kantor and H. Kenny, 'The Pov-

erty of Neo-Marxism: The Case of South Africa', *Journal of Southern African Studies*, 3 (1976).

³ D. Yudelman, 'The Quest for a Neo-Marxist Approach to Contemporary South Africa', *South African Journal of Economics*, 45 (1977). Cf. his survey of the debate in 'Industrialization, Race Relations and Change in South Africa', *African Affairs*, 74 (1975).

⁴ D. Yudelman, *The Emergence of Modern South Africa: State, Capital and the Incorporation of Organized Labour on the South African Goldfields, 1902-1939* (Cape Town, 1984).

⁵ M. Lipton, *Capitalism and Apartheid* (Aldershot, 1985).

⁶ O'Meara's major work was published in 1983 under the title *Volkskapitalisme*; some of his earlier articles are cited in the bibliography below.

⁷ F. Johnstone, '"Most Painful to Our Hearts": South Africa Through the Eyes of the New School', *Canadian Journal of African Studies*, 16 (1982), 134 and esp. note 27.

⁸ O' Meara, *Volkskapitalisme*; T. Lodge, *Black Politics in South Africa* (Johannesburg, 1983).

⁹ E.g. Hermann Giliomee, 'Eighteenth Century Cape Society and Its Historiography', *Social Dynamics*, 9 (1983).

¹⁰ His major contribution to Cape history was an edition of the letters of Sir James Rose Innes.

¹¹ David Hedges in *Africa*, 53 (1983), 88.

¹² Wright was not in fact as totally opposed to the present-mindedness of historians as some suggested: cf. H. Wright, *The Burden of the Present* (Cape Town, 1977), esp. pp. 96, 103.

¹³ Some went further than he in talking of two quite separate paradigms: J. Wright, 'Clash of Paradigms', *Reality*, 9 (1977); cf. H. Wright, '*The Burden of the Present* and Its Critics, *Social Dynamics*, 6 (1980).

¹⁴ Cf. S. Marks, 'The Faultlines of Race', *New Statesman*, 12 September 1981. She took the word from Tom Nairn, a British Marxist.

¹⁵ Cf. H. Wolpe, 'The Liberation Struggle and Research', *Review of African Political Economy*, 32 (1985), 77.

¹⁶ Cf. e.g. B. Bozzoli, 'Marxism, Feminism and South African Studies', *Journal of Southern African Studies*, 9 (2) 1983; D. Gaitskell, *et al.*, 'Historiography in the 1970s: A Feminist Perspective' in *Southern African Studies: Retrospect and Prospect* (Edinburgh, 1983).

Conclusion

¹ H. Reynolds, *The Breaking of the Great Australian Silence: Aborigines in Australian Historiography 1955-1983* (London, 1984), p.1.

² E.g. H. Reynolds, *The Other Side of the Frontier* (Townsville, Queensland, 1982); F. Jennings, *The Invasion of America* (New York, 1976).

³ Cf. Berger, *The Writing of Canadian History*.

⁴ Cf. F. A. van Jaarsveld, 'Afrikaner Historiography' , in D. Ray *et al.* (eds.), *Into the '80s* (Vancouver, 1981).

⁵ De Kiewiet, *Imperial Factor*, p. 1.

⁶ J. Higham, *History*, p. 106.

⁷ Cf. esp. L. Thompson, *The Political Mythology of Apartheid* (New Haven, 1985).

⁸ As Maureen Swan did in *Weekly Mail*, 12-18 September 1986.

⁹ B. Bozzoli (ed.), *Town and Countryside in the Transvaal*, p. 2.

¹⁰ Cf. esp. Marks and Trapido (eds.), *The Politics of Race, Class and Nationalism*.

Select bibliography

Interviews
C. W. de Kiewiet
B. Hirson
A. Keppel-Jones
M. Macmillan
L. Thompson
S. van der Horst
J. van der Poel

Archival sources
University of Cape Town Library, Manuscripts and Archives Division: M. Ballinger papers; C. W. de Kiewiet papers; H. Mandelbrote papers; L. Marquard papers; J. Stewart papers; E. Walker papers
University of Cape Town: University Archives: miscellaneous papers re History Department
Cape Archives depot: letters by G. Theal in various collections; Theal press cuttings
University of Stellenbosch Library: G. Theal papers
South African Library, Cape Town; J. X. Merriman papers; G. Stow papers; G. Theal letter
Rhodes University Library: G. Cory papers
University of the Witwatersrand Archives: J. S. Marais papers
Yew Tree Cottage, Long Wittenham, Oxfordshire: W. M. Macmillan papers
Lady Margaret Hall, Oxford: L. Sutherland papers
Rhodes House Library, Oxford: Notes by W. M. Macmillan and others on J. Philip papers
Oxford University Press: archives
Cornell University Library, Ithaca: C. W. de Kiewiet papers
Cambridge University Library: Cambridge University Press archives
In possession of J. Naidoo, Niort, France: letters from C. W. de Kiewiet.

Published sources
1. *General Non-African*
Allen, H. C. 'F. J. Turner and the Frontier in American History', in Allen, H. and Hill, C. (eds.) *British Essays in American History* (New York, 1957)

Anderson, P. *Arguments Within English Marxism* (London, 1980)

Barker, J. *The Superhistorians* (New York, 1982)

Barnes, H. E. *History of Historical Writing* (Norman, Oklahoma, 1932)

Becker, C. 'What is Historiography?', *American Historical Review*, 44 (1938)

Berger, C. *The Writing of Canadian History* (Toronto, 1976)

Bolt, C. *Victorian Attitudes to Race* (London, 1971)

Breisach, E. *Historiography Ancient, Medieval and Modern* (Chicago, 1983)

Burrow, J. W. *A Liberal Descent. Victorian Historians and the English Past* (Cambridge, 1981)

Butterfield, H. *The Whig Interpretation of History* (Cambridge, 1931)

Butterfield, H. *The Englishman and His History* (Cambridge, 1945)

Carr, E. H. *What is History?* (Harmondsworth, 1964)

Constantino, R. 'Notes on Historical Writing for the Third World', *Journal of Contemporary Asia*, 10 (1980)

Cook, R. *The Maple Leaf Forever* (Toronto, 1971)

Cunliffe, M. and Winks, R. (eds.) *Pastmasters* (New York, 1969)

Donald, D. H. 'Radical History on the Move', *New York Times Book Review*, 19 (1970)

Elton, G. R. 'Herbert Butterfield and the Study of History', *Historical Journal*, 27 (1984)

Etherington, N. *Theories of Imperialism. War, Conquest and Capital* (London, 1984)

Fehrenbacker, D. E. *History and American Society. Essays of David M. Potter* (New York, 1973)

Fitzgerald, F. *America Revised* (New York, 1980)

Fitzsimons, M. A. *The Past Recaptured. Great Historians and the History of History* (Notre Dame, 1983)

Frank, A. G. *Capitalism and Underdevelopment in Latin America* (New York, 1967)

Gay, P. *Style in History* (New York, 1974)

Genovese, E. *In Red and Black* (London, 1971)

Guha, R. (ed.) *Subaltern Studies* (New Delhi, 1980)

Hancock, W. K. *Australia* (London, 1930)

Hancock, W. K. *Country and Calling* (London, 1934)

Harte, N. B. (ed.) *The Study of Economic History* (London, 1971)

Higham, J. *History* (Englewood Cliffs, New Jersey, 1965)

Hobsbawm, E. *Worlds of Labour* (London, 1984)

Hofstadter, R. *The Progressive Historians* (New York, 1969)

Huxley, J. et al. *We Europeans. A Survey of 'Racial' Problems* (Harmondsworth, 1935)

Jennings, F. *The Invasion of America* (New York, 1976)

Johnston, R. et al. *Making Histories* (London, 1982)

Kaye, H. *The British Marxist Historians* (London, 1984)

Kenyon, J. *The History Men* (London, 1983)

King, R. H. *A Southern Renaissance* (New York, 1980)

Kirby, J. T. *Darkness at the Dawning. Race and Reform in the Progressive South* (Philadelphia, 1972)

Lorimer, D. *Colour, Class and the Victorians* (Leicester, 1978)

MacDougall, H. A. *Racial Myth in English History* (Montreal, 1982)

Madden, F. and Fieldhouse, D. (eds.) *Oxford and the Idea of Commonwealth* (London, 1982)

Montagu, A. (ed.) *The Concept of Race* (New York, 1964)

Pascoe, R. *The Manufacture of Australian History* (Melbourne, 1979)

Pole, J. R. 'The American Past: Is It Still Usable?', *Journal of American Studies*, 1 (1967)

Pole, J. R. *Paths to the American Past* (New York, 1979)

Read, C. (ed.) *The Constitution Reconsidered* (New York, 1938)

Reynolds, H. *The Other Side of the Frontier* (Townsville, 1982)

Reynolds, H. *The Breaking of the Great Australian Silence: Aborigines in Australian History 1955–1983* (London, 1984)

Rich, P. *Race and Empire in British Politics* (Cambridge, 1986)

Rodney, W. *A History of the Guyanese Working People* (London, 1982)

Smith, P. *The Historian and History* (New York, 1960)

Stepan, N. *The Idea of Race in Science* (London, 1982)

Stephenson, W. H. *Southern Historians in the Making* (Baton Rouge, 1964)

Stephenson, W. H. *The South Lives in History* (Baton Rouge, 1955)

Stone, L. *The Past and the Present* (London, 1981)

Thompson, E. P. *The Making of the English Working Class* (London, 1963; Harmondsworth, 1968)

Thompson, E. P. *The Poverty of Theory and Other Essays* (London, 1978)

Unger, I. 'The "New Left" and American History', *American Historical Review*, 72 (1967)

Van den Berghe, P. *Race and Racism* (New York, 1967)

Williams, E. *British Historians and the West Indies* (Port of Spain, 1964)

Williamson, J. *The Crucible of Race* (New York, 1984)

Winks, R. (ed.) *The Historiography of the British Empire-Commonwealth* (Durham, N.C., 1966)

Wish, J. H. *The American Historian: A Socio-Intellectual History of the Writing of the American Past* (New York, 1960)

Wynn, G. 'Reflections on the Writing of New Zealand History', *New Zealand Journal of History*, 18 (1984).

2. African and South African

Adler, T.(ed.) *Perspectives on South Africa. A Collection of Working Papers* (Johannesburg, 1977)

Agar-Hamilton, J. A. I. *The Native Policy of the Voortrekkers* (Cape Town, n.d. [1928])

Agar-Hamilton, J. A. I. *South Africa* (London, 1934)

Agar-Hamilton, J. A. I. *The Road to the North* (London, 1937)

Alexander, N. *Sow the Wind* (Johannesburg, 1985)

Andrews, W. H. *Class Struggles in South Africa* (Cape Town, 1941)

Atmore, A. and Marks, S. 'The Imperial Factor in South Africa in the Nineteenth Century: Towards a Reassessment', *Journal of Imperial and Commonwealth History*, 3 (1974)

Atmore, A. and Westlake, N. 'A Liberal Dilemma: A Critique of the Oxford History of South Africa', *Race*, 14 (1972)

Barnes, L. *Caliban in Africa. An Impression of Colour Madness* (London, 1930)

Barnett, U. *A Vision of Order. Black South African Literature in English 1914-80* (London, 1984)

Beinart, W. 'Scholarly Burdens in South Africa', *Journal of African History*, 19 (1978)

Beinart, W. *The Political Economy of Pondoland, 1870-1930* (Cambridge, 1982)

Beinart, W., Delius, P. and Trapido, S. (eds.) *Putting a Plough to the Ground. Accumulation and Dispossession in Rural South Africa 1850-1930* (Johannesburg, 1986)

Benyon, J. *et al.* (eds.) *Essays in Local History* (Cape Town, 1974)

Bernstein, H. and Depelchin, J. 'The Object of African History: A Materialist Perspective', *History in Africa*, 5 (1978) and 6 (1979)

Bird, J. (ed.) *Annals of Natal*, 2 vols. (Pietermaritzburg, 1888)

Bleek, W. and Lloyd, L. *Specimens of Bushman Folklore* (London, 1911)

Böeseken, A. J. 'Dr George McCall Theal', *Dictionary of South African Biography*, 4 (Cape Town, 1981)

Bonacich, E. 'Class Approaches to Ethnicity and Race', *The Insurgent Sociologist*, 10 (1980)

Bonacich, E. 'Capitalism and Race Relations in South Africa: A Split Labor Market Analysis' in Zeitlin, M. (ed.) *Political Power and Social Theory. A Research Annual*, 2 (1981)

Bonn, M. J. *Wandering Scholar* (New York, 1948)

Bonner, P. *Kings, Commoners and Concessionaires* (Cambridge, 1983)

Bosman, G. C. R. *The Industrialisation of South Africa* (Rotterdam, 1938)

Bosman, I. D. *Dr George McCall Theal as die Geskiedskrywer van Suid Afrika* (Amsterdam, n.d.[?1932])

Bozzoli, B. (ed.) *Labour, Townships and Protest* (Johannesburg, 1979)

Bozzoli, B. 'Capital and the State in South Africa', *Review of African Political Economy* 11 (1979)

Bozzoli, B. 'Challenging Local Orthodoxies', *Social Dynamics* 6 (1981)

Bozzoli, B. *The Political Nature of a Ruling Class* (London, 1981)

Bozzoli, B. (ed.) *Town and Countryside in the Transvaal* (Johannesburg, 1983)

Bozzoli, B. 'Marxism, Feminism and South African Studies', *Journal of Southern African Studies*, 9 (1983)

Bredekamp, H. 'Marxist History on South Africa Before the 1970s', University of the Western Cape Centre for Research in Africa, *Occasional Papers*, 1 (1985)

Brett, E. *Colonialism and Underdevelopment in East Africa* (London, 1973)

Brookes, E. *The History of Native Policy in South Africa from 1830 to the Present Day* (Cape Town, 1924; 2nd ed. Pretoria, 1927)

Brookes, E. *A History of the University of Natal* (Pietermaritzburg, 1966)

Brookes, E. *A South African Pilgrimage* (Johannesburg, 1977)

Brownlee, F.(ed.) *The Transkeian Territories: Historical Records* (Lovedale, 1923)

Bryant, A. *Olden Times in Zululand and Natal* (London, 1929)

Bryant, A. *A History of the Zulu and Neighbouring Tribes* (Cape Town, 1964)

Bundy, C. 'The Emergence and Decline of a South African Peasantry', *African Affairs*, 71 (1972)

Bundy, C. *The Rise and Fall of the South African Peasantry* (London, 1979)

Buroway, M. 'The Capitalist State in South Africa: Marxist and Sociological Perspectives on Race and Class', *Political Power and Social Theory*, 2 (1981)

Butler, G. *Bursting World* (Cape Town, 1983)

Butler, J., Elphick, R. and Welsh, D. (eds.) *Democratic Liberalism in South Africa* (Middletown, 1987)

Cameron, T. and Spies, B. (eds.) *Illustrated History of South Africa* (Johannesburg, 1986)

Cappon, J. *Britain's Title in South Africa* (London, 1901)

Cell, J. W. *The Highest Stage of White Supremacy. The Origins of Segregation in South Africa and the American South* (Cambridge, 1982)

Chainaiwa, D. 'Historiographical Traditions of Southern Africa', *Journal of Southern*

African Affairs, 3 (1978)

Charney, C. 'Challenging Liberal Orthodoxy', *The Times Higher Education Supplement*, 4 September 1981

Chase, J. C. *The Cape of Good Hope and the Eastern Province* (London, 1843)

Clarke, S. 'Capital, Fractions of Capital and the State: Neo-Marxist Analysis of the South African State', *Capital and Class*, 5 (1978)

Cloete, H. *Five Lectures on the Emigration of the Dutch Farmers* (Cape Town, 1856)

Coetzee, J. M. 'Idleness in South Africa', *Social Dynamics*, 8 (1982)

Cooper, F. 'Peasants, Capitalists and Historians', *Journal of Southern African Studies*, 7 (1981)

Cope, R. K. *Comrade Bill* (Cape Town, 1943)

Cornevin, M. *Apartheid: Power and Historical Falsification* (Paris, 1980)

Cory, G. E. *The Rise of South Africa*, 5 vols (London, 1910-30); 6 vols. (reprint, Cape Town, 1965)

Couzens, T. *The New African. A Study of the Life and Work of H. I. E.Dhlomo* (Johannesburg, 1985)

Crapanzano, V. *Waiting. The Whites of South Africa* (London, 1985)

Cronje, G. (ed.) *Aspekte van die Suid-Afrikaanse Historiografie* (Pretoria, 1967)

Crush, J. and Rogerson, C. 'New Wave African Historiography and African Historical Geography', *Progress in Human Geography*, 7 (1983)

Curtin, P. D. 'The British Empire and Commonwealth in Recent Historiography', *American Historical Review*, 65 (1959)

Davenport, T. R. H. and Hunt, K. *The Right to the Land* (Cape Town, 1974)

Davenport, T. R. H. *South Africa. A Modern History* (London, 1977)

Davies, R., Kaplan, D., Morris, M. and O'Meara, D. 'Class Struggle and the Periodisation of the State in South Africa', *Review of African Political Economy*, 7 (1976)

Davies, R. *Capital, State and White Labour in South Africa 1900-1960. An Historical Materialist Analysis* (Brighton, 1979)

De Kiewiet, C. W. *British Colonial Policy and the South African Republics* (London, 1929)

De Kiewiet, C. W. 'The Frontier and the Constitution' in Read, C. (ed.) *The Constitution Reconsidered* (New York, 1938)

De Kiewiet, C. W. *The Imperial Factor in South Africa* (Cambridge, 1937)

De Kiewiet, C.W. *A History of South Africa Social and Economic* (Oxford, 1941)

De Kiewiet, C. W. *The Anatomy of South African Misery* (London, 1956)

De Kock, M. H. *Selected Subjects in the Economic History of South Africa* (Cape Town, 1924)

Delius, P. *The Land Belongs to Us* (Johannesburg, 1983)

Denoon, D. 'Synthesising South African History', *Transafrican Journal of History*, 2 (1972)

Denoon, D. and Kuper, A. 'Nationalist Historians in Search of a Nation: The "New Historiography" in Dar es Salaam', *African Affairs*, 69 (1970)

Derricourt, R. 'Early European Travellers in the Transkei and Ciskei', *African Studies*, 35 (1976)

De Villiers, A. (ed.) *English-speaking South Africa Today* (Cape Town, 1976)

Dike, K.O. *Trade and Politics in the Niger Delta, 1830-1885* (London, 1956)

Du Bruyn, J. 'The Forgotten Factor Sixteen Years Later: Some Trends in Historical Writing on Precolonial South Africa', *Kleio* 16 (1984)

Duminy, A. and Ballard, C. (eds.) *The Anglo-Zulu War of 1879: Towards a Reassessment*

(Pietermaritzburg, 1979)

Du Toit, D. *Capital and Labour in South Africa: Class Struggles in the 1970s* (London, 1981)

Elphick, R. *Kraal and Castle* (New Haven, 1977)

Elphick, R. and Giliomee, H.(eds.) *The Shaping of South African Society* (Cape Town, 1979)

Elphick, R. 'A Comparative History of White Supremacy', *Journal of Interdisciplinary History*, 13 (1983)

Elphick, R. 'Methodology in South African Historiography: A Defence of Idealism and Empiricism', *Social Dynamics,* 9 (1983)

Etherington, N. 'Labour Supplies and the Genesis of South African Confederation', *Journal of African History*, 20 (1979)

Fage, J. 'Continuity and Change in the Writing of West African History', *African Affairs,* 70 (1971)

February, V. (ed.) *From the Arsenal* (Leiden, 1983)

Forman, L. *Chapters in the History of the March to Progress* (Cape Town, n.d.)

Forman, L. *Black and White in S. A. History,* ed. Alexander, R. (n.p., n.d.)

Fouché, L. *Die Evolutie van die Trekboer* (Pretoria, 1909)

Fouché, L. *Mapungubwe* (Cambridge, 1937)

Frankel, S. H. *Capital Investment in Africa* (Oxford, 1938)

Fredrickson, G. *White Supremacy* (New York, 1981)

Freund, B. *The Making of Contemporary Africa* (London, 1984)

Freund, W. M. 'Race in the Social Structure of South Africa 1652-1836', *Race and Class,* 17 (1976)

Fuze, M. *The Black People and Whence They Came* (Pietermaritzburg, 1979)

Fyfe, C. (ed.) *African Studies since 1945* (London, 1976)

Gaitskell, D. *et al.* 'Historiography in the 1970's: A Feminist Perspective', in *Southern African Studies: Retrospect and Prospect* (Edinburgh, 1983)

Galbraith, J. *Reluctant Empire* (Berkeley and Los Angeles, 1963)

Gann, L. H. 'Liberal Interpretations of South African History: A Review Article', *Rhodes-Livingstone Journal,* 25 (1959)

Garson, N. 'South African History: A New Look', *African Studies,* 29 (1970)

Gibson, J.Y. *The Story of the Zulus* (London, 1908)

Giliomee, H. 'Eighteenth Century Cape Society and Its Historiography: Culture, Race and Class', *Social Dynamics*, 9 (1983)

Giliomee, H. *The History in Our Politics* (Cape Town, 1986)

Godlonton, R. *A Narrative of the Irruption of the Kaffir Hordes into the Eastern Province of the Cape of Good Hope* (Grahamstown, 1835-36)

Goldberg, M. 'Capital, State and White Labour in South Africa', *Social Dynamics,* 6 (1980)

Goldberg, M. 'Formulating Worker Consciousness', *Social Dynamics,* 7 (1981)

Gomas, J. *100 Years.'Emancipation of Slaves.' Smash the Chains of Slavery!* (Cape Town, n.d.[1934])

Graaff, J. de V. 'H. M. Robertson 1905-1984', *South African Journal of Economics,* 52 (1983)

Gray, R. Reviews of M. Wilson and L. Thompson (eds.) *The Oxford History of South Africa* in *Race,* 11 (1969) and 14 (1972)

Greenberg, S. B. *Race and State in Capitalist Development: Comparative Perspectives* (New Haven, 1980)

Greenberg, S. B. Review of D. O'Meara, *Volkskapitalisme* in *Social Dynamics*, 9 (1983)

Grosskopf, J. F. W. *Rural Impoverishment and Rural Exodus* (Stellenbosch, 1932)

Grundlingh, A. 'George Orwell's Nineteen Eighty-Four: Some Reflections on Its Relevance to the Study of History in South Africa', *Kleio*, 16 (1984)

Grundlingh, A. 'Some Perspectives on the Function and Manufacturing of History in Current South African Society', *History News*, 25 (1985)

Guy, J. *The Destruction of the Zulu Kingdom* (London, 1979)

Hamilton, C. A. 'The Study of Southern African Pre-Colonial History', *Reality*, 14 (1982)

Hancock, I. R. and Markus, A. 'Race and Class: The Neo-Marxists, South Africa and Australia', *Historical Studies*, 18 (1978)

Hancock, W. K. *Survey of British Commonwealth Affairs*, 2. *Problems of Economic Policy 1918-1939*, Part 2 (London, 1942)

Harris, R. (ed.) *The Political Economy of Africa* (Cambridge, Mass., Boston, 1975)

Hirson, B. 'Revisionists, Neo-Marxists and Labour History in South Africa', *Journal of Commonwealth and Comparative Politics*, 21 (1983)

Hobson, J. A. *The War in South Africa* (London, 1900)

Hodgson, M. 'The Hottentots to 1828: A Problem in Labour and Administration', *Report of the South African Association for the Advancement of Science*, 21 (1924)

Holden, W.C. *History of the Colony of Natal* (London, 1855)

Holden, W. C. *The Past and Future of the Kaffir Races* (London, 1866)

Horwitz, R. *The Political Economy of South Africa* (London, 1967)

Houghton, D. H. *The South African Economy* (Cape Town, 1964)

Hughes, K. 'Challenges from the Past: Reflections on Liberalism and Radicalism in the Writing of South African History', *Social Dynamics*, 3 (1977)

Hughes, K. 'On the Shaping of South African Society', *Social Dynamics*, 5 (1979)

Hunt, D. R. 'An Account of the Bapedi', *Bantu Studies*, 5 (1931)

Hunter, G. (ed.) *Industrialisation and Race Relations* (London, 1965)

Hunter (Wilson), M. *Reaction to Conquest* (London, 1936)

Innes, D. *Anglo American and the Rise of Modern South Africa* (London, 1984)

Jaffe, H. *Storia del Sudafrika* (Milan, 1980)

James, W. 'Social History and Socialist Historians', *Social Dynamics*, 10 (1984)

James, W. 'Materialist History, Materialist Theory: A Reply to Charles van Onselen', *Social Dynamics*, 9 (1983)

Jewsiewicki, B. and Newbury, D. (eds.) *African Historiographies. What History for Which Africa?* (Beverly Hills, 1986)

Johnstone, F. R. 'White Prosperity and White Supremacy in South Africa Today', *African Affairs*, 69 (1970)

Johnstone, F. R. *Class, Race and Gold. A Study of Class Relations and Racial Discrimination in South Africa* (London, 1976)

Johnstone, F. R. 'The Labour History of the Witwatersrand', *Social Dynamics*, 4 (1978)

Johnstone, F. R. 'Comments', *Review*, 3 (1979)

Johnstone, F. R. '"Most Painful to Our Hearts": South Africa through the Eyes of the New School', *Canadian Journal of African Studies*, 16 (1982)

Jones, S. 'On Economic History in General and the Economic History of South Africa in Particular', *Perspectives in Economic History*, 1 (1982)

Jubber, K. 'Sociology and Its Sociological Content: The Case of the Rise of Marxist Sociology in South Africa', *Social Dynamics*, 9 (1983)

Kallaway, P. 'What Happened in South African History?', *Concept*, 6 (1975)

Kantor, B. and Kenney, H. 'The Poverty of Neo-Marxism: The Case of South Africa', *Journal of Southern African Studies*, 3 (1976)

Kaplan, D. E. 'The South African State: The Origins of a Racially Exclusive Democracy', *The Insurgent Sociologist*, 10 (1980)

Keegan, T. 'Crisis and Catharsis in South African Agriculture', *African Affairs*, 84 (1985)

Keppel-Jones, A. *When Smuts Goes* (Cape Town, 1947)

Keppel-Jones, A. *South Africa, A Short History* (London, 1949)

Keppel-Jones, A. *Friends or Foes?* (Pietermaritzburg, 1950)

Keppel-Jones, A. 'Where Did We Take the Wrong Turning?', *Race Relations Journal*, 26 (1959)

Keppel-Jones, A. 'A Case of Minority Rule: The Cape Colony, 1854-1898', *Canadian Historical Papers*, 1966

Keppel-Jones, A. 'Culture, Race and History: A Question Without an Answer' in Shaw, T. and Heard, K. (eds.) *Co-operation and Conflict in Southern Africa* (Washington, 1977)

Keppel-Jones, A. *Rhodes and Rhodesia* (Pietermaritzburg, 1983)

Kirkwood, K. (ed.) *African Affairs* (London, 1969)

Ki-Zerbo, J. (ed.) *General History of Africa* 1 (London, 1980)

Kleynhans, P. 'Interpreting and Teaching S.A. History', *Educational Journal* (1972)

Krige, E. *The Social System of the Zulus* (London, 1936)

Kuper, A. *Anthropology and Anthropologists. The British School 1922-1972* (London, 1972)

Kuper, L. *Race, Class and Power* (London, 1977)

Lau, B. '"Thank God the Germans Came": Heinrich Vedder and Namibian History', in Gottschalk, K. and Saunders, C. (eds.) *Africa Seminar. Collected Papers*, 2 (Cape Town, 1981)

Le Cordeur, B. A. 'The Reconstruction of South African History', *South African Historical Journal*, 17 (1985)

Le Cordeur, B. A. *The Power of History* (Cape Town, 1986)

Leftwich, A. (ed.) *South Africa. Economic Growth and Political Change* (London, 1974)

Legassick, M. 'The Dynamics of Modernisation in South Africa', *Journal of African History*, 13 (1972)

Legassick, M. 'South Africa: Capital Accumulation and Violence', *Economy and Society*, 3 (1974)

Legassick, M. 'Legislation, Ideology and Economy in Post-1948 South Africa', *Journal of Southern African Studies*, 1 (1974)

Legassick, M. 'Race, Industrialisation and Social Change in South Africa: The Case of R. F. A. Hoernlé', *African Affairs*, 74 (1976)

Legassick, M. 'The Concept of Pluralism: A Critique' in Gutkind, P. and Waterson, P. (eds.) *African Social Studies. A Radical Reader* (London, 1978)

Legassick, M. 'Records of Protest and Challenge', *Journal of African History*, 20 (1979)

Legassick, M. 'Apartheid and the Struggle for Workers' Democracy in South Africa', *Die Suid-Afrikaan* (1985)

Le Roux, F. J. and Van Zyl, D. (eds.) *'n Eeu van Onreg* (Cape Town, 1985)

Lewin, J. *Politics and the Law in South Africa* (London, 1963)

Lewis, J. 'The Rise and Fall of the South African Peasantry: A Critique', *Journal of Southern African Studies*, 11 (1984)

Lewsen, P. 'The Oxford History of South Africa: An Attempt at Revaluation', *South African Historical Journal*, 5 (1973)

Leyburn, J. G. *Frontier Folkways* (New Haven, 1935)

Leys, C. *Underdevelopment in Kenya: The Politics of Neo-colonialism* (London, 1975)

Liebenberg, B. 'Eric Walker's Interpretation of Recent South African History', *Historia*, 11 (1966)

Liebenberg, B. (comp.) *Opstelle oor die Suid-Afrikaanse Historiografie* (Pretoria, 1975)

Lipton, M. 'The Debate about South Africa: Neo-Marxists and Neo-Liberals', *African Affairs*, 78 (1979)

Lipton, M. *Capitalism and Apartheid* (Aldershot, 1985)

Lodge, T. *Black Politics in South Africa Since 1945* (Johannesburg, 1983)

Lodge, T. (ed.) *Resistance and Ideology in Settler Societies* (Johannesburg, 1986)

Lonsdale, J. 'From Colony to Industrial State: South African Historiography as Seen from England', *Social Dynamics*, 9 (1983)

MacCrone, I. D. *Race Attitudes in South Africa* (Johannesburg, 1937)

Macgaffey, W. 'Concepts of Race in the Historiography of Northeast Africa', *Journal of African History*, 7 (1966)

Macmillan, M. *Champion of Africa: W. M. Macmillan The Second Phase* (Long Wittenham, 1985)

Macmillan, W. M. *The South African Agrarian Problem and Its Historical Development* (Johannesburg, 1919)

Macmillan, W. M. *The Land, the Native and Unemployment* (Johannesburg, 1924)

Macmillan, W. M. 'Native Land and the Provisions of the Natives Land Act of 1913' in *European and Bantu: Papers and Addresses Read at the Conference on Native Affairs 27 to 29 September 1923* (Cape Town, 1923)

Macmillan, W. M. *The Cape Colour Question* (London, 1927)

Macmillan, W. M. *Bantu, Boer, and Briton* (London, 1929; 2nd ed. Oxford, 1963)

Macmillan, W. M. *Complex South Africa* (London, 1930)

Macmillan, W. M. *Warning from the West Indies* (Harmondsworth, 1938)

Macmillan, W. M. *Africa Emergent* (London, 1938)

Macmillan, W. M. *Democratize the Empire!* (London, 1941)

Macmillan, W. M. *The Road to Self-Rule* (London, 1959)

Macmillan, W. M. *My South African Years* (Cape Town, 1975)

Magubane, P. *The Politics of History in South Africa* (New York, 1982)

'Majeke, N.' (pseud.) *The Role of the Missionaries in Conquest* (Alexandra, 1952; new ed. Cumberwood, n.d.)

Marais, J. S. *The Cape Coloured People* (Johannesburg, 1939)

Marais, J. S. *Maynier and the First Boer Republic* (Cape Town, 1944)

Marais, J. S. *The Study of South African History* (Johannesburg, 1945)

Marais, J. S. *The Fall of Kruger's Republic* (Oxford, 1961)

Marks, S. *Reluctant Rebellion* (Oxford, 1970)

Marks, S. 'African and Afrikaner History', *Journal of African History*, 11 (1970)

Marks, S. 'Khoisan Resistance to the Dutch', *Journal of African History*, 12 (1972)

Marks, S. 'Liberalism, Social Realities and South African History', *Journal of Commonwealth Political Studies*, 8 (1972)

Marks, S. and Atmore, A. (eds.) *Economy and Society in Pre-Industrial South Africa* (London, 1980)

Marks, S. 'Towards a People's History of South Africa? Recent Developments in the Historiography of South Africa' in Samuel, R. (ed.) *People's History and Socialist*

Theory (London, 1981)

Marks, S. 'The Faultlines of Race', *New Statesman*, 12 September 1981

Marks, S. 'Scrambling for South Africa', *Journal of African History*, 22 (1982)

Marks, S. and Rathbone, R. (eds.) *Industrialisation and Social Change in South Africa* (London, 1982)

Marks, S. *The Ambiguities of Dependence. Class, Nationalism and the State in Twentieth Century Natal* (Baltimore, 1986)

Marks S. and Trapido, S. (eds.) *The Politics of Race, Class and Nationalism in Twentieth Century South Africa* (London, 1987)

Marquard, L. *The Black Man's Burden* (London, 1943)

Marwick, B. *The Swazi* (Cambridge, 1940)

Mason, D. 'Industrialisation, Race and Class Conflict in South Africa', *Ethnic and Racial Studies*, 3 (1980)

Massie, R. H. (comp.) *The Native Tribes of the Transvaal* (London, 1905)

Matthews, Z. K. *Freedom for My People* (Cape Town, 1981)

Maxwell, W. *Random Reflections on the Study of History in South Africa* (Grahamstown, 1956)

Mbeki, G. *The Peasants' Revolt* (Harmondsworth, 1964)

Mbeki, T. 'South Africa: The Historical Injustice' in Anglis, D. G., Shaw, T. M. and Widstrand, C. G. (eds.) *Conflict and Change in Southern Africa* (Washington, 1978)

McAdam, A. 'Leonard Barnes and South Africa', *Social Dynamics*, 3 (1977)

'A Member of the Late Committee'. *Remarks upon Some of the Results Depicted by the Publication of a Portion of the Cape Records* (Cape Town, 1841)

'Mnguni' (pseud.) *Three Hundred Years* (Cape Town, 1952)

Mokone, S. *Majority Rule: Some Notes* (n.p., n.d.)

Molema, S.M. *The Bantu Past and Present* (Edinburgh, 1920)

Molema, S. M. *Chief Moroka* (Cape Town, 1951)

Moodie, D. (comp.) *The Record* (Cape Town, 1838-41, reprinted Cape Town, 1960)

Morris, M. 'The Development of Capitalism in Southern African Agriculture: Class Struggle in the Countryside' *Economy and Society*, 5 (1976)

Muller, C. (ed.) *Five Hundred Years* (Pretoria, 1969; 3rd ed., 1981)

Murray, B. *Wits. The Early Years* (Johannesburg, 1982)

Neale, C. *Writing 'Independent' History. African Historiography 1960-1980* (Westport, 1985)

Nel, P. 'Recent Marxist Analyses of South Africa: The Question Concerning Explanatory Superiority', *South African Journal of Philosophy*, 2 (1983)

Neumark, S. D. *Economic Influences on the South African Frontier* (Stanford, 1957)

Newton, A. P. 'Africa and Historical Research', *Journal of the Africa Society*, 22 (1922-23)

Newton, A. P. and Benians, E. (ed.) *The Cambridge History of the British Empire*, 8 (Cambridge, 1936)

Newton-King, S. and Malherbe, C. *The Khoikhoi Rebellion in the Eastern Cape* (Cape Town, 1981)

Norton, W. A. 'Dr Theal and the Records of South-Eastern Africa', *South African Journal of Science*, 19 (1922)

'No Siswe' (pseud.) *One Azania One Nation* (London, 1980)

Odendaal, A. *Vukani Bantu!* (Cape Town, 1984)

Ogot, B. 'Towards a History of Kenya', *Kenya Historical Review*, 4 (1976)

Oliver, R. and Fage, J. *A Short History of Africa* (Harmondsworth, 1962)

Olivier, S. *The Anatomy of African Misery* (London, 1927)

Olivier, S. *White Capital and Coloured Labour* (London, 1929; 2nd ed. 1933)

O'Meara, D. 'The 1946 African Mineworkers' Strike in the Political Economy of South Africa', *Journal of Commonwealth and Comparative Politics*, 13 (1975)

O'Meara, D. 'The Afrikaner Broederbond 1927-48: Class Vanguard of Afrikaner Nationalism', *Journal of Southern African Studies*, 3 (1977)

O'Meara, D. *Volkskapitalisme. Class, Capital and Ideology in the Development of Afrikaner Nationalism* (Johannesburg, 1983)

Omer-Cooper, J. *The Zulu Aftermath* (London, 1966)

Palmer, R. and Parsons, N. (eds.) *The Roots of Rural Poverty* (London, 1977)

Parry, R. '"In a Sense Citizens but Not Altogether Citizens": Rhodes, Race and the Ideology of Segregation in the Cape in the Late Nineteenth Century', *Canadian Journal of African Studies*, 17 (1983)

Peires, J. 'On the Burden of the Present', *Social Dynamics*, 3 (1977)

Peires, J. (ed.) *Before and After Shaka* (Grahamstown, 1979)

Peires, J. 'Lovedale and Literature for the Bantu', *History in Africa*, 7 (1980)

Peires, J. *The House of Phalo* (Johannesburg, 1981)

Peregrino, F. *A Short History of the Native Tribes of South Africa* (London, 1899)

Philip, J. *Researches in South Africa*, 2 vols. (London, 1828)

Plaatje, S. T. *Native Life in South Africa* (London, 1916; new. ed. Johannesburg, n.d.[1982])

Posel, D. 'Rethinking the "Race-Class Debate" in South African Historiography', *Social Dynamics*, 9 (1983)

Preller, G. *Day Dawn in South Africa* (Pretoria, 1938)

The Prominent Men of Cape Colony, South Africa (Portland, Oregon, 1902)

Quispel, C. and Ross, R. 'Theorie en Mentaliteit in de Historiografie van Zuid-Afrika', *Tijdschrift Voor Geschiedenis*, 98 (1985)

Ranger, T. *Emerging Themes of African History* (Nairobi, 1968)

Ranger, T. 'The New Historiography in Dar es Salaam: An Answer', *African Affairs*, 70 (1971)

Reyburn, H. 'Studies in Cape Frontier History', *The Critic*, 3-4 (1934-36)

Rich, P. 'Ideology in a Plural Society: the Case of South African Segregation', *Social Dynamics*, 1 (1975)

Rich, P. *White Power and the Liberal Conscience* (Manchester, 1984)

Riemenschneider, D. (ed.) *The History and Historiography of Commonwealth Literature* (Tübingen, 1983)

Roberts, A. 'The Historiography of Central Africa', *History in Africa*, 5 (1978)

Roberts, M. and Trollip, A. *The South African Opposition* (Cape Town, 1947)

Robertson, H. M. '150 Years of Economic Contact Between Black and White', *South African Journal of Economics*, 2-3 (1934-35)

Robertson, H. M. *South Africa. Economic and Political Aspects* (Durham, N.C., 1957)

Rodney, W. *How Europe Underdeveloped Africa* (Dar-es-Salaam, 1972)

Ross, A. *John Philip (1775-1851). Missions, Race and Politics in South Africa* (Aberdeen, 1986)

Ross, R. 'The First Two Centuries of Colonial Agriculture in the Cape Colony : A Historiographical Review', *Social Dynamics*, 9 (1983)

Ross, R. 'Pre-Industrial and Industrial Racial Stratification in South Africa' in Ross, R. (ed.), *Racism and Colonialism* (The Hague, 1982)

Roux, E. *S. P. Bunting* (Cape Town, 1944)

Roux, E. *Time Longer Than Rope* (London, 1948; 2nd ed. Madison, 1964)

Roux, E. and W. *Rebel Pity* (London, 1971)

Saunders, C. 'Tile and the Thembu Church', *Journal of African History*, 10 (1970)

Saunders, C. 'U.C.T. Historians 1: L. M. Thompson', *Janus* (1977)

Saunders, C. 'James Read: Towards a Reassessment', Institute of Commonwealth Studies, *Collected Seminar Papers*, 7 (1977)

Saunders, C. 'F. Z. S. Peregrino and the *South African Spectator*', *Quarterly Bulletin of the South African Library*, 33 (1978)

Saunders, C. 'The Missing Link in Theal's Career: The Historian as Labour Agent', *History in Africa*, 7 (1980)

Saunders, C. 'George McCall Theal and Lovedale', *History in Africa*, 8 (1981)

Saunders, C. 'The Making of an Historian: The Early Years of George McCall Theal', *South African Historical Journal*, 13 (1981)

Saunders, C. 'South African Historiography in English', in Ray, D. *et al.* (eds.) *Into the '80s* (Vancouver, 1981)

Saunders, C. '"Mnguni" and *Three Hundred Years* Revisited', *Kronos*, 11 (1986)

Saunders, C. *C. W. de Kiewiet. Historian of South Africa* (Cape Town, 1986)

Saunders, C. 'The Writing of C. W. de Kiewiet's *A History of South Africa Social and Economic*', *History in Africa*, 13 (1986)

Saunders, C. 'Our Past as Literature: Notes on Style in South African History in English', *Kleio*, 18 (1986)

Saunders, C. 'Jean van der Poel, Historian', *Quarterly Bulletin of the South African Library*, 41 (1986)

Schapera, I. *The Khoisan Peoples* (London, 1930)

Schapera, I. (ed.) *Western Civilization and the Natives of South Africa* (London, 1933)

Schapera, I. (ed.) *The Bantu-speaking Tribes of South Africa* (London, 1937)

Schapera, I. (ed.) *David Livingstone. South African Papers* (Cape Town, 1974)

Scher, D. 'Margaret Ballinger', *Kleio*, 13 (1981)

Schreuder, D. M. 'The Imperial Historian as Colonial Nationalist: George McCall Theal and the Making of South African History', in Martel, G. (ed.) *Studies in Imperial History* (London, 1986)

Scully, W. C. 'Fragments of Native History', *The State*, 1 and 2 (1909)

Simons, H. J. *African Women. Their Legal Status in South Africa* (London, 1968)

Simons, H. J. and R. E. *Class and Colour in South Africa* (Harmondsworth, 1969)

Skota, T. D. M. *The African Yearly Register* (Johannesburg, 1930)

Slovo, J. 'South Africa. No Middle Road' in Davidson, B., Slovo, J. and Wilkinson, A. *Southern Africa. The New Politics of Revolution* (Harmondsworth, 1976)

Soga, J. H. *The South-Eastern Bantu* (Johannesburg, 1930)

Soga, J. H. *The Ama-Xosa. Life and Customs* (Lovedale, n.d.[1932])

Stasiulis, D. K. 'Pluralist and Marxist Perspectives on Racial Discrimination in South Africa', *British Journal of Sociology*, 31 (1980)

Stow, G. *The Native Races of South Africa* (London, 1905)

Stuart, J. *A History of the Zulu Rebellion, 1906* (London, 1913)

Temu, A. and Swai, B. *Historians and Africanist History: A Critique* (London, 1981)

Theal, G. M. *South Africa As It Is* (King William's Town, 1871)

Theal, G. M. *Compendium of South African History and Geography* (Lovedale, 1873; 2nd ed. 1876; 3rd ed. 1877)

Theal, G. M. *Kaffir Folk-lore* (London, 1882)

Theal, G. M. *Basutoland Records*, 3 vols. (Cape Town, 1883; reprint Cape Town,

1964)

Theal, G. M. *History of the Emigrant Boers in South Africa* (London, 1887; 2nd ed. 1888)

Theal, G. M. *History of South Africa under the Administration of the Dutch East India Company*, 2 vols. (London, 1888; rev. ed., 1897)

Theal, G. M. *Korte Geschiedenis van Zuid-Afrika, 1486-1835* (Cape Town, 1891)

Theal, G. M. *South Africa* (London, 1894; 3rd ed. 1897; 8th ed. 1917)

Theal, G. M. *Notes on Canada and South Africa* (Cape Town, 1895)

Theal, G. M. *The Prospect in South Africa* (London, n.d.[1900])

Theal, G. M. *Progress of South Africa in the Century* (Toronto and Philadelphia, 1902)

Theal, G. M. *Records of the Cape Colony*, 36 vols. (London, 1897-1905)

Theal, G. M. *The Beginning of South African History* (London, 1902)

Theal, G. M. *History of South Africa from 1828 to 1846* (London, 1904)

Theal, G. M. *The Yellow and Dark-Skinned Peoples of Africa South of the Zambesi* (London, 1910)

Theal, G. M. *Willem Adriaan van der Stel and Other Historical Sketches* (Cape Town, 1913)

Theal, G. M. *History of South Africa*, 11 vols (London, 1892-1919; reprint Cape Town, 1964)

Thompson, L. M. *Democracy in Multi-Racial Societies* (Johannesburg, 1949)

Thompson, L. M. 'Afrikaner Nationalist Historiography and the Policy of Apartheid', *Journal of African History*, 3 (1962)

Thompson, L. M. 'The South African Dilemma' in Hartz, L. (ed.) *The Founding of New Societies* (New York, 1964)

Thompson, L. M. 'South Africa' in Winks, R. (ed.) *The Historiography of the British Empire-Commonwealth* (Durham, N.C., 1966)

Thompson, L. M. *Politics in the Republic of South Africa* (Boston, 1966)

Thompson, L. M. (ed.) *African Societies in Southern Africa* (London, 1969)

Thompson, L. M. *et al. Southern African History before 1900: A Select Bibliography of Articles* (Stanford, 1971)

Thompson, L. M. *Survival in Two Worlds* (Oxford, 1975)

Thompson, L. M. *The Political Mythology of Apartheid* (New Haven, 1985)

Thornton, R. '"This Dying Out Race": W. H. I. Bleek's Approach to the Languages of Southern Africa', *Social Dynamics*, 9 (1983)

Trapido, S. (ed.) *My Life and the I.C.U.* by Kadalie, C. (London, 1970)

Trapido, S. 'South Africa in a Comparative Study of Industrialization', *Journal of Development Studies*, 7 (1971)

Trapido, S. 'South Africa and the Historians', *African Affairs*, 71 (1972)

Trapido, S. 'Landlord and Tenant in a Colonial Economy', *Journal of Southern African Studies*, 5 (1978)

Tsotsi, W. *From Chattel to Wage Slavery* (Maseru, 1981)

UNESCO. *The Historiography of Southern Africa* (Paris, 1980)

Uys, C. J. *In the Era of Shepstone* (Lovedale, 1933)

Van den Berghe, P. *South Africa. A Study in Conflict* (Berkeley, 1967)

Van den Berghe, P. (ed.) *The Liberal Dilemma in South Africa* (London, 1979)

Van der Horst, S. *Native Labour in South Africa* (Cape Town, 1942)

Van der Poel, J. *Education and the Native* (Cape Town, 1934)

Van Heyningen, E. *The History of Shawco* (Cape Town, 1975)

Van Jaarsveld, F. A. *The Afrikaner's Interpretation of South African History* (Cape Town, 1964)

Van Jaarsveld, F. A. *Geskiedkundige Verkenninge* (Pretoria, 1974)

Van Jaarsveld, F. A. *From Van Riebeeck to Vorster, 1652-1974* (Pretoria, 1975)

Van Jaarsveld, F. A. *Wie en Wat is die Afrikaner?* (Cape Town, 1981)

Van Jaarsveld, F. A. 'Afrikaner Historiography' in Ray, D. *et al.* (eds.) *Into the '80s* (Vancouver, 1981)

Van Jaarsveld, F. A. *Die Afrikaners se Groot Trek na die Stede* (Johannesburg, 1982)

Van Jaarsveld, F. A. *Omstrede Suid-Afrikaanse Verlede: Geskiedenisideologie en die Historiese Skuldvraagstuk* (Johannesburg, 1984)

Van Onselen, C. *Chibaro. African Mine Labour in South Africa, 1900-33* (London, 1976)

Van Onselen, C. *Studies in the Social and Economic History of the Witwatersrand*, 2 vols (Johannesburg, 1982)

Vansina, J. *Oral Tradition: A Study in Historical Methodology* (Chicago, 1965)

Verhoef, G. 'Die Neo-Marxistiese Historiografie oor Suid-Afrika', *Historia*, 30 (1985)

Walker, E. *A History of South Africa* (London, 1928; rev. ed. 1935; 2nd ed. 1940; 3rd ed. 1957)

Walker, E. *The Frontier Tradition in South Africa* (Oxford, 1930)

Walker, E. 'A Zulu View of the Retief Massacre', *The Critic*, 3 (1935)

Walker, E. 'Of Franchises', *The Critic*, 4 (1936)

Walker, E. *The Cape Native Franchise* (Cape Town, 1936)

Walker, E. (ed.) *South Africa* 2nd ed. of *The Cambridge History of the British Empire*, 8 (Cambridge, 1963)

Walker, J. *Skin Deep. The Autobiography of a Woman Doctor* (Kommetjie, 1977)

Walshe, P. *The Rise of African Nationalism in South Africa* (London, 1971)

Webb, C. *History in a Time of Crisis* (Cape Town, 1977)

Webb, C. and Wright, J.(eds.) *The James Stuart Archive* (Pietermaritzburg, 1977—)

Welsh, D. 'Social Research in a Divided Society: The Case of South Africa', *Social Dynamics*, 1 (1975)

Welsh, D. 'The Nature of Racial Conflict in South Africa', *Social Dynamics*, 4 (1978)

Welsh, D. *South Africa: Power, Process and Prospect* (Cape Town, 1982)

West, M. and Whisson, M. (eds.) *Religion and Social Change* (Cape Town, 1975)

Wickins, P. *The Industrial and Commercial Workers' Union of South Africa* (Cape Town, 1974)

Wickins, P. 'Hector Monteith Robertson', *Cabo*, 3 (1985)

Wilmot, A. and Chase, J. C. *History of the Colony of the Cape of Good Hope* (Cape Town, 1869)

Wilmot, A. *The History of Our Times in South Africa*, 2 vols. (Cape Town, 1897)

Wilson, G and M. *The Analysis of Social Change* (Cambridge, 1945)

Wilson, M. 'The Early History of the Ciskei and Transkei', *African Studies*, 18 (1959)

Wilson, M. and Majeke, A. *Langa* (Cape Town, 1963)

Wilson, M. and Thompson, L. (eds.) *The Oxford History of South Africa*, 2 vols (Oxford, 1969, 1971)

Wolpe, H. 'Industrialisation and Race in South Africa' in Zubaida, S. (ed.) *Race and Racialism* (London, 1970)

Wolpe, H. 'Capitalism and Cheap Labour-Power in South Africa: From Segregation to Apartheid', *Economy and Society*, 1 (1972)

Wolpe, H. 'The "White Working Class" in South Africa', *Economy and Society*, 5 (1976)

Wolpe, H. 'A Comment on "The Poverty of Neo-Marxism"', *Journal of Southern African Studies*, 4 (1978)

Wolpe, H. 'The Liberation Struggle and Research', *Review of African Political Economy*,

32 (1985)

Wright, H. M. *The Burden of the Present: Liberal-Radical Controversy over Southern African History* (Cape Town, 1977)

Wright, H. M. 'The Burden of the Present and Its Critics', *Social Dynamics*, 6 (1980)

Wright, J. 'Clash of Paradigms', *Reality*, 9 (1977)

Wrigley, C. 'Historicism in Africa: Slavery and State Formation', *African Affairs*, 70 (1971)

Yudelman, D. 'Industrialization, Race Relations and Change in South Africa', *African Affairs*, 74 (1975)

Yudelman, D. 'The Quest for a Neo-Marxist Approach', *South African Journal of Economics*, 45 (1977)

Yudelman, D. 'Capital, Capitalists and Power in South Africa: Some Zero-Sum Fallacies', *Social Dynamics*, 6 (1980)

Yudelman, D. 'Dan O'Meara's Afrikaner Nationalism', *Social Dynamics*, 9 (1983)

Yudelman, D. *The Emergence of Modern South Africa: State, Capital and the Incorporation of Organized Labor on the South African Goldfields, 1902-1939* (Cape Town, 1984)

Unpublished secondary sources

Ambler, S. 'Social Structure and Race Attitudes: A Critique of the Liberal Interpretation of South African History', University of Calgary Honours essay, 1977

Babrow, M. 'A Critical Assessment of the Work of George McCall Theal', University of Cape Town, M.A. thesis, 1963

Boucher, M. 'Eric Walker', *Dictionary of South African Biography*, 5 (forthcoming)

Edgar, R. 'The Fifth Seal: Enoch Mgijima, the Israelites and the Bulhoek Massacre, 1921', University of California, Los Angeles, Ph.D thesis, 1977

Jeeves, A. 'Arthur Keppel-Jones: A Tribute', Queen's University, 1982

Johnstone, F. R. 'Class and Race Relations in the South African Gold Mining Industry 1910-26', Oxford University, D.Phil. thesis, 1972

Legassick, M. 'The Griqua, the Sotho-Tswana and the Missionaries', University of California, Los Angeles, Ph.D thesis, 1969

Legassick, M. 'The Making of South African "Native Policy" 1903-1923: The Origins of Segregation', University of London, 1972

Legassick, M. 'The Rise of Modern South African Liberalism', University of London, 1973

Legassick, M. 'British Hegemony and the Origins of Segregation, 1901-14', University of London, 1974

Le Roux, H. J. 'Die Toestand, Verspreiding en Verbrokkeling van die Hottentotstamme in Suid-Afrika 1652-1713', Stellenbosch University, M.A. thesis, 1945

Marquard, J. 'W. C. Scully', University of the Witwatersrand, Ph.D. thesis, 1984

Martin, S. J. R.'British Images of the Zulu, c.1820-1879', Cambridge University, Ph.D thesis, 1982

Naidoo, J. 'W. M. Macmillan, South African Historian', University of South Africa, M.A. thesis, 1983

Robertson, H. M. 'Some Trends in South African History of the 1920s and 1930s', University of Cape Town, c.1975

Robertson, H. M. 'History of the University of Cape Town', University of Cape Town, n.d.

Thompson, L. M. 'Interest, Ideology and History: The South African Case', Yale University, c.1978

Thornton, R. 'Wilhelm Immanuel Bleek's Discovery of Southern African Literatures', University of Cape Town, 1983

Index

185
Wodehouse, Sir P., 83
Wolpe, H., 169, 171–2, 175–6, 187–9
Woodward, C. V., 157, 186
Wright, H. M., 4, 5, 189
Xhosa, 28, 34, 68, 85, 108–9, 115, 117, 134, 152, 183; *see also* Cattle-killing,

Gcaleka, Ngqika
Yudelman, D., 169, 187
Zimbabwe (Great Zimbabwe), 36, 108
Zulu, 36, 105, 109–11, 156, 183; *The Zulu Aftermath*, 150–3, 183; *see also* Anglo–Zulu War
Zuurveld, 39, 113

DATE DUE

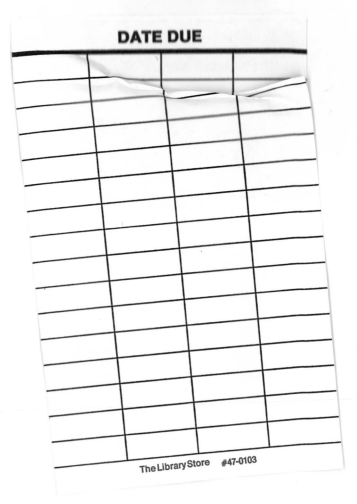

The Library Store   #47-0103